MEXICAN SPANISH

A ROUGH GUIDE PHRASEBOOK

Compiled by

LEXUS

Credits

Compiled by Lexus with Mike Gonzalez
Lexus Series Editor: Sally Davies
Rough Guides Phrase Book Editor: Jonathan Buckley
Rough Guides Series Editor: Mark Ellingham

First edition published in 1995 by Rough Guides Ltd,
62–70 Shorts Gardens, London WC2H 9AB.
Reprinted in 1995, 1996, 1998 and 1999.

Distributed by the Penguin Group.

Penguin Books Ltd, 27 Wrights Lane, London W8 5TZ
Penguin Books USA Inc., 375 Hudson Street, New York 10014, USA
Penguin Books Australia Ltd, 487 Maroondah Highway,
PO Box 257, Ringwood, Victoria 3134, Australia
Penguin Books Canada Ltd, Alcorn Avenue,
Toronto, Ontario, Canada M4V 1E4
Penguin Books (NZ) Ltd, 182–190 Wairau Road,
Auckland 10, New Zealand

Typeset in Bembo and Helvetica to an original design by Henry Iles.
Printed in Spain by Graphy Cems.

British Library Cataloguing in Publication Data
A catalogue for this book is available from the British Library.

ISBN 1-85828-609-3

HELP US GET IT RIGHT

Lexus and Rough Guides have made great efforts to be accurate and
informative in this Rough Guide Mexican Spanish phrasebook. However, if
you feel we have overlooked a useful word or phrase, or have any other
comments to make about the book, please let us know. All contributors
will be acknowledged and the best letters will be rewarded with a free
Rough Guide phrasebook of your choice. Please write to 'Mexican Spanish
Phrasebook Update', at either Shorts Gardens (London) or Hudson Street
(New York) – for full addresses see above. Alternatively you can email us at
mail@roughguides.co.uk

Online information about Rough Guides can be found at our website
www.roughguides.com

CONTENTS

Introduction

The Rough Guide Mexican Spanish phrasebook is a highly practical introduction to the contemporary language. Laid out in clear A-Z style, it uses key-word referencing to lead you straight to the words and phrases you want – so if you need to book a room, just look up 'room'. The Rough Guide gets straight to the point in every situation, in bars and shops, on trains and buses, and in hotels and banks.

The main part of the Rough Guide is a double dictionary: English-Spanish then Spanish-English. Before that, there's a section called **Basics**, which sets out the fundamental rules of the language, with plenty of practical examples. You'll also find here other essentials like numbers, dates, telling the time and basic phrases.

Forming the heart of the guide, the **English-Spanish** section gives easy-to-use transliterations of the Spanish words wherever pronunciation might be a problem, and to get you involved quickly in two-way communication, the Rough Guide includes dialogues featuring typical responses on key topics – such as renting a car and asking directions. Feature boxes fill you in on cultural pitfalls as well as the simple mechanics of how to make a phone call, what to do in an emergency, where to change money, and more. Throughout this section, cross-references enable you to pinpoint key facts and phrases, while asterisked words indicate where further information can be found in the Basics.

In the **Spanish-English** dictionary, we've given not just the phrases you're likely to hear (starting with a selection of slang and colloquialisms), but also all the signs, labels, instructions and other basic words you might come across in print or in public places.

Finally the Rough Guide rounds off with an extensive **Menu Reader**. Consisting of food and drink sections (each starting with a list of essential terms), it's indispensable whether you're eating out, stopping for a quick drink, or browsing through a local food market.

¡buen viaje!
have a good trip!

Basics

Pronunciation

In this phrasebook, the Spanish has been written in a system of imitated pronunciation so that it can be read as though it were English, bearing in mind the notes on pronunciation given below:

air	as in hair
ay	as in may
e, eh	as in get
g	always hard as in goat
H	a harsh 'ch' as in the Scottish way of pronouncing loch
ī	as the 'i' sound in might
o	as in not
ow	as in now
s	as in miss
y	as in yes

Letters given in bold type indicate the part of the word to be stressed.

As i and u are always pronounced 'ee' and 'oo' in Spanish, pronunciation has not been given for all words containing these letters unless they present other problems for the learner. Thus María is pronounced 'maree-a' and fútbol is 'footbol'.

Abbreviations

adj	adjective	pl	plural
f	feminine	pol	polite
fam	familiar	sing	singular
m	masculine		

Note

In the Spanish-English section and Menu Reader, the letter ñ is treated as a separate letter, as is customary in Spanish. Alphabetically, it comes after n.

Nouns

All nouns in Spanish have one of two genders: masculine or feminine. Generally speaking, those ending in **-o** are masculine:

el zapato
el sap**a**to
the shoe

Those ending in **-a**, **-d**, **-z** or **-ión** are usually feminine:

la cama	**la pensión**
la k**a**ma	la pens-y**o**n
the bed	the boarding house, the guesthouse

Nouns ending in **-or** are masculine. To form the feminine, add **-a**:

el señor	**la señora**
el sen-y**or**	la sen-y**o**ra
the man	the woman

el profesor	**la profesora**
the (male) teacher	the (female) teacher

A small number of nouns ending in **-o** and **-a** (usually professions) can be either masculine or feminine:

el/la guía	**el/la violinista**
el/la g**ee**-a	el/la bee-oleen**ee**sta
the guide	the violinist

Plural Nouns

If the noun ends in a vowel, the plural is formed by adding **-s**:

el camino	**los caminos**
el kam**ee**no	los kam**ee**nos
the path	the paths

la mesera	**las meseras**
la mes**ai**ra	las mes**ai**ras
the waitress	the waitresses

If the noun ends in a consonant, the plural is formed by adding **-es**:

el chofer	**los choferes**
el chof**ai**r	los chof**ai**r-es
the driver	the drivers
la recepción	**las recepciones**
la reseps-y**o**n	las reseps-y**o**n-es
the reception desk	the reception desks

If the noun ends in a **-z**, change the **-z** to **-ces** to form the plural:

la luz	**las luces**
la l**oo**s	las l**oo**s-es
the light	the lights

Articles

The different articles ('the' and 'a') in Spanish vary according to the number (singular or plural) and gender of the noun they refer to.

The Definite Article

The definite article 'the' is as follows:

	singular	plural
masculine	el	los
feminine	la	las

el cuchillo/los cuchillos	**la mesa/las mesas**
el kooch**ee**-yo/los kooch**ee**-yos	la m**e**sa/las m**e**sas
the knife/the knives	the table/the tables

11

When the article **el** is used in combination with **a** (to) or **de** (of) it changes as follows:

a + el = al
de + el = del

vamos al museo	**cerca del hotel**
vamos al moos**eh**-o	sairka del otel
let's go to the museum	near the hotel

The Indefinite Article

The indefinite article (a, an, some), also changes according to the gender and number of the accompanying noun:

	singular	plural
masculine	**un**	**unos**
	oon	**oo**nos
feminine	**una**	**unas**
	oona	**oo**nas

un sello	**unos sellos**
oon **seh**-yo	**oo**nos **seh**-yos
a stamp	some stamps
una chica	**unas chicas**
oona cheeka	**oo**nas cheekas
a girl	some girls

Adjectives and adverbs

Adjectives must agree in gender and number with the noun they refer to. Unlike English, Spanish adjectives usually follow the noun. In the English-Spanish section of this book, all adjectives are given in the masculine singular. Adjectives ending in **-o** change as follows for the plural:

el precio alto	**los precios altos**
el pres-yo **a**lto	los pres-yos **a**ltos
the high price	the high prices

The feminine singular of the adjective is formed by changing the masculine endings as follows:

masculine	feminine
-o	-a
-or	-ora
-és	-esa

un cocinero estupendo
oon koseen**ai**ro estoopendo
a wonderful cook

una cocinera estupenda
oona koseen**ai**ra estoopenda
a wonderful cook

un señor encantador
oon sen-y**o**r enkantad**o**r
a nice man

una señora encantadora
oona sen-y**o**ra enkantad**o**ra
a nice woman

un chico inglés
oon ch**ee**ko eeng-l**e**s
an English boy

una chica inglesa
oona ch**ee**ka eengl**e**sa
an English girl

For other types of adjective, the feminine forms are the same as the masculine:

un hombre agradable
oon h**o**mbreh agrad**a**bleh
a nice man

una mujer agradable
oona moo**H**air agrad**a**bleh
a nice woman

The plurals of adjectives are formed in the same way as the plurals of nouns, by adding an **-s**:

una silla roja
oona s**ee**-ya ro**H**a
a red chair

dos sillas rojas
dos s**ee**-yas ro**H**as
two red chairs

Comparatives

The comparative is formed by placing **más** (more) or **menos** (less) before the adjective or adverb:

lindo
l**ee**ndo
beautiful

más lindo
mas l**ee**ndo
more beautiful

tranquilo	**menos tranquilo**
trank**ee**lo	m**e**nos trank**ee**lo
quiet	less quiet

este hotel es más/menos caro que el otro
esteh ot**e**l es mas/m**e**nos k**a**ro keh el **o**tro
this hotel is more/less expensive than the other one

¿tiene un cuarto más soleado?
t-y**e**neh **oo**n kw**a**rto mas soleh-**a**do
do you have a sunnier room?

¿podría ir más de prisa, por favor?
podr**ee**-a **ee**r mas deh pr**ee**sa por fab**o**r
could you go faster please?

Superlatives

Superlatives are formed by placing one of the following before the adjective: **el más**, **la más**, **los más** or **las más** (depending on the noun's gender and number):

¿cuál es el más divertido?
kwal es el mas deebairt**ee**do
which is the most entertaining?

el carro más rápido
el k**a**rro mas r**a**peedo
the fastest car

la casa más linda
la k**a**sa mas l**ee**nda
the prettiest house

las mujeres más inteligentes
las mooн**ai**r-es mas eenteleeн**e**nt-es
the most intelligent women

The following adjectives have irregular comparatives and superlatives:

bueno	mejor	el mejor
bweno	meнor	el meнor
good	better	the best

grande	mayor	el mayor
grandeh	mī-yor	el mī-yor
big	bigger	the biggest
old	older	the oldest

malo	peor	el peor
malo	peh-or	el peh-or
bad	worse	the worst

pequeño	menor	el menor
peken-yo	menor	el menor
small	smaller	the smallest
	younger	the youngest

'As ... as ...' is translated as follows:

Oaxaca está tan linda como siempre!
waнaka esta tan leenda komo s-yempreh
Oaxaca is as beautiful as ever!

The superlative form ending in **-ísimo** indicates that something is 'very/extremely ...' without actually comparing it to something else:

guapo	guapísimo
gwapo	gwapeeseemo
attractive	very attractive

Adverbs

There are two ways to form an adverb. If the adjective ends in **-o**, take the feminine and add **-mente** to form the corresponding adverb:

exacto	exactamente
eksakto	eksaktamente
accurate	accurately, exactly

If the adjective ends in any other letter, add **-mente** to the basic form:

feliz
felees
happy

felizmente
feleesmenteh
happily

Possessive Adjectives

Possessive adjectives, like other Spanish adjectives, agree with the noun in gender and number:

	singular		plural	
	masculine	feminine	masculine	feminine
my	**mi**	**mi**	**mis**	**mis**
	mee	mee	mees	mees
your	**tu**	**tu**	**tus**	**tus**
(sing, fam)	too	too	toos	toos
his/her/its/your	**su**	**su**	**sus**	**sus**
(sing, pol)	soo	soo	soos	soos
our	**nuestro**	**nuestra**	**nuestros**	**nuestras**
	nwestro	nwestra	nwestros	nwestras
your (pl)/their	**su**	**su**	**sus**	**sus**
	soo	soo	soos	soos

tu bolsa
too bolsa
your bag

sus pastillas
soos pastee-yas
his/her/your tablets

su maleta
soo maleta
your suitcase

nuestros trajes de baño
nwestros traHes deh ban-yo
our swimming costumes

If when using **su/sus**, it is unclear whether you mean 'his', 'her', 'your' or 'their', you can use the following after the noun instead:

de él	his	**de ellos**	their (m)
deh el		deh **eh**-yos	
de ella	her	**de ellas**	their (f)
deh **eh**-ya		deh **eh**-yas	
de Usted	your (sing, pol)	**de Ustedes**	your (pl)
deh oost**eh**		deh oosted-es	

el dinero de Usted
el deen**ai**ro deh oost**eh**
your money

el dinero de ella
el deen**ai**ro deh **eh**-ya
her money

el dinero de él
el deen**ai**ro deh el
his money

Possessive pronouns

To translate 'mine', 'yours', 'theirs' etc, use one of the following forms. Like possessive adjectives, possessive pronouns must agree in gender and number with the object or objects referred to:

	singular		plural	
	masculine	feminine	masculine	feminine
mine	**el mío**	**la mía**	**los míos**	**las mías**
	el **mee**-o	la **mee**-a	los **mee**-os	las **mee**-as
yours	**el tuyo**	**la tuya**	**los tuyos**	**las tuyas**
(sing, fam)	el **too**-yo	la **too**-ya	los **too**-yos	las **too**-yas
his/hers/yours	**el suyo**	**la suya**	**los suyos**	**las suyas**
(sing, pol)	el **soo**-yo	la **soo**-ya	los **soo**-yos	las **soo**-yas
ours	**el nuestro**	**la nuestra**	**los nuestros**	**las nuestras**
	el **nwe**stro	la **nwe**stra	los **nwe**stros	las **nwe**stras
yours (pl)/theirs	**el suyo**	**la suya**	**los suyos**	**las suyas**
	el **soo**-yo	la **soo**-ya	los **soo**-yos	las **soo**-yas

ésta es su llave y ésta es la mía
esta es soo y**a**beh ee **e**sta es la m**ee**-a
this is your key and this is mine

no es la suya, es de sus amigos
no es la **soo**-ya es deh soos ame**ee**gos
it's not his, it's his friends'

Personal pronouns

Subject Pronouns

yo	I	**nosotros**	we (m)
yo		nos**o**tros	
tú	you (sing, fam)	**nosotras**	we (f)
too		nos**o**tras	
él	he/it	**ellos**	they (m)
el		**eh**-yos	
ella	she/it	**ellas**	they (f)
eh-ya		**eh**-yas	
Usted	you (sing, pol)	**Ustedes**	you (pl)
oost**eh**		oosted-es	

Tú is used when speaking to one person and is the familiar form generally used when speaking to family, friends and children.
Usted is the polite form of address to be used when talking to someone you don't know or an older person.
Ustedes is the plural form used in Mexico whoever you are speaking to. The third person of verbs is used with **Usted** and **Ustedes**: **Usted** takes the same verb form as 'he/she/it'; **Ustedes** takes the same verb form as 'they'.

In Spanish the subject pronoun is usually omitted:

no saben	**está cansado**
no s**a**ben	est**a** kansado
they don't know	he is tired

although it may be retained for emphasis or to avoid confusion:

18

¡soy yo!
soy yo
it's me!

¡somos nosotros!
somos nosotros
it's us!

yo pago los tacos, tú pagas las cervezas
yo pago los takos too pagas las sairbesas
I'll pay for the tacos, you pay for the beers

él es inglés y ella es americana
el es eeng-les ee eh-ya es amaireekana
he's English and she's American

Subject pronouns are also used after prepositions:

para Usted
para oosteh
for you

con él
kon el
with him

sin ella
seen eh-ya
without her

detrás de Usted
detras deh oosteh
behind you

después de nosotros
despwes deh nosotros
after us

The exceptions are **yo**, which is replaced by **mí**, and **tú** which is replaced by **tí**:

eso es para mí/tí
eso es para mee/tee
that's for me/you

After **con** (with), **mí** and **tí** change as follows:

conmigo
konmeego
with me

contigo
konteego
with you

Object pronouns

me	[meh]	me	nos	[nos]	us
te	[teh]	you (sing, fam)	los	[los]	them (m), you (mpl)
lo	[lo]	him/it, you (sing, pol)	las	[las]	them (f), you (fpl)
la	[la]	her/it, you (sing, pol)			

19

Object pronouns usually precede the verb:

me la dio ayer
meh la dee-o ī-yair
she gave it to me yesterday

las compré para ella
las kompreh para eh-ya
I bought them for her

cada viernes la compro flores
kada b-yairn-es la kompro flor-es
every Friday I buy her flowers

los vi ayer
los bee a-yair
I saw them yesterday

When used with infinitives, pronouns are added to the end of the infinitive:

¿puede llevarme al aeropuerto?
pwedeh yebarmeh al airopwairto
can you take me to the airport?

intentaré recordarlo
eententareh rekordarlo
I'll try and remember it

When used with commands, pronouns are added to the end of the imperative form. See **Imperatives** page 34.

If you are using an indirect pronoun to mean 'to me', 'to you' etc (although 'to' might not always be necessarily said in English), you generally use the following:

me	[meh]	to me
te	[teh]	to you (sing, fam)
le/lo	[leh/lo]	to him, to you (sing, pol)
le/la	[leh/la]	to her, to you (sing, pol)
nos	[nos]	to us
les/los	[les/los]	to them (m), to you (mpl)
les/las	[les/las]	to them (f), to you (fpl)

me enseñó el camino
meh ensen-yo el kameeno
he showed me the way

le pedí su dirección
leh pedee soo deereks-yon
I asked him/her for his/her address

Reflexive Pronouns

These are used with reflexive verbs like **lavarse** 'to wash (oneself)', that is where the subject and the object are one and the same person:

me	[meh]	myself (used with I)
te	[teh]	yourself (used with singular, familiar 'you')
se	[seh]	him/her/itself (used with singular, polite 'you')
nos	[nos]	ourselves (used with 'we')
se	[seh]	themselves (used with 'they' and plural 'you')

presentarse to introduce oneself
> **me presento: me llamo Richard**
> meh pres**e**nto: meh y**a**mo Richard
> may I introduce myself? my name's Richard

divertirse to enjoy oneself
> **nos divertimos mucho en la fiesta**
> nos deebairt**ee**mos m**oo**cho en la f-y**e**sta
> we enjoyed ourselves a lot at the party

Demonstratives

The English demonstrative adjective 'this' is translated by the Spanish **este**. 'That' is translated by **ese** or **aquel**. **Ese** refers to something near to the person being spoken to. **Aquel** refers to something further away.

Like other adjectives, they agree with the noun they qualify in gender and number but they are placed in front of the noun. Their forms are:

masculine singular			feminine singular		
este	**ese**	**aquel**	**esta**	**esa**	**aquella**
esteh	**e**seh	ak**e**l	**e**sta	**e**sa	ak**e**-ya

masculine plural			feminine plural		
estos	**esos**	**aquellos**	**estas**	**esas**	**aquellas**
estos	**e**sos	ak**e**-yos	**e**stas	**e**sas	ak**e**-yas

este restaurante	**ese mesero**	**aquella playa**
esteh restow**ran**teh	**e**seh mes**ai**ro	ak**eh**-ya plī-ya
this restaurant	that waiter	that beach (in the distance)

'This one', 'that one', 'those', 'these' etc (as pronouns) are translated by the same words as above only they are spelt with an **é**:

éste	**ése**	**aquél**
esteh	**e**seh	ak**el**
this one	that one	that one (over there)

quisiera éstos/ésos/aquéllos
kees-y**ai**ra **e**stos/**e**sos/ak**eh**-yos
I'd like these/those/those (over there)

The neuter forms **esto/eso/aquello** are used when no particular noun is being referred to:

esto	**eso**	**aquello**
esto	**e**so	ak**eh**-yo

eso no es justo	**¿qué es esto?**
eso no es н**oo**sto	keh es **e**sto
that's not fair	what is this?

Verbs

The basic form of the verb given in the **English-Spanish** and **Spanish-English** sections is the infinitive (e.g. to drive, to go etc). There are three verb types in Spanish which can be recognized by their infinitive endings: **-ar**, **-er** or **-ir**. For example:

hablar	[ab**l**ar]	to talk
comer	[kom**air**]	to eat
abrir	[ab**reer**]	to open

Present Tense

The present tense corresponds to 'I leave' and 'I am leaving' in English. To form the present tense for the three main types of verb in Spanish, remove the -ar, -er or -ir and add the following endings:

hablar to speak

habl-o	[**a**blo]	I speak
habl-as	[**a**blas]	you speak (sing, fam)
habl-a	[**a**bla]	he/she speaks, you speak (sing, pol)
habl-amos	[abl**a**mos]	we speak
habl-an	[**a**blan]	they speak, you speak (pl)

comer to eat

com-o	[k**o**mo]	I eat
com-es	[k**o**m-es]	you eat (sing, fam)
com-e	[k**o**meh]	he/she eats, you eat (sing, pol)
com-emos	[kom**e**mos]	we eat
com-en	[k**o**men]	they eat, you eat (pl)

abrir to open

abr-o	[**a**bro]	I open
abr-es	[**a**b-res]	you open (sing, fam)
abr-e	[**a**breh]	he/she opens, you open (sing, pol)
abr-imos	[abr**ee**mos]	we open
abr-en	[**a**bren]	they open, you open (pl)

Some common verbs are irregular:

dar to give

doy	[doy]	I give
das	[das]	you give (sing, fam)
da	[da]	he/she gives, you give (sing, pol)
damos	[d**a**mos]	we give
dan	[dan]	they give, you give (pl)

ir to go

voy	[boy]	I go
vas	[bas]	you go (sing, fam)
va	[ba]	he/she goes, you go (sing, pol)
vamos	[bamos]	we go
van	[ban]	they go, you go (pl)

poder can, to be able

puedo	[pwedo]	I can
puedes	[pwed-es]	you can (sing, fam)
puede	[pwedeh]	he/she can, you can (sing, pol)
podemos	[podemos]	we can
pueden	[pweden]	they can, you can (pl)

querer to want

quiero	[k-yairo]	I want
quieres	[k-yair-es]	you want (sing, fam)
quiere	[k-yaireh]	he/she wants, you want (sing, pol)
queremos	[kairemos]	we want
quieren	[k-yairen]	they want, you want (pl)

tener to have

tengo	[tengo]	I have
tienes	[t-yen-es]	you have (sing, fam)
tiene	[t-yeneh]	he/she has, you have (sing, pol)
tenemos	[tenemos]	we have
tienen	[t-yenen]	they have, you have (pl)

venir to come

vengo	[bengo]	I come
vienes	[b-yen-es]	you come (sing, fam)
viene	[b-yeneh]	he/she comes, you come (sing, pol)
venimos	[beneemos]	we come
vienen	[b-yenen]	they come, you come (pl)

The first person singular (the 'I' form) of the following verbs is irregular in some verbs:

decir to say	**digo**	[deego]
hacer to do, to make	**hago**	[a-go]
poner to put	**pongo**	[pongo]
saber to know	**sé**	[seh]
salir to go out	**salgo**	[salgo]

See page 31 for the present tense of the verbs **ser** and **estar** 'to be'.

Past Tense:

Preterite

The preterite is the tense normally used to talk about the past:

habl-é	[ableh]	I spoke
habl-aste	[ablasteh]	you spoke (sing, fam)
habl-ó	[ablo]	he/she spoke, you spoke (sing, pol)
habl-amos	[ablamos]	we spoke
habl-aron	[ablaron]	they spoke, you spoke (pl)

com-í	[komee]	I ate
com-iste	[komeesteh]	you ate (sing, fam)
com-ió	[komee-o]	he/she ate, you ate (sing, pol)
com-imos	[komeemos]	we ate
com-ieron	[kom-yairon]	they ate, you ate (pl)

abr-í	[abree]	I opened
abr-iste	[abreesteh]	you opened (sing, fam)
abr-ió	[abree-o]	he/she opened, you opened (sing, pol)
abr-imos	[abreemos]	we opened
abr-ieron	[abr-yairon]	they opened, you opened (pl)

¿quién te dijo eso?
k-yen teh deeʜo eso
who told you that?

nos conocimos en Mérida
nos konoseemos en mereeda
we met each other in Mérida

lo compramos el año pasado
lo kompramos el an-yo pasado
we bought it last year

The verbs **ser** (to be) and **ir** (to go) are irregular and have the same form in the preterite:

fui	[fwee]	I was; I went
fuiste	[fweesteh]	you were; you went (sing, fam)
fue	[fweh]	he/she/it was; you were (sing, pol);
		he/she/it went; you went (sing, pol)
fuimos	[fweemos]	we were; we went
fueron	[fwairon]	they were; you were (pl);
		they went; you went (pl)

Perfect Tense

The perfect tense corresponds to the English past tense using 'have' – i.e. 'I have seen', 'he has said' etc. It is formed by combining the appropriate person of the present tense of **haber** with the past participle of the other verb. The present tense of **haber** is as follows:

he	[eh]	I have
has	[as]	you have (sing, fam)
ha	[a]	he/she/it has; you have (sing, pol)
hemos	[emos]	we have
han	[an]	they have; you have (pl)

The past participle is formed by removing the infinitive ending (**-ar**, **-er** or **-ir**) and adding **-ado** or **-ido** as follows:

infinitive	past participle	
hablar	hablado	[ablado]
comer	comido	[komeedo]
vivir	vivido	[beebeedo]

hemos dado una propina
emos dado oona propeena
we have given a tip

hemos comido bien
emos komeedo b-yen
we've eaten well, we've had a good meal

he encendido la luz
eh ensendeedo la loos
I (have) put the light on

Some verbs have irregular past participles:

hacer to do, to make	**hecho**	[echo]
abrir to open	**abierto**	[ab-yairto]
decir to say	**dicho**	[deecho]
volver to return	**vuelto**	[bwelto]
poner to put	**puesto**	[pwesto]
ver to see	**visto**	[beesto]

Imperfect Tense

This tense is used to describe something or someone in the past, or to describe activities that were habitual in the past. It is also the tense you would use to talk about something that was going on over a period of time. It is formed as follows:

hablar to talk

habl-**aba**	[abl**aba**]	I was speaking
habl-**abas**	[abl**abas**]	you were speaking (sing, fam)
habl-**aba**	[abl**aba**]	he/she was speaking, you were speaking (sing, pol)
habl-**ábamos**	[abl**abamos**]	we were speaking
habl-**aban**	[abl**aban**]	they were speaking, you were speaking (pl)

comer to eat

com-**ía**	[kom**ee**-a]	I was eating
com-**ías**	[kom**ee**-as]	you were eating (sing, fam)
com-**ía**	[kom**ee**-a]	he/she/it was eating, you were eating (sing, pol)
com-**íamos**	[kom**ee**-amos]	we were eating
com-**ían**	[kom**ee**-an]	they were eating, you were eating (pl)

abrir to open

abr-ía	[abr**ee**-a]	I was opening
abr-ías	[abr**ee**-as]	you were opening (sing, fam)
abr-ía	[abr**ee**-a]	he/she/it was opening, you were opening (sing, pol)
abr-íamos	[abr**ee**-amos]	we were opening
abr-ían	[abr**ee**-an]	they were opening, you were opening (pl)

Other useful verbs in the imperfect tense are:

estar to be

estaba	[est**a**ba]	I was
estabas	[est**a**bas]	you were (sing, fam)
estaba	[est**a**ba]	he/she/it was, you were (sing, pol)
estábamos	[est**a**bamos]	we were
estaban	[est**a**ban]	they were, you were (pl)

tener to have

tenía	[ten**ee**-a]	I had
tenías	[ten**ee**-as]	you had (sing, fam)
tenía	[ten**ee**-a]	he/she/it had, you had (sing, pol)
teníamos	[ten**ee**-amos]	we had
tenían	[ten**ee**-an]	they had, you had (pl)

The following are irregular in the imperfect tense:

ir to go

iba	[**ee**ba]	I was going
ibas	[**ee**bas]	you were going (sing, fam)
iba	[**ee**ba]	he/she/it was going, you were going (sing, pol)
íbamos	[**ee**bamos]	we were going
iban	[**ee**ban]	they were going, you were going (pl)

ser to be (see page 31 for more on this)

era	[aira]	I was
eras	[airas]	you were (sing, fam)
era	[aira]	he/she/it was, you were (sing, pol)
éramos	[airamos]	we were
eran	[airan]	they were, you were (pl)

todos los viernes salíamos a dar un paseo

todos los b-yairn-es sal**ee**-amos a dar oon pas**eh**-o

every Friday we used to go for a walk, every Friday we went for a walk

era alto y delgado

aira **a**lto ee delg**a**do

he was tall and slim

viajaban de México a Veracruz

bee-a**н**aban deh me**н**eeko a bai**r**akr**oo**s

they were travelling from Mexico to Veracruz

Future Tense

To form the future tense in Spanish (I will do, you will do etc) add the following endings to the infinitive. The same endings are used whether verbs end in **-ar**, **-er** or **-ir**:

hablar-é	[ablar**eh**]	I will speak
hablar-ás	[ablar**as**]	you will speak (sing, fam)
hablar-á	[ablar**a**]	he/she/you will speak (sing, pol)
hablar-emos	[ablar**emos**]	we will speak
hablar-án	[ablar**an**]	they/you will speak (pl)

llamaré más tarde

yamar**eh** mas **ta**rdeh

I'll call later

The immediate future can also be translated by **ir** + **a** + infinitive:

vamos a comprar una botella de vino tinto
bamos a komprar **oo**na boteh-ya deh **vee**no **tee**nto
we're going to buy a bottle of red wine

iré a recogerlo
eer**eh** a reкон**air**lo
I'll fetch him, I'll go and fetch him

In Spanish, as in English, the future can sometimes be expressed by the present tense:

tu avión sale a la una
too ab-y**o**n s**a**leh a la **oo**na
your plane takes off at one o'clock

However, Spanish often uses the present tense where the future would be used in English:

le doy ochocientos pesos
leh doy ochos-y**e**ntos p**e**sos
I'll give you 800 pesos

The following verbs are irregular in the future tense:

decir	to say	diré	I will say
hacer	to do	haré	I will do
poder	to be able	podré	I will be able
poner	to put	pondré	I will put
querer	to want	querré	I will want
saber	to know	sabré	I will know
salir	to leave	saldré	I will leave
tener	to have	tendré	I will have
venir	to come	vendré	I will come

The Verb 'To Be'

There are two verbs 'to be' in Spanish: **ser** and **estar**. The present tense is as follows:

ser

soy	[soy]	I am
eres	[air-es]	you are (sing, fam)
es	[es]	he/she/it is, you are (sing, pol)
somos	[somos]	we are
son	[son]	they are, you are (pl)

estar

estoy	[estoy]	I am
estás	[estas]	you are (sing, fam)
está	[esta]	he/she/it is, you are (sing, pol)
estamos	[estamos]	we are
están	[estan]	they are, you are (pl)

Ser

Ser is generally used to describe a permanent state, for example, what something or someone looks like or what their nature is:

la nieve es blanca
la n-yebeh es blanka
snow is white

Ser is also used with occupations, nationalities, the time and to indicate possession:

somos escoceses	**mi madre es profesora**
somos eskoses-es	mi madreh es profesora
we are Scottish	my mother is a teacher

éste es nuestro carro	**son las cinco de la tarde**
esteh es nwestro karro	son las seenko deh la tardeh
this is our car	it's five o'clock in the afternoon

Estar

Estar, on the other hand, is used above all to answer the question 'where?':

el libro está en la mesa
el **lee**bro esta en la **me**sa
the book is on the table

Nuevo Laredo está en el norte del país
nw**e**vo lar**e**do esta en el n**o**rteh del pa-**ee**s
Nuevo Laredo is in the north of the country

It also describes the temporary or passing qualities of something or someone:

estoy enojado
est**oy** eno**н**ado
I'm angry

estoy cansado
est**oy** kans**a**do
I'm tired

este filete está frío
esteh feel**e**teh esta **free**-o
this steak is cold

Note the difference between the following two phrases:

Isabel es muy guapa
Isabel es mwee gw**a**pa
Isabel is very pretty

Isabel está muy guapa (esta noche)
Isabel esta mwee gw**a**pa **e**sta n**o**cheh
Isabel looks pretty (tonight)

soy inglés
soy eeng-l**e**s
I am English

estoy en México
est**oy** en me**н**eeko
I am in Mexico

Negatives

To express a negative in Spanish, to say 'I don't want', 'it's not here' etc, place the word **no** in front of the verb:

entiendo
ent-y**e**ndo
I understand

no entiendo
no ent-y**e**ndo
I don't understand

me gusta este helado
meh g**oo**sta **e**steh el**a**do
I like this ice cream

no me gusta este helado
no meh g**oo**sta **e**steh el**a**do
I don't like this ice cream

lo alquilé aquí
lo alkeel**eh** ak**ee**
I rented it here

no lo alquilé aquí
no lo alkeel**eh** ak**ee**
I didn't rent it here

van a cantar
ban a kan**tar**
they're going to sing

no van a cantar
no ban a kan**tar**
they're not going to sing

To use negative words like:

nadie	**nada**	**nunca**
n**a**d-yeh	n**a**da	n**oo**nka
no-one, nobody	nothing	never

you can either place them before the verb, or put them after
the verb with **no** in front, thus:

no llegó nadie/nadie llegó
no yeg**o** n**a**d-yeh/n**a**d-yeh yeg**o**
nobody came

no hay nadie ahí
no ī n**a**d-yeh a-**ee**
there's no-one there

no compramos nada
no kompr**a**mos n**a**da
we didn't buy anything

no sabemos nada de ella
no sab**e**mos n**a**da deh **eh**-ya
we don't know anything
about her

To say 'there's no ...', 'I've no ...' etc, make the accompanying
verb negative:

no hay vino
no ī b**ee**no
there's no wine

no tengo cerillas
no t**e**ngo sair**ee**-yas
I've no matches

To say 'not him', 'not her' etc just use the personal pronoun
followed by **no**:

nosotros, no	**ella, no**	**yo, no**
nos**o**tros no	**eh**-ya no	yo no
not us	not her	not me

Imperatives

When giving a command to people you would normally address with **Usted** or **Ustedes**, you form the imperative by taking the first person singular of the present tense and changing the endings as follows:

	first person singular	singular	plural
hablar to speak	hablo	habl-e	habl-en
		ableh	ablen
comer to eat	como	com-a	com-an
		koma	koman
abrir to open	abro	abr-a	abr-an
		abra	abran
venir to come	vengo	ven-ga	ven-gan
		benga	bengan

coma despacio
koma despas-yo
eat slowly

When you are telling someone not to do something, use the forms above and place **no** in front of the verb:

no me moleste, por favor
no meh molesteh por fabor
please don't disturb me

¡no beba alcohol!
no beba alkol
don't drink alcohol!

¡no venga esta noche!
no benga esta nocheh
don't come tonight!

To give a command to people you would normally address as **tú**, remove the endings **-ar**, **-er**, and **-ir** from the verb and add these endings:

hablar to speak	habl-a	[abla]
comer to eat	com-e	[komeh]
abrir to open	abr-e	[abreh]

To form a negative imperative to people addressed as **tú, no** is placed in front of the verb and the endings change:

habla   no habl-es   [no ab-les]
come   no com-as   [no komas]
abre   no abras   [no abras]

por favor, no hables tan rápido (to one person)
por fabor no ab-les tan rapeedo
please don't speak so quickly

Pronouns are added to the end of the imperative form:

despiérteme a las ocho, por favor
desp-yairtemeh a las ocho por fabor
wake me up at eight o'clock, please

bébelo	**ciérralas**	**ayúdeme, por favor**
bebelo	s-yairalas	a-yoodemeh por fabor
drink it	close them	help me please

but when the imperative is negative, they are placed in front of it:

no lo bebas	**no las cierres**
no lo bebas	no las s-yair-res
don't drink it	don't close them

The imperatives of the verb **ir** 'to go' are irregular:

forms	Usted	Ustedes	tú
	vaya	vayan	ve
	bī-a	bī-an	beh

Questions

Often the word order remains the same in a question, but the intonation changes, the voice rising at the end of the question:

¿quieres bailar?   ¿quieres ir al cine?
k-**yair**-es bilar   k-**yair**-es eer al **seen**eh
do you want to dance?   do you want to go to the cinema?

Dates

Use the numbers on page 38 to express the date:

el uno de septiembre [el **oo**no deh set-**yem**breh] the first of
September
el dos de diciembre [dos deh dees-**yem**breh] the second of
December
el treinta de mayo [**tray**nta deh mī-yo] the thirtieth of May
el treinta y uno de mayo [**tray**ntī **oo**no deh mī-yo] the thirty-first of
May

Days

Sunday domingo
Monday lunes [**loo**n-es]
Tuesday martes [**mart**-es]
Wednesday miércoles [m-**yair**kol-es]
Thursday jueves [**ʜweb**-es]
Friday viernes [b-**yairn**-es]
Saturday sábado

Months

January enero [e**nair**o]
February febrero [fe**brair**o]
March marzo [**marso**]
April abril
May mayo [mī-yo]
June junio [**ʜoon**-yo]
July julio [**ʜool**-yo]

August agosto
September septiembre [set-yembreh]
October octubre [oktoobreh]
November noviembre [nob-yembreh]
December diciembre [dees-yembreh]

Time

what time is it? ¿qué hora es? [keh ora]
one o'clock la una
two o'clock las dos
it's one o'clock es la una
it's two o'clock son las dos
it's ten o'clock son las diez [d-yes]
five past one la una y cinco [ee seenko]
ten past two las dos y diez
quarter past one la una y cuarto [ee kwarto]
quarter past two las dos y cuarto
half past ten las diez y media [d-yes ee med-ya]
twenty to ten veinte para las diez [baynteh]
quarter to ten cuarto para las diez
at eight o'clock a las ocho [ocho]
at half past four a las cuatro y media [kwatro ee med-ya]
2 a.m. las dos de la mañana [deh la man-yana]
2 p.m. las dos de la tarde [tardeh]
6 a.m. las seis de la mañana [seh-ees deh la man-yana]
6 p.m. las seis de la tarde
noon mediodía [med-yo-dee-a]
midnight medianoche [med-ya-nocheh]
an hour una hora [ora]
a minute un minuto
two minutes dos minutos
a second un segundo
a quarter of an hour un cuarto de hora [kwarto deh ora]
half an hour media hora [med-ya]
three quarters of an hour tres cuartos de hora [kwartos deh ora]

Numbers

0	cero [**sai**ro]
1	**u**no, **u**na
2	dos
3	tres
4	cuatro [**kwa**tro]
5	cinco [**seen**ko]
6	seis [**says**]
7	siete [s-**ye**teh]
8	ocho [**o**cho]
9	nueve [**nwe**beh]
10	diez [d-**yes**]
11	once [**on**seh]
12	doce [**do**seh]
13	trece [**tre**seh]
14	catorce [ka**tor**seh]
15	quince [**keen**seh]
16	dieciséis [d-yese**se**-ees]
17	diecisiete [d-yesees-**ye**teh]
18	dieciocho [d-yesee-**o**cho]
19	diecinueve [d-yesee**nwe**beh]
20	veinte [**bay**nteh]
21	veintiuno [bayntee-**oo**no]
22	veintidós [baynteed**os**]
23	veintitrés [baynteetr**es**]
30	treinta [**tray**nta]
31	treinta y uno [**tray**nti **oo**no]
40	cuarenta [kwa**ren**ta]
50	cincuenta [seenk**wen**ta]
60	sesenta
70	setenta
80	ochenta [o**chen**ta]
90	noventa [no**ben**ta]
100	cien [s-**yen**]

120	ciento veinte [s-**yen**to b**ayn**teh]
200	doscientos, doscientas [dos-**yen**tos]
300	trescientos, trescientas [tres-**yen**tos]
400	cuatrocientos, cuatrocientas [kwatros-**yen**tos]
500	quinientos, quinientas [keen-**yen**tos]
600	seiscientos, seiscientas [says-**yen**tos]
700	setecientos, setecientas [setes-**yen**tos]
800	ochocientos, ochocientas [ochos-**yen**tos]
900	novecientos, novecientas [nobes-**yen**tos]
1,000	mil
2,000	dos mil
5,000	cinco mil [**seen**ko]
10,000	diez mil [d-**yes**]
1,000,000	un millón [meel-**yon**]

When **uno** is used with a masculine noun, the final **-o** is dropped:

un carro
oon karo
a/one car

una is used with feminine nouns:

una bicicleta
oona beeseek**le**ta
a/one bike

With multiples of a hundred, the **-as** ending is used with feminine nouns:

trescientos hombres
tres-y**e**ntos **o**mb-res
300 men

quinientas mujeres
keen-y**e**ntas mooн**ai**r-es
500 women

Ordinals

1st	primero	[preem**ai**ro]
2nd	seg**u**ndo	
3rd	tercero	[tairs**ai**ro]
4th	cuarto	[**kw**arto]
5th	quinto	[**keen**to]
6th	sexto	[**s**esto]
7th	s**é**ptimo	
8th	octavo	[**o**ktabo]
9th	noveno	[nob**e**no]
10th	d**é**cimo	[**d**eseemo]

Basic Phrases

yes
sí

no
no

OK
bueno
bweno

hello!/hi!
¡hola!
ola

good morning
buenos días
bwenos

good evening
buenas tardes
bwenas

good night
buenas noches
noches

goodbye/see you
hasta luego
asta lwego

please
por favor
fabor

yes please
sí, por favor

thanks, thank you
gracias
gras-yas

no thanks, no thank you
no gracias

thank you very much
muchas gracias
moochas

don't mention it
no hay de qué
ī deh keh

how do you do?
¡mucho gusto!
moocho

how are you?
¿cómo le va?
leh

fine, thanks
bien gracias
b-yen gras-yas

nice to meet you
encantado de conocerle
deh konosairleh

excuse me
(to get past) con permiso
(to get attention) ¡por favor!
fabor

(I'm) sorry
disculpe
deeskoolpeh

sorry?/pardon (me)?
(didn't understand) ¿mande?
mandeh

what did you say?
¿qué dijo?
keh dee**H**o

I see/I understand
entiendo
ent-**y**endo

I don't understand
no entiendo

do you speak English?
¿habla inglés?
abla

I don't speak Spanish
no hablo español
ablo espan-**yo**l

could you speak more slowly?
¿podría hablar mas lento?
abl**a**r

could you repeat that?
¿puede repetir eso?
pw**e**deh

could you write it down?
¿puede escribírmelo?

I'd like a ...
quisiera un/una ...
kees-y**ai**ra

I'd like to ...
me gustaría ...
meh

can I have ...?
¿me da ...?

how much is it?
¿cuánto vale?
kw**a**nto b**a**leh

cheers!
(<u>toast</u>) ¡salud!
sal**oo**

it is ...
es ...; está ...

where is it?
¿dónde está?
d**o**ndeh

where are the ...?
¿dónde están los/las ...?

how far is it to ...?
¿cuánto hay de aquí a ...?
kw**a**nto ī deh ak**ee**

is it far?
¿queda lejos?
k**e**da le**H**os

how long does it take?
¿cuánto dura?
kw**a**nto

at what time ...?
¿a qué hora ...?
keh **o**ra

when is ...?
cuándo es ...?
kw**a**ndo

Conversion Tables

1 centimetre = 0.39 inches	1 inch = 2.54 cm
1 metre = 39.37 inches = 1.09 yards	1 foot = 30.48 cm
1 kilometre = 0.62 miles = 5/8 mile	1 yard = 0.91 m
	1 mile = 1.61 km

km	1	2	3	4	5	10	20	30	40	50	100
miles	0.6	1.2	1.9	2.5	3.1	6.2	12.4	18.6	24.8	31.0	62.1

miles	1	2	3	4	5	10	20	30	40	50	100
km	1.6	3.2	4.8	6.4	8.0	16.1	32.2	48.3	64.4	80.5	161

1 gram = 0.035 ounces	1 kilo = 1000 g = 2.2 pounds		

g	100	250	500	1 oz = 28.35 g
oz	3.5	8.75	17.5	1 lb = 0.45 kg

kg	0.5	1	2	3	4	5	6	7	8	9	10
lb	1.1	2.2	4.4	6.6	8.8	11.0	13.2	15.4	17.6	19.8	22.0

kg	20	30	40	50	60	70	80	90	100
lb	44	66	88	110	132	154	176	198	220

lb	0.5	1	2	3	4	5	6	7	8	9	10	20
kg	0.2	0.5	0.9	1.4	1.8	2.3	2.7	3.2	3.6	4.1	4.5	9.0

1 litre = 1.75 UK pints / 2.13 US pints

1 UK pint = 0.57 l	1 UK gallon = 4.55 l
1 US pint = 0.47 l	1 US gallon = 3.79 l

centigrade / Celsius $°C = (°F - 32) \times 5/9$

°C	-5	0	5	10	15	18	20	25	30	36.8	38
°F	23	32	41	50	59	64	68	77	86	98.4	100.4

Fahrenheit $°F = (°C \times 9/5) + 32$

°F	23	32	40	50	60	65	70	80	85	98.4	101
°C	-5	0	4	10	16	18	21	27	29	36.8	38.3

English

→

Spanish

A

a, an* un [oon], una [oona]
about: about 20 unos veinte
  it's about 5 o'clock son
  aproximadamente las cinco
  [aprokseemadamenteh]
  a film about Mexico una
  película sobre México
  [sobreh]
above ... arriba de ... [arreeba
  deh]
abroad en el extranjero
  [estranHairo]
absolutely! (I agree) ¡claro!
accelerator el acelerador
  [aselairador]
accept aceptar [aseptar]
accident el accidente
  [akseedenteh]
  there's been an accident
  hubo un accidente [oobo]
accommodation alojamiento
  [aloHam-yento]
  see room and hotel
accurate exacto
ache el dolor
  my back aches me duele la
  espalda [meh dweleh]
across: across the road al
  otro lado de la calle [ka-yeh]
adapter el adaptador
address la dirección [deereeks-
  yon]
  what's your address? ¿cuál
  es su dirección? [kwal]

Addresses are frequently
written using just the
street name and number,
for example **Doctores 83**;
sometimes the names of the streets
themselves are numbers, which can
be confusing – although if this is the
case the word **calle**, which means
street, will usually be included.
Avenida, **Calzada** and **Paseo** are
common names for streets, and you
may sometimes see the words
callejón (lane, alley) and **cerrada**
(cul-de-sac). An address may be
written like this: **Hidalgo, 39, 8o 2a**
meaning number 39, Hidalgo Street,
8th floor, apartment 2. You might
also see **planta baja** (PB), meaning
ground floor, **sótano** (basement) or
even **azotea** (roof). In some towns,
streets may be laid out on a grid and
have **Ote.** (**Oriente** east), **Pte.**
(**Poniente** west), **Nte.** (**Norte** north)
or **Sur** (south) added to the street
name to show which side of two
central dividing streets it is on. A
typical address is as follows:

Sr. José Gómez Ruiz
Tacubaya, 38, 4o 2a
Mexico D.F.
2P 00020

address book la libreta de
  direcciones [deh deereeks-
  yon-es]
admission charge la entrada
adult el/la adulto [adoolto],
  el/la persona mayor [mī-yor]

advance: in advance por adelantado

aeroplane el avión [ab-yon]

after después (de) [despwes (deh)]

after you pase Usted [paseh oosteh]

after lunch después de comer

afternoon la tarde [tardeh]

in the afternoon por la tarde

this afternoon esta tarde

aftershave el aftershave

aftersun cream la crema para después del sol [despwes]

afterwards luego [lwego]

again otra vez [bes]

against contra

age la edad [eda]

ago: a week ago hace una semana [aseh]

an hour ago hace una hora

agree: I agree de acuerdo [deh akwairdo]

AIDS el SIDA [seeda]

air el aire [īreh]

by air en avión [ab-yon]

air-conditioned con clima artificial [arteefees-yal]

air-conditioning el aire acondicionado [īreh akondees-yonado]

airmail: by airmail por avión [ab-yon]

airmail envelope el sobre aéreo [sobreh a-aireh-o]

airplane el avión [ab-yon]

airport el aeropuerto [īropwairto]

to the airport, please al aeropuerto, por favor [fabor]

airport bus el camión del aeropuerto [kam-yon]

aisle seat el asiento de pasillo [as-yento deh pasee-yo]

alarm clock el despertador

alcohol el alcohol [alkol]

alcoholic alcohólico

all: all the boys todos los chicos

all the girls todas las chicas

all of it todo

all of them todos

that's all, thanks eso es todo, gracias [gras-yas]

allergic: I'm allergic to ... tengo alergia a ... [alairHee-a]

alligator el caimán [kiman]

allowed: is it allowed? ¿se permite? [seh pairmeeteh]

all right! ¡bueno! [bweno]

I'm all right estoy bien [b-yen]

are you all right? (fam) ¿estás bien?

(pol) ¿se encuentra bien? [seh enkwentra]

almond la almendra

almost casi

alone solo

alphabet el alfabeto

a a	g Heh
b beh larga	h acheh
c seh	i ee
ch cheh	j Hota
d deh	k ka
e eh	l eleh
f efeh	m emeh

n **e**neh	t teh
ñ **e**n-yeh	u oo
o 0	v beh **chee**ka
p peh	w **oo**beh
q koo	x e**kees**
r **ai**rreh	y ee gr-**ye**ga
s **e**seh	z **se**ta

already ya

also también [tamb-**yen**]

although aunque [a-**oon**keh]

altogether del todo

always siempre [s-**yem**preh]

am*: I am soy; est**oy**

a.m.: at seven a.m. a las siete de la mañana [deh la man-**ya**na]

amazing (surprising) increíble [eenkreh-**ee**bleh]
(very good) extraordinario [estra-ordeen**ar**-yo]

ambulance la ambulancia [amboo**lans**-ya]
call an ambulance! ¡llame a una ambulancia! [**ya**meh]

 Most phone booths give the number for the local Red Cross (**Cruz Roja**).

America Estados Unidos

American (adj) norteamericano [norteh-amaireek**a**no]
I'm American (man/woman) soy norteamericano/ norteamericana

among entre [**en**treh]

amount la cantidad [kanteed**a**]
(money) la suma

amp: a 13-amp fuse el fusible de trece amperios [foos**ee**bleh deh – amp**ai**ree-os]

and y [ee]

angry enojado [eno**Ha**do]

animal el animal

ankle el tobillo [tob**ee**-yo]

anniversary (wedding) el aniversario de boda [anee-bairsar-yo deh]

annoy: this man's annoying me este hombre me está molestando [esteh **o**mbreh meh]

annoying molesto

another otro
can we have another room? ¿puede darnos otro cuarto? [pwedeh – kw**ar**to]
another beer, please otra cerveza, por favor [fab**or**]

antibiotics los antibióticos [anteeb-y**o**teekos]

antifreeze el anticongelante [anteekon**He**lanteh]

antihistamines los antihistamínicos [antee-eestam**ee**-neekos]

antique: is it an antique? ¿es antiguo? [ant**ee**gwo]

antique shop la tienda de antigüedades [t-**yen**da deh anteegwed**a**d-es]

antiseptic el antiséptico

any: have you got any bread/tomatoes? ¿tiene pan/jitomates? [t-**yen**eh]
do you have any? ¿tiene?
sorry, I don't have any lo

siento, no tengo [s-yento]
anybody cualquiera [kwalk-yaira]
   does anybody speak English? ¿habla alguien inglés? [abla alg-yen eeng-les]
   there wasn't anybody there (allí) no había nadie [(a-yee) no abee-a nad-yeh]
anything algo
   (negative) nada

dialogues

anything else? ¿algo más?
nothing else, thanks nada más, gracias [gras-yas]

would you like anything to drink? ¿quiere algo de beber? [k-yaireh – deh bebair]
I don't want anything, thanks no quiero nada, gracias [k-yairo]

apart from aparte de [aparteh deh]
apartment el departamento, el piso
appendicitis la apendicitis [apendeeseetees]
appetizer la botana
aperitif el aperitivo [apereeteebo]
apologize: I apologize disculpe [deeskoolpeh]
apology la disculpa
apple la manzana [mansana]
appointment la cita [seeta]

dialogue

good afternoon, sir, how can I help you? buenas tardes, señor, ¿en qué puedo servirle? [bwenas tard-es sen-yor, en keh pwedo sairbeerleh]
I'd like to make an appointment quisiera hacer cita [kees-yaira asair seeta]
what time would you like? ¿a qué hora le conviene? [keh ora leh konb-yeneh]
three o'clock a las tres
I'm afraid that's not possible, is four o'clock all right? lamento que no será posible, ¿está bien a las cuatro? [keh no saira poseebleh – b-yen]
yes, that will be fine sí, está bien
the name was ...? ¿su nombre ...? [nombreh]

apricot el chabacano, el damasco
April abril
are*: we are somos; estamos
   you are (fam) eres [air-es]; estás
   (pol) es; está
   they are son; están
area la zona [sona]
area code el prefijo [prefeeHo]
arm el brazo [braso]
arrange: will you arrange it for

us? ¿nos lo organiza Usted? [organeesa oosteh]

arrival la llegada [yegada]

arrive llegar [yegar]

when do we arrive? ¿cuándo llegamos? [kwando yegamos]

has my fax arrived yet? ¿llegó ya mi fax? [yego]

we arrived today llegamos hoy [yegamos oy]

art el arte [arteh]

art gallery la galería de arte [galeree-a deh]

artist (man/woman) el pintor, la pintora

as: as big as tan grande como

as soon as possible lo más pronto posible [poseebleh]

ashtray el cenicero [seneesairo]

ask preguntar

to ask for pedir

I didn't ask for this no pedí esto

could you ask him to ...? ¿puede decirle que ...? [pwedeh deseerleh keh]

asleep: she's asleep está dormida

aspirin la aspirina

asthma el asma

astonishing increíble [eenkreh-eebleh]

at: at the hotel en el hotel

at the station en la estación

at six o'clock a las seis

at Pedro's en casa de Pedro [deh]

athletics el atletismo

Atlantic Ocean el Océano Atlántico [oseh-ano]

attractive atractivo [atrakteebo]

aubergine la berenjena [berenHena]

August agosto

aunt la tía

Australia Australia [owstral-ya]

Australian (adj) australiano

I'm Australian (man/woman) soy australiano/australiana

automatic automático [owtomateeko]

automatic teller el cajero automático [kaHairo]

autumn el otoño [oton-yo]

in the autumn en otoño

avenue la avenida [abeneeda]

average (ordinary) mediano [med-yano]

(not good) regular [regoolar]

on average por término medio [tairmeeno med-yo]

avocado el aguacate [agwakateh]

awake: is he awake? ¿está despierto? [desp-yairto]

away: go away! ¡lárguese! [largeseh]

he's gone away se ha ido fuera [seh a eedo fwaira]

is it far away? ¿está lejos? [leHos]

awful horrible [oreebleh]

axle el eje [eHeh]

Aztec (adj) azteca [asteka]

B

baby el bebé [beh-**beh**]
baby food la comida de bebé
[deh]
baby's bottle el biberón [bee-
bairon]
baby-sitter la niñera [neen-
yaira]
back (of body) la espalda
(back part) la parte de atrás
[**parteh deh**]
at the back en la parte de
atrás
can I have my money back?
¿me devuelve el dinero?
[meh debwelbeh el deenairo]
to come/go back regresar
backache el dolor de espalda
[deh]
bacon el jamón [Hamon], el
tocino [tos**ee**no]
bad malo
a bad headache un fuerte
dolor de cabeza [fwairteh –
deh kabesa]
badly mal
(injured) gravemente
[grabementeh]
bag la bolsa
(handbag) el bolso
(suitcase) la maleta, la petaca
baggage el equipaje
[ekeepaHeh]
baggage check la consigna
[kons**ee**gna], la paquetería
[paketair**ee**-a]
baggage claim la recogida de

equipajes [rekoHeeda deh
ekeepaH-es]
bakery la panadería
[panadair**ee**-a]
balcony el balcón
a room with a balcony un
cuarto con balcón [kwarto]
bald calvo [kalbo]
ball (large) la pelota, el balón
(small) la bola
ballet el ballet
banana el plátano
band (musical) la orquesta
[ork**e**sta]
bandage la venda [benda]
Bandaid® la tirita
bandit el bandido

You should be aware of
the danger of bandits
when driving in Mexico,
especially in a foreign vehicle.
Sometimes robbers pose as police
or hitchhikers so be wary of offering
a lift or a helping hand. On the other
hand, there are plenty of legitimate
police checkpoints along the main
roads, where you must stop. The US
embassy in Mexico advises never
driving after dark.

bank (money) el banco

The easiest kind of
foreign currency to
change in Mexico is US
dollars; US dollar travellers' cheques
are the second easiest to exchange.
Canadian dollars and other major

50

international currencies such as sterling and Deutschmarks are harder to exchange and sometimes refused. In general it is usually only the larger branches of the main banks (and some other banks in main tourist resorts) that are willing to change anything other than dollars.

Banks are generally open Monday to Friday from 9. 30 a.m. until 1.30 p.m., though sometimes with shorter hours for exchange. The commission varies from bank to bank but the exchange rate is the same, fixed daily by the government. Cashpoints/ATMs are becoming more and more common. In some border towns, they pay out in US dollars. **Casas de cambio** (bureaux de change) are open longer hours and at weekends and have varying exchange rates and commission charges. Many hotels, shops and restaurants in tourist areas are prepared to change dollars or accept them as payment but the rate will be very low.

bank account la cuenta bancaria [kwenta]
bar el bar
  a bar of chocolate una barra de chocolate [deh chokolateh]

The least heavy atmosphere is in hotel bars, tourist areas, or

anything that describes itself as a 'ladies' bar'. Traditional **cantinas** are for serious and excessive drinking, have a thoroughly threatening, macho atmosphere, and there's almost inevitably a sign above the door prohibiting entry to 'women, members of the armed forces and anyone in uniform' (**se prohibe la entrada a mujeres, uniformados e integrantes de las fuerzas armadas**). Special bars called **pulquerías** [poolkair**ee**-as] sell **pulque** [**poo**lkeh], a mildly alcoholic milky beer made from cactus, but these too will be male preserves monopolized by serious drinkers.

barber's la peluquería [pelookair**ee**-a]
bargain regatear [regateh-**ar**]

dialogue

> **how much is this?** ¿a cómo está?
> **100 pesos** a cien pesos
> **that's too expensive, how about 50?** es muy caro, ¿me lo deja en cincuen- ta? [mwee – de**Ha**]
> **I'll let you have it for 80** se lo dejo en ochenta [seh lo de**Ho**]
> **can't you reduce it a bit more, to 70 ?** ¿me lo rebaja un poco más, en setenta? [re**ba**ha]

51

that's the lowest I'll go es lo último
OK de acuerdo [deh akwairdo]

If you're buying handicrafts in markets you're expected to bargain fiercely. But don't try bargaining in supermarkets. Most shops have fixed prices and don't take kindly to being offered half (though you might get a small discount), while even in markets produce and household goods usually have their prices clearly marked.
Bargaining and haggling are very much a matter of personal style, highly dependent on your command of Spanish but to some extent on experience. Even if you intend to buy, never show the least enthusiasm or interest: walking away will often cut the price dramatically. Decide what you want in advance, find out what a reasonable price would be and decide how much you are prepared to pay. If you start to haggle then it is assumed that you genuinely want to buy.

baseball el béisbol [baysbol]
basement el sótano
basket la canasta
 (in shop) la cesta [sesta]
bath el baño [ban-yo], la tina
 can I have a bath? ¿puedo

bañarme? [pwedo ban-yarmeh]
bathroom el cuarto de baño [kwarto]
 with a private bathroom con baño privado [preebado]
bath towel la toalla de baño [to-a-ya deh]
battery la pila
 (car) la batería [batairee-a]
bay la bahía [ba-ee-a]
be* ser [sair]; estar
beach la playa [plī-ya]
 on the beach en la playa

Mexico has thousands of miles of wonderful beaches, on many of which you can camp if you want to. For your own safety, however, you should check with locals before camping anywhere, and avoid very isolated situations. Some of the bigger resorts like **Acapulco**, **Puerto Vallarta** or **Cancún** will have stretches of beach to which access is restricted, but by and large the beaches are open and accessible.
see **campsite**

beach umbrella la sombrilla [sombree-ya]
beans los frijoles [freeHol-es]
 runner beans los ejotes [eHot-es]
 broad beans las habas [abas]
beard la barba
beautiful lindo
because porque [porkeh]

because of ... debido a ...
bed la cama
  I'm going to bed now me voy a acostar ahora [meh boy – a-**o**ra]
bed and breakfast cuarto y desayuno [k**wa**rto ee desī-**yoo**no]
bedroom la recámara
beef la carne de res [**ka**rneh deh]
beer la cerveza [sair**be**sa]
  two beers, please dos cervezas, por favor [fa**bor**]

Mexican beer is excellent. Most is light, lager-style beer, fine examples being **Bohémia**, **Superior**, **Dos Equis** and **Tecate** (the last normally served with lime and salt); but you can also get dark beers of which the best are **Negra Modelo** and **Tres Equis**, or the fine **Nochebuena** (literally: Christmas Eve) which is normally only produced around the year's end. Locally-bottled beers, such as **Sol** on the east coast or **Pacífico** on the west, are often even better than the national labels. Beer is also sold in most shops, supermarkets and, cheapest of all, **agencias** (agents for just one brand). When buying from these places, it is normal to pay a deposit and bring your empties back to the same store.

Some useful terms:
cerveza clara light lager-style beer

cerveza oscura dark beer
cerveza de barril draught beer
una mediana a bottle of beer

before antes
begin empezar [empe**sar**]
  when does it begin? ¿cuándo empieza? [k**wa**ndo emp-**ye**sa]
beginner el/la principiante [preenseep-**ya**nteh]
beginning: at the beginning al principio [preen**see**p-yo]

behaviour
At heart Mexico is still a conservative, Catholic place and there are obvious ways to avoid hurting local sensibilities, for example: dressing 'decently' in public and covering up in church. It is especially important to be careful in rural areas, where it's unwise even to enter a church without permission, or to take photographs without asking first.

behind atrás
  behind me detrás de mí [deh]
beige beige [baysh]
believe creer [kreh-**air**]
Belize Belice [be**lee**seh]
below abajo [aba**Ho**]
belt el cinturón [seentoo**ron**]
bend (in road) la curva [**koo**rba]
berth (on ship) el camarote [kama**ro**teh]

beside: beside the ... al lado
  de la ... [deh]
best el mejor [meHor]
better mejor
  are you feeling better? ¿se
  siente mejor? [seh s-yenteh]
between entre [entreh]
beyond más allá [a-ya]
bicycle la bicicleta [beeseekle-
  ta]
big grande [grandeh]
  too big demasiado grande
  [demas-yado]
  it's not big enough no es lo
  suficientemente grande
  [soofees-yentementeh]
big game fishing la pesca
  mayor [mī-yor]
bike la bicicleta [beeseekleta]
  (motorbike) la moto
bikini el bikini
bill la cuenta [kwenta]
  (US: banknote) el billete [bee-
  yeteh]
  could I have the bill, please?
  me pasa la cuenta, por
  favor [meh – fabor]
bin el bote de la basura
  [boteh deh]
bin liners las bolsas de basura
binding (ski) la atadura
bird el pájaro [paHaro]
biro® el bolígrafo
birthday el cumpleaños
  [koompleh-an-yos]
  happy birthday! ¡feliz
  cumpleaños! [felees]
biscuit la galleta [ga-yeta]
bit: a little bit un poquito

[pokeeto]
  a big bit un pedazo grande
  [pedaso grandeh]
  a bit of ... un pedazo de ...
  [deh]
  a bit expensive un poco
  caro
bite (by insect) la picadura
  (by dog) la mordedura
bitter (taste etc) amargo
black negro [neh-gro]
black coffee el café
  americano [kafeh]
  (strong) el café solo
blanket la cobija [kobeeHa], la
  frazada [frasada]
bleach (for toilet) la lejía [leHee-
  a]
bless you! ¡Jesús! [Hesoos]
blind ciego [s-yego]
blinds las persianas [pers-
  yanas]
blister la ampolla [ampo-ya]
blocked (road, pipe) bloqueado
  [blokeh-ado]
  (sink) atascado
block (city) la cuadra [kwadra]
  block of flats el edificio de
  departamentos [edeefees-yo
  deh]
blond guero [gwairo]
blood la sangre [sangreh]
  high blood pressure la
  tensión alta [tens-yon]
blouse la blusa
blow-dry (verb) secar a
  mano
  I'd like a cut and blow-dry
  quisiera un corte y un

marcado [kees-yaira oon korteh ee]
blue azul [asool]
blusher el colorete [koloreteh]
boarding house la pensión [pens-yon], la hostería [ostairee-a]
boarding pass la tarjeta de embarque [tarHeta deh embarkeh]
boat el barco
body el cuerpo [kwairpo]
boiled egg el huevo pasado (por agua) [webo pasado por agwa]
boiler la caldera [kaldaira]
bone el hueso [weso]
bonnet (of car) el capó, el cofre [kofreh]
book el libro
(verb) reservar [resairbar]
can I book a seat? ¿puedo reservar un asiento? [pwedo – as-yento]

dialogue

I'd like to book a table for two quisiera reservar una mesa para dos personas [kees-yaira]
what time would you like it booked for? ¿para qué hora la quiere? [keh ora la k-yaireh]
half past seven las siete y media
that's fine de acuerdo [deh akwairdo]

and your name? ¿y su nombre ...? [ee soo nombreh]

bookshop, bookstore la librería [leebrairee-a]
boot (footwear) la bota
(of car) la maleta, la cajuela [kaHwela]
border (of country) la frontera [frontaira]
bored: I'm bored (said by man/woman) estoy aburrido/aburrida
boring aburrido, pesado
born: I was born in Manchester nací en Manchester [nasee]
I was born in 1960 nací en mil novecientos sesenta
borrow pedir prestado
may I borrow ...? ¿puede prestarme ...? [pwedeh prestarmeh]
both los dos
both... and... tanto ... como ...
bother: sorry to bother you siento molestarlo [s-yento]
bottle la botella [boteh-ya], el frasco
a bottle of house red una botella de tinto de la casa [deh]
bottle-opener el abrebotellas [abreboteh-yas]
bottom (of person) el trasero [trasairo], el culo
at the bottom of the ...

(hill/road) al pie del/de la ...
[p-yeh del/deh]

(sea) al fondo de ...

box la caja [ka**Ha**]

box office la taquilla [tak**ee**-
ya], la boletería [boletair**ee**-a]

boy el chico, el joven
[**Ho**ven], el chavo [**cha**bo]

boyfriend el novio [n**ob**-yo]

bra el brassiere [bras-y**air**]

bracelet la pulsera [pools**ai**ra]

brake el freno

brandy el coñac [kon-**yak**]

bread el pan

  white bread el pan blanco

  brown bread el pan de
  centeno [deh sent**e**no]

  wholemeal bread el pan
  integral [eentegr**al**]

break (verb) romper [romp**air**]

  I've broken the ... rompí
  el ...

  I think I've broken my ... creo
  que me he roto el ... [kr**eh**-o
  keh meh eh]

break down descomponerse
[deskompon**air**seh]

  I've broken down se me ha
  descompuesto el carro [seh
  meh a deskomp**we**sto]

breakdown (mechanical) la
descompostura

If you have a breakdown,
there is a free highway
mechanics service known
as the **Angeles Verdes** (Green
Angels). As well as patrolling all
major routes looking for stranded

motorists, they can be reached by
phone (AT 02-684-9715/9761) and
speak English. They don't operate
inside the capital; there you should
call the AAM (AA or AAA equivalent).
Should you have a minor accident,
try to come to some arrangement
with the other party – involving the
police will only make matters worse
and Mexican drivers are anxious
to do the same. Also, if you witness
an accident, don't get involved –
witnesses can get locked up along
with those responsible to prevent
them leaving before the case comes
up.

breakdown service el
servicio de grúa [serb**ee**s-yo
deh gr**oo**-a]

breakfast el desayuno [desï-
y**oo**no]

break-in: I've had a break-in
entraron en mi casa a robar

breast el pecho

breathe respirar

breeze la brisa

bribe la mordida

bridge (over river) el puente
[p**wen**teh]

brief breve [br**eb**eh]

briefcase la cartera [kart**ai**ra]

bright (light etc) brillante [bree-
y**an**teh]

  bright red rojo vivo [r**o**Ho
  b**ee**bo]

brilliant (idea, person) brillante
[bree-y**an**teh]

bring traer [tra-**air**]

I'll bring it back later lo devolveré luego [debolbaireh lwego]

Britain Gran Bretaña [bretan-ya]

British británico

I'm British (man/woman) soy británico/británica

brochure el folleto [fo-yeto]

broken roto

bronchitis la bronquitis [bronkeetees]

brooch el broche [brocheh]

broom la escoba

brother el hermano [airmano]

brother-in-law el cuñado [koon-yado]

brown color café [kafeh]

brown hair el pelo castaño [kastan-yo]

brown eyes los ojos castaños [oHos]

bruise el moretón

brush (for hair, cleaning) el cepillo [sepee-yo]
(artist's) el pincel [peensel]

bucket el cubo [koobo], el balde [baldeh]

buffet car el vagón–restaurante [bagon-restowranteh]

buggy (for child) el carrito de niño [deh neen-yo]

building el edificio [edeefees-yo]

bulb (light bulb) el foco

bull el toro

bullfight la corrida

bullring la plaza de toros [plasa deh]

bumper la defensa

bunk la litera [leetaira]

bureau de change el cambio [kamb-yo], la casa de cambio [deh]
see bank

burglary el robo con allanamiento de morada [a-yanam-yento]

burn la quemadura [kemadoo-ra]
(verb) quemar [kemar]

burnt: this is burnt está quemado [kemado]

burst: a burst pipe la cañería rota [kan-yairee-a]

bus el camión [kam-yon]
(long-distance) el autobús [owtoboos]

what number bus is it to ...? ¿qué número tomo para ...? [keh noomairo]

when is the next bus to ...? ¿cuándo sale el próximo camión/autobús para ...? [kwando saleh]

what time is the last bus? ¿a qué hora sale el último camión? [keh ora – oolteemo]

could you let me know when we get there? ¿puede avisarme cuando llegamos [pwedeh abeesarmeh kwando yegamos]

Within Mexico, long-distance buses (called **camiones** or **autobuses**) are by far the most common and efficient form of transport. There are basically two classes of bus, first (**primera**) and second (**segunda**), though on major long-distance routes, there's often little to differentiate the two. The main differences are that second-class buses make more stops and first-class buses are more expensive. In addition there are luxury buses with comfortable seats and air-conditioning – particularly on the long-distance routes from the US border. These are called **pullman**. Most large towns have a 'central' bus station (**central camionera** or **central de autobuses**), which is often a long way from the town centre.

Often the main terminals in towns are for local bus lines only. Wherever possible, you should reserve your seat in advance at the terminal or the bus company office. If you cannot book, you may be able to stand on second-class buses, but most first-class buses will not take standing passengers. It's worth remembering, too, that while trains are quite leisurely about times, buses almost always depart exactly on time.

Public transport within towns and cities is always plentiful and inexpensive, though also very crowded and not very comfortable. You may need to shout loudly to the driver if you want him to stop (the cry is ¡**bajan!** [baHan] – 'people

getting off'). Usually, you'll be relying on buses, although Mexico City has a vast and excellent **metro** system and there are smaller metros in Guadalajara and Monterrey.
see **taxi**

dialogue

does this bus go to ...?
¿este camión va a ...?
[**e**steh kam-y**o**n ba]
no, you need a number ...
no, tiene que tomar el ...
[t-y**e**neh keh]

business el negocio [neg**o**s-yo]
bus station la central camionera [s**e**ntral kam-yon**ai**ra], la estación de auto-buses [estas-y**o**n deh owtob**oo**s-es]
bus stop la parada de camión [kam-y**o**n]
bust el pecho
busy (restaurant etc) concurrido
I'm busy tomorrow (said by man/woman) est**o**y ocup**a**do/ocup**a**da mañana [man-y**a**na]
but pero [p**ai**ro]
butcher's la carnicería [karneesair**ee**-a]
butter la mantequilla [mante-k**ee**-ya]
button el bot**ó**n
buy (verb) compr**a**r

where can I buy ...? ¿dónde puedo comprar ...? [dondeh pwedo]

buzzard el buitre [bweetreh]

by: by bus/car en camión/ carro

written by ... escrito por ...

by the window junto a la ventana [Hoonto]

by the sea a orillas del mar [oree-yas]

by Thursday para el jueves

bye! ¡hasta luego! [asta lwego]

C

cabbage el repollo [repo-yo]

cabin (on ship) el camarote [kamaroteh]

cable car el teleférico [telefaireeko], el funicular [fooneekoolar]

cactus el cacto

café la cafetería [kafetairee-a] see **restaurant**

cagoule el chubasquero [choobaskairo]

cake el pastel

cake shop la pastelería [pastelairee-a]

call (verb) llamar [yamar] (to phone) llamar (por teléfono)

what's it called? ¿cómo se llama ? [seh yama]

he/she is called ... se llama ...

please call the doctor llame

al médico, por favor [yameh – fabor]

please give me a call at 7.30 a.m. tomorrow por favor, llámeme mañana a las siete y media de la mañana [yamameh man-yana]

please ask him to call me por favor, dígale que me llame [deegaleh keh meh yameh]

call back: I'll call back later regresaré más tarde [regresareh mas tardeh] (phone back) volveré a llamar [bolbaireh a yamar]

call round: I'll call round tomorrow mañana paso

camcorder la videocámara [beedeh-o-kamara]

camera la cámara

camera shop la tienda fotográfica [t-yenda]

camp (verb) acampar

can we camp here? ¿se puede acampar aquí? [seh pwedeh – akee]

camping gas canister la bomba de butano [deh bootano]

Kerosene or paraffin oil for camping stoves is called **petróleo para lámparas** and can normally be bought from an **expendio** or **despacho de petróleo** or from the **tlapaleria** (hardware store); it cannot be bought at petrol stations. Camping gas is widely available.

campsite el camping

There is not usually much alternative to staying in hotels. Camping is easy enough if you are hiking in the back country or happy to crash on the beach. However, robberies are common, especially in places with a lot of tourists. There are few organized campsites and those that do exist are first and foremost trailer parks. In a lot of less official campsites, you can rent a hammock and a place to sling it. Beach huts (**cabañas** [kaban-yas]) are found at the more rustic, backpacker-oriented beach resorts, and sometimes inland. Usually just a wooden or palm-frond shack with a hammock or hooks to hang your own, they often do not have electricity. In less touristy areas that don't have cabañas, you should still be able to sling a hammock somewhere (probably the local bar or restaurant).

can la lata
 a can of beer una lata de cerveza [deh sairbesa]
can*: can you ...? ¿puede ...? [pwedeh]
 can I have ...? ¿me da ...? [meh]
 I can't ... no puedo ... [pwedo]
Canada el Canadá
Canadian (adj) canadiense

[kanad-yenseh]
 I'm Canadian soy canadiense
canal el canal
cancel cancelar [kanselar]
candies los dulces [dool-ses]
candle la vela [bela]
canoe la canoa
canoeing el piragüismo [peeragweesmo]
can-opener el abrelatas
canyon el cañón [kan-yon], la cañada [kan-yada]
cap (hat) la gorra
 (of bottle) el tapón
car el carro, el auto [owto], el automóvil
 by car en carro
caravan la caravana [karabana]
caravan site el camping
carburettor el carburador
card (birthday etc) la tarjeta [tarнeta]
 here's my (business) card aquí tiene mi tarjeta (de visita) [akee t-yeneh – deh beeseeta]
cardigan la chamarra
cardphone el teléfono de tarjeta [deh tarнeta]
careful cauteloso [kowteloso]
 be careful! ¡cuidado! [kweedado]
caretaker el portero [portairo]
car ferry el ferry, el transbordador de carros [deh]
car hire el alquiler de carros [alkeelair deh]
 see car rental
car park el estacionamiento

[estas-**yo**nam-**ye**nto]

carpet la alfombra, el tapete [ta**pe**teh]

car rental el alquiler de carros [alkee**lair** deh]

Renting a car avoids many of the problems associated with driving in Mexico. Local operators normally charge less than the well-known chains. Check the rates carefully and make sure that insurance, tax and mileage are included. Weekly rates are usually better value and unlimited mileage is almost always a bargain. For shorter distances, mopeds and motorbikes are also available in most resorts.
see **driving** and **rent**

carriage (of train) el vagón [ba**gon**]

carrier bag la bolsa de plástico [deh]

carrot la zanahoria [sana-**or**-ya]

carry llevar [ye**bar**]

carry-cot el capazo [ka**pa**so]

carton la caja [**ka**Ha]

carwash el lavado de carros [la**ba**do deh]

case (suitcase) la maleta

cash el dinero [dee**nai**ro], la plata

to pay (in) cash pagar en efectivo [efek**tee**bo], pagar al contado

will you cash this for me? ¿podría hacerme efectivo un cheque? [a**sair**meh – **che**keh]

see **bank** and **cheque**

cash desk la caja [**ka**Ha]

cash dispenser el cajero automático [ka**Hai**ro owto**ma**teeko]

cassette la cassette [ka**set**]

cassette recorder el cassette

castle el castillo [kas**tee**-yo]

casualty department emergencias [emair**Hen**s-yas]

cat el gato

catch (verb) agarrar

where do we catch the bus to ...? ¿dónde se toma el camión para ...? [**don**deh seh]

cathedral la catedral

Catholic (adj) católico

cauliflower el coliflor

cave la cueva [**kwe**ba]

ceiling el techo

celery el apio [**ap**-yo]

cellar (for wine) la bodega

cellular phone el teléfono celular [seloo**lar**]

cemetery el cementerio [semen**tair**-yo], el panteón [panteh-**on**]

centigrade* centígrado [sen**tee**grado]

centimetre* el centímetro [sen**tee**metro]

central central [sen**tral**]

Central America Centroamérica [sentro-a**mai**reeka]

Central American (adj) centroamericano

central heating la
  calefacción central [kalefaks-
  yon sentral]
centre el centro [sentro]
  how do we get to the city
  centre? ¿cómo se llega al
  centro? [seh yega]
cereals los cereales [sereh-al-
  es]
certainly por supuesto
  [soopwesto]
  certainly not de ninguna
  manera [deh neengoona
  manaira]
chair la silla [see-ya]
champagne el champán
change (loose) el suelto
  [swelto]
  (after payment) el vuelto
  [bwelto]
  (verb) cambiar [kamb-yar]
  can I change this for ...?
  ¿puedo cambiar esto
  por ...? [pwedo]
  I don't have any change no
  tengo suelto
  can you give me change for a
  1,000 peso note? ¿puede
  cambiarme un billete de
  mil? [pwedeh kamb-yarmeh oon
  bee-yeteh deh meel]

dialogue

  do we have to change
  (trains)? ¿tenemos que
  hacer correspondencia?
  [keh aser korrespondens-ya]
  yes, change at Xalapa/no

  it's a direct train sí, haga
  trasbordo en Xalapa/no,
  es directo [aga – Halapa]

changed: to get changed
  cambiarse [kamb-yarseh]
chapel la capilla [kapee-ya]
charge (verb) cobrar
charge card see credit card
cheap barato
  do you have anything
  cheaper? ¿tiene algo más
  barato? [t-yeneh]
check (US) el cheque
  [chekeh]
  (US: bill) la cuenta [kwenta]
  see bank and cheque
check (verb) revisar [rebeesar]
  could you check the ...,
  please? ¿puede revisar el
  ..., por favor? [pwedeh – fabor]
check book el libro de
  cheques [deh chek-es]
check-in la facturación
  [faktooras-yon]
check in facturar
  where do we have to check
  in? ¿dónde se factura?
  [dondeh seh]
cheek la mejilla [meHee-ya]
cheerio! ¡hasta luego! [asta
  lwego]
cheers! (toast) ¡salud! [saloo]
cheese el queso [keso]
cheesecake el pay de queso
  [pī deh keso]
chemist's la farmacia
  [farmas-ya]
  see pharmacy

cheque el cheque [chekeh]
do you take cheques?
¿aceptan cheques? [aseptan
chek-es]

Although travellers'
cheques are obviously
safer in case of theft or
loss, it is best to bring some cash in
dollars with you as sometimes you
won't be able to change anything
else. It's a good idea to have a
mixture of denominations, including
some one-dollar bills, and to change
a small amount into pesos before
you leave home. When buying
travellers' cheques you should
also get a mixture of denominations
and stick to the established
names.
see **bank**

cheque book la chequera
[chekaira]
cheque card la tarjeta de
banco [tarHeta deh]
cherry la cereza [sairesa]
(black) la guinda [geenda]
chess el ajedrez [aHed-res]
chest el pecho [pecho]
chewing gum el chicle
[cheekleh]
chicken el pollo [po-yo], la
gallina [ga-yeena]
chickenpox la varicela
[bareesela]
child (male/female) el niño
[neen-yo], la niña
children los niños

Children under 18 require
the permission of both
parents to enter Mexico. If
you are travelling with your child or
children on your own, you will need
a notarized letter from the other
parent giving permission for you to
take the child abroad. When
travelling with children bear in mind
that climate and diet might create
some problems at first but that
children adapt quickly. Mexicans are
generally well disposed towards
kids and there are not many
restrictions on where you take them
other than bars and other obviously
adult places.

child minder la niñera [neen-
yaira]
children's pool la alberca
infantil [albairka eenfanteel]
children's portion la ración
pequeña (para niños) [ras-
yon peken-ya – neen-yos]
chilli el chile [cheeleh]

Chillies are in most kinds
of Mexican food. **Chiles
jalapeños** or **rajas** (strips
of pickled green chillies) are often
on restaurant tables as a garnish.
They are hot, but in the wide
spectrum of Mexican chillies they
are mild compared with, for
example, the small green **chile de
Pekin** or the innocent looking white
chile rubio, whose effects are
brutal. If you want to know if it is hot

ask **¿pica mucho?** [peeka moocho] or **¿es muy picante?** [es mwee peekanteh]. It may still be hot for tourist tastes but it is worth persevering to enjoy Mexico's wonderful cooking. If you do burn, water doesn't really help; try salt on the lips or bread.

chin la barba
china la porcelana [porselana]
Chinese (adj) chino [cheeno]
chips las papas fritas
chocolate el chocolate [chokolateh]
  milk chocolate el chocolate con leche [lecheh]
  plain chocolate el chocolate negro [neh-gro]
  a hot chocolate una taza de chocolate [tasa deh]
choose elegir [eleHeer], escoger [eskoHair]
Christian name el nombre de pila [nombreh deh]
Christmas Navidad [nabeeda]
  Christmas Eve Nochebuena [nocheh-bwena]
  merry Christmas! ¡Felices Pascuas! [felees-es paskwas]
  see **holiday**
church la iglesia [eegles-ya]
cider la sidra
cigar el puro [pooro]
cigarette el cigarro [seegarro]

Mexican brand cigarettes are cheap but generally dark and strong. Most American brands are readily available – there are hundreds of sellers in the street in addition to tobacconists' – but are much more expensive than local brands.

cigarette lighter el mechero [mechairo]
cinema el cine [seeneh]

Cinema is enormously popular in Mexico, particularly in the capital. Cinemas show all the latest Hollywood releases as well as Mexican films, and 'art films' are shown in most towns and cities. Last showings tend to begin at around 9.30 or 10 p.m.

circle el círculo [seerkoolo]
  (in theatre) el anfiteatro [anfeeteh-atro]
city la ciudad [s-yooda]
city centre el centro de la ciudad [sentro deh]
clean (adj) limpio [leemp-yo]
  can you clean these for me? ¿puede limpiarme estos? [pwedeh leemp-yarmeh]
cleaning solution (for contact lenses) el líquido limpiador para las lentillas [leekeedo leemp-yador – lentee-yas]
cleansing lotion la crema limpiadora
clear claro
clever listo
cliff el acantilado

cliff-diving el clavado de acantilado [deh]

climbing el montañismo [montan-**yee**smo]

cling film el plástico de envolver [deh embolb**air**]

clinic la clínica

cloakroom el guardarropa [gwardarr**o**pa]

clock el reloj [rel**o**H]

close (verb) cerrar [serr**ar**]

dialogue

what time do you close?
¿a qué hora cierran? [keh **o**ra s-y**ai**rran]
we close at 8 p.m. on weekdays and 1.30 p.m. on Saturdays cerramos a las ocho de la tarde entre semana y a la una y media los sábados [serr**a**mos – deh la t**a**rdeh entr**eh**]
do you close for lunch?
¿cierra a mediodía?
[s-y**ai**rra]
yes, between 1 and 3.30 p.m. sí, de la una hasta las tres y media de la tarde [deh – **a**sta]

closed cerrado [sairr**a**do]

cloth (fabric) la tela

(for cleaning etc) el trapo

clothes la ropa

clothes line la cuerda para tender [kw**ai**rda para tend**air**]

clothes peg la pinza de la

ropa [p**ee**nsa deh]

cloud la nube [n**oo**beh]

cloudy nublado

clutch el embrague [embr**a**geh]

coach (bus) el autobús [owtob**oo**s]

(on train) el vagón [bag**o**n]

coach station la estación de camiones [estas-y**o**n deh kam-y**o**n-es]

coach trip la excursión (en autobús) [eskoors-y**o**n]

coast la costa

on the coast en la costa

coat (long coat) el abrigo

(jacket) el saco

coathanger la percha [p**ai**rcha]

cockroach la cucaracha [kookar**a**cha]

cocoa el cacao [kak**a**-o]

coconut el coco

code (for phoning) el prefijo [pref**ee**Ho], el código

what's the (dialling) code for Veracruz? ¿cuál es el prefijo de Veracruz? [kwal – deh bairakr**oo**s]

coffee el café [kaf**eh**]

two coffees, please dos cafés, por favor [fab**o**r]

A great deal of coffee is grown in Mexico, and in the growing areas and the coffee houses in the capital, you will be served excellent coffee. If you ask for just café you will be given black coffee. Some useful terms:

café americano weaker, black coffee or instant coffee
café con leche [lecheh] coffee made with milk and no water
café cortado or café con un poquito de leche [pokeeto deh] white coffee
café de olla [oh-ya] coffee stewed in the pot with cinnamon and sugar
café solo or negro black coffee, usually strong and often sweet
Nescafe instant coffee
sin azúcar [asookar] without sugar

coin la moneda
Coke® la Coca-Cola
cold frío
  I'm cold tengo frío
  I have a cold tengo resfriado [resfr-yado]
collapse: he's collapsed se desmayó [seh desmi-yo]
collar el cuello [kweh-yo]
collect recoger [rekoHair]
  I've come to collect ... vine a recoger ... [beeneh]
collect call la llamada por cobrar [yamada]
college la Universidad [ooneebairseeda]
colour el color
  do you have this in other colours? ¿tiene otros colores? [t-yeneh – kolor-es]
colour film la película en color
comb el peine [payneh]
come venir [beneer]

dialogue

where do you come from?
¿de dónde es? [deh dondeh]
I come from Edinburgh
soy de Edimburgo

come back regresar
  I'll come back tomorrow regreso mañana
come in entrar
  come in! ¡pase! [paseh]
comfortable cómodo
compact disc el compact disc
company (business) la compañía [kompan-yee-a]
compartment (on train) el compartimento
compass la brújula [brooHoola]
complain quejarse [keh-Harseh]
complaint la queja [keHa]
  I have a complaint tengo queja
completely completamente [kompletamenteh]
computer la computadora
concert el concierto [kons-yairto]
concussion la conmoción cerebral [konmos-yon sairebral]
conditioner (for hair) el acondicionador de pelo [akondees-yonador deh]
condom el condón
condor el cóndor
conference el congreso
confirm confirmar

congratulations! ¡felicidades! [feleeseedad-es]

connecting flight el vuelo de conexión [bwelo deh koneks-yon]

connection el enlace [enlaseh]

conscious consciente [kons-yenteh]

constipation el estreñimiento [estren-yeem-yento]

consulate el consulado

contact (verb) ponerse en contacto con [ponairseh]

contact lenses las lentes de contacto [lent-es deh], las lentillas [lentee-yas]

contraceptive el anticonceptivo [anteekonsepteebo]

convenient a mano

that's not convenient no conviene [konb-yeneh]

cook (verb) cocinar [koseenar]

not cooked poco hecho [echo]

cooker el horno [orno]

cookie la galleta [ga-yeta]

cooking utensils los utensilios de cocina [ootenseel-yos deh koseena]

cool fresco

cork el corcho

corkscrew el sacacorchos

corner: on the corner en la esquina [eskeena]

in the corner en el rincón

cornflakes los cornflakes

correct (right) correcto

corridor el pasillo [pasee-yo]

cosmetics los cosméticos

cost (verb) costar, valer [balair]

how much does it cost? ¿cuánto vale? [kwanto baleh]

cot la cuna

cotton el algodón

cotton wool el algodón

couch (sofa) el sofá

couchette la litera [leetaira]

cough la tos

cough medicine la medicina para la tos [medeeseena]

could: could you ...? ¿podría ...?

could I have ...? ¿quisiera ...? [kees-yaira]

I couldn't ... no podría ...

country (nation) el país [pa-ees]

(countryside) el campo

countryside el campo

couple (two people) la pareja [pareHa]

a couple of ... un par de ... [deh]

courgette la calabacita [kalabaseeta], el calabacín [kalabaseen]

courier el/la guía turístico [gee-a]

course (main course etc) el plato

of course por supuesto [soopwesto]

of course not! ¡claro que no! [keh]

cousin (male/female) el primo, la prima

cow la vaca [baka]

crab la jaiba [Hiba]
cracker (biscuit) la galleta salada [ga-yeta]
craft shop la tienda de artesanías [t-yenda deh]
crash el accidente [akseedenteh]
(verb) chocar
I've had a crash tuve un accidente [toobeh]
crazy loco
cream la crema
(colour) color crema
creche la guardería infantil [gwardairee-a]
credit card la tarjeta de crédito [tarHeta deh kredeeto]

Major credit cards are widely accepted. Visa and Mastercard are the best; American Express and other charge cards are usually only accepted by expensive places. Credit cards are not accepted in the cheapest hotels and restaurants, or for most bus tickets, but you can use them to get cash advances from banks. You can also use credit cards from home to get cash 24 hours a day from cashpoint/ATM machines in larger towns. Machines are erratic, however, and sometimes debit your account without giving you any cash so keep all receipts for checking. Many cashpoints/ATMs also accept debit cards from the Cirrus and PLUS systems, which enable customers to withdraw money from their accounts back home. You may get preferential exchange rates this way.

dialogue

> **can I pay by credit card?**
> ¿puedo pagar con tarjeta? [pwedo – kon tarHeta]
> **which card do you want to use?** ¿qué tarjeta quiere usar? [keh – k-yaireh oosar]
> **yes, sir** sí, señor [sen-yor]
> **what's the number?** ¿qué número tiene? [noomairo t-yeneh]
> **and the expiry date?** ¿y la fecha de caducidad? [deh kadooseeda]

crisps las patatas fritas (de bolsa)
crockery la loza [losa]
crocodile el caimán [kiman]
crossing (by sea) la travesía [trabesee-a]
crossroads el cruce [krooseh]
crowd la muchedumbre [moocheh-doombreh]
crowded atestado
crown (on tooth) la funda [foonda]
cruise el crucero [kroosairo]
crutches las muletas
cry (verb) llorar [yorar]
Cuban (adj) cubano
cucumber el pepino
cup la taza [tasa]
a cup of ..., please una taza

de ..., por favor [deh – fabor]
cupboard el armario [armar-yo]
cure la cura [koora]
curly rizado [reesado]

currency
Since 1993 and the revaluation of the peso, the national currency has been the **nuevo peso**, sometimes expressed as **N$**; you may also see **M.N.** for **moneda nacional** (national currency).

current la corriente [korr-yenteh]
curtains las cortinas
cushion el cojín [koHeen]
custom la costumbre [kostoombreh]
Customs la aduana [adwana]

Crossing the border, especially on foot, it's easy to go straight past the immigration and Customs checks. Make sure that you get your tourist card (**FMT – Folleto de Migración Turística**) stamped and your bags checked though, otherwise you'll be stopped after some 20km and sent back to complete the formalities. It is equally important to have a properly stamped tourist card on leaving the country, since you can be refused exit from the country without it. It's also wise to have receipts for any major items you are carrying into the country – radios, TVs, jewellery, cameras etc – to make sure that you are not charged duty on exit. It is illegal to take antiquities out of the country. The penalties for contravention are severe.
see **passport**

cut el corte [korteh]
 (verb) cortar
 I've cut myself me corté [meh korteh]
cutlery los cubiertos [koob-yairtos]
cycling el ciclismo [seekleesmo]
cyclist el/la ciclista [seekleesta]

D

dad el papá
daily cada día [dee-a], todos los días
 (adj) diario [d-yar-yo], de cada día [deh]
damage: damaged dañado [dan-yado]
damn! ¡caramba!
damp (adj) húmedo [oomedo]
dance el baile [bīleh]
 (verb) bailar [bīlar]
 would you like to dance? ¿quiere bailar? [k-yaireh]
dangerous peligroso
Danish danés [dan-es]
dark (adj: colour) oscuro

[os**koo**ro]

(hair) moreno

it's getting dark está
oscureciendo [os**koo**res-yendo]

date* la fecha

what's the date today? ¿qué
fecha es hoy? [keh – oy]

let's make a date for next
Monday quedamos para el
próximo lunes [ked**a**mos –
pr**o**kseemo]

dates (fruit) los dátiles

daughter la hija [**ee**Ha]

daughter-in-law la nuera
[nw**ai**ra]

dawn el amanecer
[amanes**air**]

at dawn al amanecer

day el día

the day after el día siguiente
[seeg-y**e**nteh]

the day after tomorrow
pasado mañana [man-y**a**na]

the day before el día
anterior [antair-y**o**r]

the day before yesterday
anteayer [anteh-ī-y**ai**r]

every day todos los días

all day todo el día

in two days' time dentro de
dos días [deh]

have a nice day! ¡que pase
buen día! [keh p**a**seh bwen]

day trip la excursión
[ekskoors-y**o**n]

dead muerto [mw**ai**rto]

deaf sordo

deal (business) el negocio
[neg**o**s-yo]

it's a deal trato hecho
[**e**cho]

death la muerte [mw**ai**rteh]

decaffeinated coffee el café
descafeinado [kaf**eh** deskafay-
een**a**do]

December diciembre [dees-
y**e**mbreh]

decide decidir [desee**deer**]

we haven't decided yet
todavía no hemos
decidido [todab**ee**-a no **e**mos
desee**dee**do]

decision la decisión [desees-
y**o**n]

deck (on ship) la cubierta
[koob-y**ai**rta]

deckchair la tumbona

deduct descontar

deep profundo

definitely (certainly) sin
duda

definitely not ni hablar
[**a**blar]

degree (qualification) el título

delay la demora

the train was delayed se
demoró el tren [seh]

deliberately a propósito

delicatessen la charcutería
[charkootair**ee**-a]

delicious delicioso [delees-
y**o**so]

deliver entregar

delivery (of mail) el reparto

Denmark Dinamarca

dental floss el hilo dental
[**ee**lo]

dentist el/la dentista

dialogue

it's this one here es ésta
de aquí [deh ak**eh**-ya]
this one? ¿ésta?
no, that one no, aquélla
[ak**eh**-ya]
here? ¿aquí?
yes sí
see doctor

dentures la dentadura postiza
[post**ee**sa]
deodorant el desodorante
[desodor**anteh]
department el departamento
department store la tienda
de departamentos [t-y**e**nda
deh]
departure la salida
departure lounge la sala de
embarque [deh emb**ar**keh]
depend: it depends depende
[dep**e**ndeh]
it depends when según
cuándo [kw**a**ndo]
it depends on ... depende de
... [deh]
deposit (as security) la fianza
[fee-**a**nsa]
(as part payment) el enganche
[eng**a**ncheh]
description la descripción
[deskreeps-y**on**]
desert el desierto [des-y**air**to]
dessert el postre [p**o**streh]
destination el destino
develop (photos) revelar
[rebel**ar**]

dialogue

could you develop these
films? ¿puede revelar
estos carretes? [pw**e**deh –
karr**et**-es]
when will they be ready?
¿cuándo estarán listos?
[kw**a**ndo]
tomorrow afternoon
mañana por la tarde
[man-y**a**na – t**ar**deh]
how much is the four-hour
service? ¿cuánto es el
servicio de cuatro horas?
[kw**a**nto – sairb**ee**s-yo deh kw**a**-
tro **o**ras]

diabetic (man/woman) el
diabético [dee-ab**e**teeko], la
diabética
diabetic foods la comida
para diabéticos
dial (verb) marcar
dialling code el prefijo
[pref**ee**Ho], el código

Calling from long-
distance (**Ladatel**) phones
dial the codes below,
followed by the area code and
number:

Mexico inter-state: 91
US and Canada: 95

Omit the initial zero of the area code
when dialling the following:

UK: 98 44
Ireland: 98 353
Australia: 98 61
New Zealand: 98 64

To call collect or person-to-person
outside Mexico, dial 09.

diamond el diamante
[d-yam**a**nteh]
diaper el pañal [pan-y**a**l]
diarrhoea la diarrea
[d-yarr**eh**-a]
diary (business etc) la agenda
[aHenda]
(for personal experiences) el
diario [d-y**a**r-yo]
dictionary el diccionario
[deeks-yon**a**r-yo]
didn't see **not**
die morir
diesel el gasoil, el diesel
[d**ee**sel]
diet la dieta [d-y**e**ta]
I'm on a diet estoy a
régimen [reHeemen]
I have to follow a special diet
tengo que seguir una dieta
especial [keh seg**ee**r – espes-
y**a**l]
difference la diferencia
[deefair**e**ns-ya]
what's the difference? ¿cuál
es la diferencia? [kwal]
different distinto
this one is different éste es
distinto [**e**steh]
a different table otra mesa
difficult difícil [deef**ee**seel]

difficulty la dificultad
[deefeekoolt**a**]
dinghy el bote [b**o**teh]
dining room el comedor
dinner (evening meal) la cena
[s**e**na]
to have dinner cenar
[sen**a**r]
direct (adj) directo
is there a direct train? ¿hay
un tren directo? [ī]
direction la dirección
[deereks-y**o**n], el sentido
which direction is it? ¿en
qué dirección está? [keh]
is it in this direction? ¿es por
aquí? [ak**ee**]
directory enquiries
información [eenformas-y**o**n]

For directory enquiries
ring 01 for Mexico, 04 for
the Federal District, 07 for
other information.

dirt la suciedad [soos-yed**a**], la
mugre [m**oo**greh]
dirty sucio [s**oo**s-yo]
disabled minusválido
[meenoosb**a**leedo]
**is there access for the dis-
abled?** ¿hay acceso para
minusválidos? [ī aks**e**so]
disappear desaparecer
[desapares**air**]
it's disappeared desapareció
[desapares-y**o**]
disappointed decepcionado
[deseps-yon**a**do]

disappointing decepcionante [deseps-yonanteh]
disaster el desastre [desastreh]
disco la discoteca
discount el descuento [deskwento]
 is there a discount? ¿hay descuento? [i]
disease la enfermedad [enfairmeda]
disgusting repugnante [repoognanteh]
dish (meal) el plato
dishcloth el trapo de cocina [deh koseena]
disinfectant el desinfectante [deseenfektanteh]
disk (for computer) la disqueta [deesketa]
disposable diapers/nappies los pañales desechables [pan-yal-es desechab-les]
distance la distancia [deestans-ya]
 in the distance a lo lejos [leHos]
distilled water el agua destilada [agwa]
district el barrio
disturb molestar, estorbar
diversion (detour) el desvío [desbee-o]
diving board el trampolín
divorced divorciado [deebors-yado]
dizzy: I feel dizzy (said by man/woman) estoy mareado/mareada [mareh-ado]
do hacer [asair]

what shall we do? ¿qué hacemos? [keh asemos]
how do you do it? ¿cómo se hace? [seh aseh]
will you do it for me? ¿me lo puede hacer Usted? [meh lo pwedeh asair oosteh]

dialogues

how do you do? ¿cómo está? [komo]
nice to meet you encantado de conocerle [deh konosairleh]
what do you do? (work) ¿a qué se dedica? [keh seh]
I'm a teacher, and you? soy profesor, ¿y Usted? [ee oosteh]
I'm a student soy estudiante [estood-yanteh]
what are you doing this evening? ¿qué hace esta tarde? [aseh]
we're going out for a drink; do you want to join us? salimos a tomar una copa, ¿nos acompaña? [akompan-ya]

do you want cream? ¿quiere crema? [k-yaireh]
I do, but she doesn't yo sí, pero ella no [pairo eh-ya]

doctor el/la médico

we need a doctor
necesitamos un médico
[neseseetamos]
please call a doctor por
favor, llame a un médico
[fabor yameh]

There are no reciprocal
health arrangements
between Mexico and any
other country, so travel and health
insurance is essential. You can get a
list of English-speaking doctors from
your government's nearest
consulate. Big hotels and tourist
offices may also be able to
recommend someone. Every border
town has hundreds of doctors and
dentists experienced in treating
English-speaking tourists. In every
reasonably-sized town, you should
be able to find a state- or Red
Cross-run health centre (**centro de
salud**), where emergency treatment
is free but very elementary. The
State Social Security System (IMSS)
also has emergency facilities which
may be of a slightly higher standard,
but you will need to pay for anything
beyond the most basic attention.
If you suffer from any chronic
condition it is important to carry
with you clear and legible
documentation from your own
doctor and if possible some of your
normal medication, since the brand
name may not be familiar to a
Mexican pharmacist.

dialogue

where does it hurt?
¿dónde le duele? [dondeh
leh dweleh]
right here justo aquí
[Hoosto akee]
does that hurt now? ¿le
duele ahora? [leh dweleh
a-ora]
yes sí
take this to the chemist's
lleve esto a la farmacia
[yebeh – farmas-ya]

document el documento
[dokoomento]
dog el perro [pairro]
doll la muñeca [moon-yeka]
domestic flight el vuelo
nacional [bwelo nas-yonal]
donkey el burro [boorro]
don't! ¡no lo haga! [aga]
 don't do that! ¡no haga eso!
 see not
door la puerta [pwairta]
doorman el portero [portairo]
double doble [dobleh]
double bed la cama
matrimonial [matreemon-yal]
double room el cuarto doble
[kwarto dobleh]
doughnut la dona
down: down here aquí abajo
[akee abaHo]
 downwards hacia abajo [as-
ya]
 put it down over there déjelo
 ahí [deh-Helo a-ee]

it's down there on the right
está ahí a la derecha
[dair**e**cha]

it's further down the road
está bajando la calle
[ba**H**ando la ka-yeh]

downhill skiing el esquí
alpino [esk**ee** alp**ee**no]

downmarket (restaurant etc)
popular [popoo**l**ar]

downstairs abajo [aba**H**o]

dozen la docena [dos**e**na]

half a dozen media docena
[med-ya]

drain (in sink, road) el desagüe
[des**a**gweh]

draught beer la cerveza de
barril [sairb**e**sa deh]

draughty: it's draughty hay
corriente [**i** korr-y**e**nteh]

drawer el cajón [ka**H**on]

drawing el dibujo [deeb**oo**Ho]

dreadful horrible [orr**ee**bleh]

dream el sueño [sw**e**n-yo]

dress el vestido [best**ee**do]

dressed: to get dressed
vestirse [best**ee**rseh]

dressing (for cut) el vendaje
[bend**a**Heh]

salad dressing el aliño
[al**ee**n-yo]

dressing gown la bata

drink (alcoholic) la copa
(non-alcoholic) la bebida
(verb) beber [beb**air**]

a cold drink una bebida fría

can I get you a drink?
¿quiere beber algo?
[k-y**ai**reh]

**what would you like (to
drink)?** ¿qué le apetece
beber? [keh leh apet**e**seh]

no thanks, I don't drink no
gracias, no bebo alcohol
[gras-yas – alk**o**l]

I'll just have a drink of water
sólo agua [**a**gwa]

Apart from beer and wine,
Mexico produces its own
alcoholic specialities; the
agave cactus (**maguey**) produces
tequila and **mezcal** as well as
pulque (a type of milky beer) which
is less familiar and takes some
getting used to. **Puro de caña** (also
called **posh** in the south) is the local
sugar cane liquor. There is a wide
variety of non-alcoholic drinks from
fizzy soft drinks (**refrescos**) to the
wonderful fruit juices (**jugos**) or
milkshakes (**licuados**) to be found in
specialist shops or on pavement
stalls. **Aguas de fruta** are delicious
but are made with water, so tourists
should beware.
see **water**

drinking water agua potable
[**a**gwa pot**a**bleh]

is this drinking water? ¿esto
es agua potable?

drive (verb) manejar [mane**H**ar]

we drove here vinimos en
carro [been**ee**mos]

I'll drive you home te llevaré
a casa en carro [teh yebar**eh**]

driver (man/woman) el/la

chofer [cho**fair**]

driving
To drive your own car in Mexico (apart from in Baja and the free zone), you must obtain a vehicle permit from the **Delegación de Servicios Migratorios** at the border. This will cover you for a period of 180 days, but remember to insist that you are given the maximum time. And make sure, too, that you are given (and always display) the windscreen sticker that comes with it. If you drive without renewal you can then become subject to large fines. The permit must be paid using a major credit card, otherwise you'll be asked for a minimum $500 refundable bond plus non-refundable tax and commission. To make sure you don't sell the car in Mexico, you'll also be required either to post a cash bond equal to the vehicle's book value or give the imprint of a major credit card. You must also have Mexican insurance, available from dozens of places on either side of the border.
Drivers from the US, Canada, Britain, Ireland, Australia and New Zealand will find their licences are valid in Mexico, though an international one is still advisable. You are required to have all your documents with you when driving.
Traffic circulates on the right, and the normal speed limit is 40km/h (25mph) in built-up areas, 70km/h (43mph) in open country, and 110km/h (68mph) on the motorway. Some of the new motorways are excellent and the toll motorways (**cuota**) are better still, though extremely expensive. Away from the major centres, roads are often narrow, winding and potholed, with livestock wandering across them. Keep out of the way of Mexican bus and truck drivers (and remember that if you signal left to them on a stretch of open road, it means it's clear to overtake). One convention to be aware of is that the first driver to flash their lights at a junction or where only one vehicle can pass has right of way, so someone who flashes you is not inviting you to go first. Most people recommend that you avoid driving at night for reasons of road safety and because of bandits.
see **rent** and **breakdown**

driving licence el carnet de chofer [kar**neh** deh cho**fair**]
drop: just a drop, please (of drink) un poquito nada más [po**kee**to]
drug la medicina [medee**see**na]
drugs (narcotics) la droga
drunk (adj) borracho
drunken driving manejar en estado de embriaguez [mane**Har** – deh embr-yag-**es**]
dry (adj) seco
dry-cleaner la tintorería [teen-torai**ree**-a]

duck el pato

due: he was due to arrive
yesterday tenía que llegar
ayer [keh yegar ī-yair]

when is the train due? ¿a
qué hora llega el tren? [ora
yega]

dull (pain) sordo
(weather) gris [grees]

dummy (baby's) el chupete
[choopeteh]

during durante [dooranteh]

dust el polvo [polbo]

dustbin el bote de la basura
[boteh deh]

dusty polvoriento [polbor-
yento]

duty-free (goods) (los
productos) sin impuestos
[seen eempwestos]

duty-free shop el duty free

 Duty-free allowances in
Mexico are three bottles
of liquor (including wine),
plus 400 cigarettes or two boxes of
cigars or a 'reasonable quantity' of
tobacco for your own use, plus
twelve rolls of camera film or
camcorder tape.

duvet el edredón

E

each cada

how much are they each? ¿a
cómo está cada uno?

ear el oído [o-eedo]

earache: I have earache
tengo dolor de oídos [deh]

early pronto

early in the morning de
madrugada

I called by earlier pasé antes
[paseh ant-es]

earring el arete [areteh]

earthquake el temblor

east oriente [or-yenteh]

in the east en el oriente

Easter la Semana Santa
see holiday

easy fácil [faseel]

eat comer [komair]

we've already eaten, thanks
ya comimos, gracias [gras-
yas]

 eating habits
Traditionally, Mexicans eat
a light breakfast very
early, a snack of tacos or eggs mid-
morning, lunch (the main meal of the
day) around two o'clock or later – in
theory followed by a siesta – and a
late, light supper. Eating a large set-
menu meal (comida corrida) at
lunchtime can be a great
moneysaver.
Breakfast (desayuno) might simply
be coffee and pan dulce (sweet
rolls and pastries that usually come
in a basket); you pay for as many as
you eat. Alternatively, breakfast can
consist of eggs in any number of
forms, or a licuado (fruit drink)
fortified with raw egg (blanquillo).

Freshly-squeezed orange juice (**jugo de naranja**) is always available from street stalls in the early morning. Snack meals mostly consist of some variation on the **taco/enchilada** theme (stalls selling them are called **taquerías**), but **tortas** – rolls heavily filled with meat or cheese or both, garnished with avocado or chilli and toasted on request – are also wonderful, and you'll see take-away torta stands everywhere.
see **restaurant**

eau de toilette el agua de baño [**a**gwa deh ban-yo]
economy class la clase turista [kl**a**seh]
Edinburgh Edimburgo [edeemb**oo**rgo]
egg el huevo [w**e**bo], el blanquillo [blank**ee**-yo]
eggplant la berenjena [beren**He**na]
either: either ... or ... o ... o ...
either of them cualquiera de los dos [kwalk-y**ai**ra deh]
elastic el elástico
elastic band la gomita
elbow el codo
electric eléctrico
electrical appliances los electrodomésticos
electric fire la estufa eléctrica
electrician el electricista [elektrees**ee**sta]
electricity la electricidad [elektreesee**da**]
see **voltage**

elevator el ascensor [asens**o**r]
else: something else otra cosa
somewhere else en otra parte [**pa**rteh]

dialogue

would you like anything else? ¿algo más?
no, nothing else, thanks nada más, gracias [gr**a**s-yas]

embassy la embajada [emba**Ha**da]
emergency la emergencia [emair**He**ns-ya]
this is an emergency! ¡es una emergencia!
emergency exit la salida de emergencia [deh]
empty vacío [bas**ee**-o]
end el final [f**ee**nal]
(verb) terminar [tairmeen**a**r]
at the end of the street al final de la calle [deh la k**a**-yeh]
when does it end? ¿cuándo termina? [kw**a**ndo]
engaged (toilet) ocupado
(telephone) comunicando
(to be married) prometido
engine (car) el motor
England Inglaterra [eenglat**ai**rra]
English inglés [eeng-l**e**s]
I'm English (man/woman) soy inglés/inglesa
do you speak English?

¿habla inglés? [**abla**]
enjoy disfrutar
  to enjoy oneself divertirse
  [deebairt**eer**seh]

dialogue

how did you like the film?
¿le gustó la película? [leh
goos**to**]
I enjoyed it very much, did
you enjoy it? me gustó
mucho, ¿le gustó a Usted?
[meh – **moo**cho – leh – oost**eh**]

enjoyable divertido
  [deebairt**ee**do]
enlargement (of photo) la
  ampliación [ampl-yas-**yon**]
enormous enorme [en**or**meh]
enough bastante [bast**an**teh]
  there's not enough no hay
  bastante [ī]
  it's not big enough no es lo
  suficientemente grande
  [soofees-yentem**en**teh]
  that's enough basta
entrance la entrada
envelope el sobre [**so**breh]
epileptic (adj) epiléptico
error el error
especially sobre todo [**so**breh]
essential imprescindible
  [eempreseend**ee**bleh]
  it is essential that ... es
  imprescindible que ... [keh]
Europe Europa [eh-oor**o**pa]
European europeo [eh-

ooroep**eh**-o]
even incluso [eenkl**oo**so]
  even if ... incluso si ...
evening (early evening) la tarde
  [**tar**deh]
  (after nightfall) la noche
  [**no**cheh]
  this evening esta tarde/
  noche
  in the evening por la tarde/
  noche
evening meal la cena [**se**na]
eventually finalmente
  [feenalm**en**teh], por fin [feen]
ever alguna vez [bes]

dialogue

have you ever been to
Monterrey? ¿estuvo
alguna vez en
Monterrey? [est**oo**bo –
montair**ray**]
yes, I was there two years
ago sí, estuve allí hace
dos años [est**oo**beh a-**yee**
aseh – an-yos]

every cada
  every day todos los días
  [**dee**-as]
everyone todos
everything todo
everywhere en todas partes
  [part-es]
exactly! ¡exactamente! [eksak-
tam**en**teh]
exam el examen
example el ejemplo [e**Hem**plo]

for example por ejemplo
excellent excelente
[ekselenteh]
excellent! ¡estupendo!
except excepto [eksepto]
excess baggage el exceso de
equipaje [ekseso deh
ekeepaHeh]
exchange rate el tipo de
cambio [teepo deh kamb-yo]
exciting emocionante [emos-
yonanteh]
excuse me (to get past) con
permiso
(to get attention) ¡por favor!
[fabor]
(to say sorry) disculpe
[deeskoolpeh]
exhaust (pipe) el tubo de
escape [toobo deh eskapeh]
exhausted (tired) agotado
exhibition la exposición
[eksposees-yon]
exit la salida
where's the nearest exit?
¿cuál es la salida más
cercana? [kwal – sairkana]
expect esperar [espairar]
expensive caro
experienced con experiencia
[espair-yens-ya]
explain explicar [espleekar]
can you explain that?
¿puede explicármelo?
[pwedeh]
express (mail) urgente
[oorHenteh]
(train) el exprés
extension (phone) extensión

[estens-yon], interno
[eentairno]
extension 221, please
extensión doscientos
veintiuno, por favor [fabor]
extension lead el alargador
extra: can we have an extra
one? ¿nos puede dar otro?
[pwedeh]
do you charge extra for that?
¿cobra extra para esto?
extraordinary extraordinario
[ekstra-ordeenar-yo]
extremely extremadamente
[estremadamenteh]
eye el ojo [oHo]
will you keep an eye on my
suitcase for me? ¿me cuida
la maleta? [meh kweeda]
eyebrow pencil el lápiz de
cejas [lapees deh seHas]
eye drops el colirio [koleer-
yo]
eyeglasses las gafas
eyeliner el lápiz de ojos
[lapees deh oHos]
eye make-up remover el
desmaquillador de ojos
[desmakee-yador]
eye shadow la sombra de
ojos

F

face la cara
factory la fábrica
Fahrenheit* Fahrenheit
faint (verb) desmayarse [desmī-

yarseh]

she's fainted se desmayó
[seh desmī-**yo**]

I feel faint (said by man/woman)
est**oy** mareado/marea**da**
[mareh-**a**do]

fair la feria [**fair**-ya]

(adj: just) justo [**Hoo**sto]

fairly bastante [**bas**tanteh]

fake (thing) la imitación
[eemeetas-**yon**]

(adj) falsificado

fake fur el piel de imitación
[p-y**el**]

fall (verb) caerse [ka-**air**seh]

she's had a fall se cayó [seh
kī-**yo**]

fall (US: noun) el otoño [oton-
yo]

in the fall en otoño

false falso [**fal**-so]

family la familia [fam**eel**-ya]

famous famoso

fan (electrical) el ventilador
[benteela**dor**]

(handheld) el abanico

(sports) el/la hincha [**een**cha]

fan belt la correa del
ventilador [ko**rreh**-a del bentee-
la**dor**]

fantastic fantástico

far lejos [**le**Hos]

dialogue

is it far from here? ¿está
lejos de aquí? [deh a**kee**]

no, not very far no, no
muy lejos [mwee]

well how far? bueno, ¿qué
tan lejos? [**bweno** keh]

it's about 20 kilometres
son **u**nos v**ei**nte
kil**ó**metros

fare el pasaje [pasa**Heh**]

farm (large) la hacienda [as-
yenda]

(small) la finca

fashionable de moda [deh]

fast rápido

fat (person) gordo

(on meat) la grasa

father el padre [**padreh**]

father-in-law el suegro
[**swegro**]

faucet la llave [la **ya**beh]

fault el defecto

sorry, it was my fault
disculpe, fue culpa mía
[dees**kool**peh fweh]

it's not my fault no es mi
culpa

faulty defectuoso [defekt**wo**so]

favourite preferido
[prefair**ee**do]

fax el fax

(verb: person) mandar un fax a

(document) mandar por fax

February febrero [feb**rai**ro]

feel sentir

I feel hot tengo calor

I feel unwell no me siento
bien [meh s-y**en**to b-yen]

I feel like going for a walk se
me antoja un paseo [seh meh
anto**Ha**]

how are you feeling today?

¿cómo se encuentra hoy? [enkwentra oy]

I'm feeling better me siento mejor [meHor]

felt-tip (pen) el rotulador

fence la cerca [sairka]

fender la defensa

ferry el ferry

festival el festival [festeebal], la fiesta

fetch: I'll fetch him lo pasaré a recoger [pasareh a rekoHair]

will you come and fetch me later? ¿vendrás a buscarme más tarde? [bendras a booskarmeh mas tardeh]

feverish con fiebre [f-yebreh]

few: a few unos pocos

a few days unos días

fiancé el novio [nob-yo]

fiancée la novia [nob-ya]

field el campo

fight la pelea [peleh-a]

figs los higos [eegos]

fill (verb) llenar [yenar]

fill in rellenar [reh-yenar]

do I have to fill this in? ¿tengo que rellenar esto? [keh]

fill up llenar [yenar]

fill it up, please lleno, por favor [yeno por fabor]

filling (in cake, sandwich) el relleno [reh-yeno]

(in tooth) el empaste [empasteh]

film (movie, for camera) la película

dialogue

do you have this kind of film? ¿tiene películas de este tipo? [t-yeneh – deh esteh teepo]

yes, how many exposures? sí, ¿de cuántas fotos? [kwantas]

36 treinta y seis

film processing el revelado [rebelado]

filter coffee el café de filtro [kafeh deh feeltro]

filter papers los papeles de filtro [papel-es]

filthy muy sucio [mwee soos-yo]

find (verb) encontrar

I can't find it no lo encuentro [enkwentro]

I've found it ya lo encontré [enkontreh]

find out enterarse [enterarseh]

could you find out for me? ¿me lo puede averiguar? [meh lo pwedeh abaireegwar]

fine (noun) la multa [moolta]

it's fine today hoy hace buen tiempo [oy aseh bwen t-yempo]

dialogues

how are you? ¿cómo estás?

I'm fine, thanks bien, gracias [b-yen gras-yas]

is that OK? ¿va bien así? [ba]

that's fine, thanks está bien, gracias

finger el dedo

finish (verb) terminar [tairmeenar], acabar

I haven't finished yet no he terminado todavía [eh tairmeenado todabee-a]

when does it finish? ¿cuándo termina? [kwando tairmeena]

fire el fuego [fwego]

(blaze) el incendio [eensend-yo]

fire! ¡fuego!

can we light a fire here? ¿se puede prender fuego aquí? [seh pwedeh prendair – akee]

it's on fire está ardiendo [ard-yendo]

fire alarm la alarma de incendios [deh eensend-yos]

fire brigade los bomberos [bombairos]

In the event of a fire, the number to ring is 08.

fire escape la salida de incendios [deh eensend-yos]

fire extinguisher el extintor [esteentor]

first primero [preemairo]

I was first (said by man/woman) fui el primero/la primera [fwee]

at first al principio [preenseep-yo]

the first time la primera vez [bes]

first on the left la primera a la izquierda [eesk-yairda]

first aid primeros auxilios [owkseel-yos]

first aid kit el botiquín [boteekeen]

first class (travel etc) de primera (clase) [preemaira (klaseh)]

first floor la primera planta (US) la planta baja [baHa]

first name el nombre de pila [nombreh deh]

fish el pez [pes]

(food) el pescado

(verb) pescar

fishing village el pueblo de pescadores [pweblo deh peskador-es]

fishmonger's la pescadería [peskadairee-a]

fit (attack) el ataque [atakeh]

fit: it doesn't fit me no me viene bien [b-yeneh b-yen]

fitting room el probador

fix (repair) arreglar

(arrange) fijar [feeHar]

can you fix this? ¿puede arreglar esto? [pwedeh]

fizzy con gas

flag la bandera [bandaira]

flannel la manopla

flash (for camera) el flash

flat (noun: apartment) el departamento

(adj) llano [yano]
I've got a flat tyre se me ponchó la llanta [seh meh – yanta]
flavour el sabor
flea la pulga
flight el vuelo [bwelo]
flight number el número de vuelo [noomairo deh]
flippers las aletas
flood la inundación [eenoon-das-yon]
floor el piso
florist la florería [florairee-a]
flour la harina [areena]
flower la flor
flu el gripe [greepeh]
fluent: he speaks fluent Spanish domina el español [espan-yol]
fly la mosca
(verb) volar [bolar]
can we fly there? ¿podemos ir en avión? [eer en ab-yon]
fly in llegar en avión [yegar]
fly out irse en avión [eerseh]
fog la niebla [n-yebla]
foggy: it's foggy hay niebla [ī]
folk dancing el baile tradicional [bīleh tradees-yonal]
folk music la música folklórica [mooseeka]
follow seguir [segeer]
follow me sígame [seegameh]
food la comida
food poisoning la intoxicación alimenticia [eentokseekas-yon aleementees-ya]

food shop/store la tienda de alimentos [t-yenda deh], el ultramarinos [ooltramareenos]
foot* (of person, measurement) el pie [p-yeh]
on foot a pie
football (game) el fútbol
(ball) el balón
football match el partido de fútbol
for para, por
do you have something for ...? (headache/diarrhoea etc) ¿tiene algo para ...? [t-yeneh]

dialogues

who's the mole poblano for? ¿para quién es el mole poblano? [k-yen]
that's for me es para mí
and this one? ¿y éste? [ee esteh]
that's for her ése es para ella [eseh – eh-ya]

where do I get the bus for Puebla? ¿dónde se toma el autobús para Puebla? [dondeh seh – pwebla]
the bus for Puebla leaves from the Zócalo el autobús para Puebla sale del Zócalo [saleh del sokalo]

how long have you been here for? ¿cuánto tiempo lleva aquí? [kwanto t-yempo

yeba akee]
**I've been here for two
days, how about you?**
llevo aquí dos días, ¿y
Usted? **[yebo – ee ooste**h**]**
I've been here for a week
llevo aquí una semana

forehead la frente [fr**e**nteh]
foreign extranjero [estran**H**airo]
foreigner (man/woman) el
extranjero, la extranjera
forest el bosque [b**o**skeh]
forget olvidar [olbeed**a**r]
I forget no me acuerdo [meh
akw**ai**rdo]
I've forgotten se me olvidó
[seh meh olbeed**o**]
fork el tenedor
(in road) la bifurcación
[beefoorkas-y**o**n]
form (document) el formulario
[formoolar-yo]
formal (dress) de etiqueta [deh
eteek**e**ta]
fortnight quince días [k**ee**nseh
d**ee**-as], la quincena
[keens**e**na]
fortunately por suerte
[sw**ai**rteh]
**forward: could you forward
my mail?** ¿puede enviarme
el correo? [pw**e**deh emb-y**a**rmeh
el korr**e**h-o]
forwarding address la nueva
dirección [nw**e**ba deereks-y**o**n]
foundation (make-up) la crema
base [b**a**seh]
fountain la fuente [fw**e**nteh]

foyer el vestíbulo [besteeb**oo**lo]
fracture la fractura [frakt**oo**ra]
France Francia [fr**a**ns-ya]
free libre [l**ee**breh]
(no charge) gratuito [grat**wee**to]
is it free (of charge)? ¿es
gratis?
freeway la autopista
[owtop**ee**sta]
freezer el congelador
[kon**H**elad**o**r]
French francés [frans-**e**s]
French fries las papas fritas
frequent frecuente
[frek**we**nteh]
**how frequent is the bus to
Monterrey?** ¿cada cuánto
tiempo hay autobús a
Monterrey [kw**a**nto t-y**e**mpo ī –
montairr**ay**]
fresh fresco
fresh orange el jugo de
naranja [**H**oo**go de naran**H**a]
Friday viernes [b-y**ai**rn-es]
fridge la refrigeradora
[refree**H**airad**o**ra]
fried frito
fried egg el huevo frito [w**e**bo]
friend (male/female) el amigo,
la amiga
friendly simpático
from de [deh], desde [d**e**sdeh]
**when does the next train
from Guadalajara arrive?**
¿cuándo llega el próximo
tren de Guadalajara?
[kw**a**ndo y**e**ga – deh gwadala**H**ara]
from Monday to Friday de
lunes a viernes [deh]

from next Thursday a partir del próximo jueves [par**teer**]

dialogue

> **where are you from?** ¿de dónde es Usted? [**do**ndeh es oos**teh**]
> **I'm from Los Angeles** soy de Los Angeles [an**Hel**-es]

front la parte delantera [**par**teh delant**air**a]
in front delante [de**lan**teh]
in front of the hotel delante del hotel
at the front en la parte de delante [deh]
frost la escarcha
frozen congelado [konHe**la**do]
frozen food los congelados
fruit la fruta
fruit juice el jugo de frutas [**Hoo**go deh]
fry freír [freh-**eer**]
frying pan la sartén
full lleno [**yeno**]
it's full of ... está lleno de ... [deh]
I'm full (said by man/woman) est**oy** lleno/llena
full board pensión completa [pens-**yon**]
fun: it was fun fue muy divertido [fweh mwee deebairt**eedo**]
funeral el funeral [foo**nairal**]
funny (strange) raro
  (amusing) divertido

[deebairt**eedo**]
furniture los muebles [**mweb**-les]
further más allá [a-**ya**]
  it's further down the road está más adelante [ade**lan**teh]

dialogue

> **how much further is it to Cuernavaca?** ¿cuánto falta para Cuernavaca? [**kwanto** – kwairna**baka**]
> **about 5 kilometres** unos cinco kilómetros

fuse el fusible [foo**see**bleh]
  the lights have fused se fundieron los plomos [seh foond-**yairon**]
fuse box la caja de fusibles [**kaHa** deh foo**seeb**-les]
fuse wire el plomo
future el futuro [foo**tooro**]
  in the future en el futuro

G

gallon* el galón
game (cards etc) el juego [**Hwego**]
  (match) el partido
  (meat) la caza [**casa**]
garage (for fuel) la gasolinera [gasolee**naira**]
  (for repairs) el taller (de reparaciones) [ta-**yair** (deh reparas-**yon**-es)]

(for parking) el garaje
[garaHeh], la cochera
[kochaira]

Unless your car is a basic VW, Ford or Dodge, parts are likely to be expensive and hard to come by. Bring a spares kit. Tyres can suffer badly so you should carry a good spare with you. Roadside **vulcanizadoras** and **llanteros** can do temporary tyre repairs. New tyres are expensive. If you do need help look for a **taller mecánico**.
see **petrol**

garden el jardín [Hardeen]
garlic el ajo [aHo]
gas el gas
(US) la gasolina
see **petrol**
gas cylinder (camping gas) la bomba de gas
gasoline la gasolina
see **petrol**
gas permeable lenses las lentillas porosas [lentee-yas]
gas station la gasolinera [gasoleenaira]
see **petrol**
gate la puerta [pwairta]
(at airport) la puerta de embarque [deh embarkeh]
gay gay
gay bar el bar gay
gearbox la caja de cambios [kaHa deh kamb-yos]
gear lever el cambio

gears la marcha
general general [Heneral]
gents (toilet) el servicio de señores [sairbees-yo deh sen-yor-es]
genuine (antique etc) auténtico [owtenteeko]
German (adj, language) alemán
German measles la rubeola [roobeh-ola]
Germany Alemania [aleman-ya]
get (fetch) traer [tra-air]
will you get me another one, please? me trae otro, por favor [meh tra-eh – fabor]
how do you get to ...? ¿cómo se va a ...? [seh ba]
do you know where I can get them? ¿sabe dónde las puedo conseguir? [sabeh dondeh las pwedo konsegeer]

dialogue

can I get you a drink? ¿puedo ofrecerle algo de beber? [pwedo ofresairleh – deh bebair]
no, I'll get this one – what would you like? no, yo invito – ¿qué se le antoja? [eenbeeto keh seh leh antoHa]
a glass of red wine una copa de vino tinto [deh]

get back (return) regresar
get in (arrive) llegar [yegar]

get off bajarse [baHarseh]
where do I get off? ¿dónde
tengo que bajarme? [dondeh
– keh baHarmeh]
get on (to train etc) subirse
[soobeerseh]
get out (of car etc) bajarse
[baHarseh]
get up (in the morning)
levantarse [lebantarseh]
gift el regalo
gift shop la tienda de regalos
[t-yenda]
gin la ginebra [Heenebra]
a gin and tonic, please un
gintónic, por favor
[jeentoneek – fabor]
girl la chica [cheeka], la
joven [Hoben], la chava
[chaba]
girlfriend la novia [nob-ya]
give dar
can you give me some
change? ¿me da suelto?
[meh]
I gave it to him se lo dí (a
él) [seh]
will you give this to ...?
¿podría entregarle esto a ...?
[entregarleh]

dialogue

> how much do you want for
> this? ¿cuánto vale esto?
> [kwanto baleh]
> 1,000 pesos mil pesos
> I'll give you 800 le doy
> ochocientos [leh]

give back devolver [debolbair]
glad feliz [felees]
glass (material) el vidrio
[beedr-yo]
(tumbler) el vaso [baso]
(wine glass) la copa
a glass of wine una copa de
vino [deh]
glasses las gafas
gloves los guantes [gwant-es]
glue el pegamento
go (verb) ir [eer]
we'd like to go to the
swimming-pool nos gustaría
ir a la alberca
where are you going?
¿adónde va? [adondeh ba]
where does this bus go?
¿adónde va este autobús?
[esteh]
let's go! ¡vamos! [bamos]
she's gone (left) se fue [seh
fweh]
where has he gone? ¿dónde
se ha ido? [dondeh seh a]
I went there last week estuve
la semana pasada [estoobeh]
go away irse [eerseh]
go away! ¡lárguese! [largeh-
seh]
go back (return) regresar
go down (the stairs etc) bajar
[baHar]
go in entrar
go out (in the evening) salir
do you want to go out
tonight? ¿quiere salir esta
noche? [k-yaireh – nocheh]
go through pasar por

go up (the stairs etc) subir
goat la cabra
God Dios [d-yos]
goggles las gafas protectoras
gold el oro
golf el golf
golf course el campo de golf
[deh]
good bueno [bweno]
 good! ¡muy bien! [mwee
 b-yen]
 it's no good es inútil
 [eenooteel]
goodbye hasta luego [asta
 lwego]
good evening buenas tardes
 [bwenas tard-es]
Good Friday el Viernes Santo
 [b-yairn-es]
 see holiday
good morning buenos días
 [bwenos]
good night buenas noches
 [bwenas noch-es]
goose el ganso
got: we've got to ... tenemos
 que ... [keh]
 have you got any apples?
 ¿tiene manzanas? [t-yeneh]
government el gobierno
 [gob-yairno]
gradually poco a poco
grammar la gramática
gram(me) el gramo
granddaughter la nieta [n-yeta]
grandfather el abuelo [abwelo]
grandmother la abuela
 [abwela]
grandson el nieto [n-yeto]

grapefruit la toronja [toronHa]
grapefruit juice el jugo de
 toronja [Hoogo deh]
grapes las uvas [oobas]
grass el pasto, el césped
 [sesped]
grateful agradecido
 [agradeseedo]
gravy la salsa
great (excellent) muy bueno
 [mwee bweno]
 that's great! ¡estupendo!
 [estoopendo]
 a great success un gran
 éxito [ekseeto]
Great Britain Gran Bretaña
 [bretan-ya]
greedy guloso
green verde [bairdeh]
green card (car insurance) la
 carta verde
greengrocer's la frutería
 [frootairee-a]
grey gris [grees]
grill la parrilla [parree-ya]
grilled a la parrilla, a la
 plancha
grocer's (la tienda de)
 abarrotes [(t-yenda deh) abarot-
 es]
ground el piso
 on the ground en el piso
ground floor la planta baja
 [baHa]
group el grupo
guarantee la garantía
 is it guaranteed? ¿lleva
 garantía? [yeva]
Guatemalan (adj)

guatemalteco [gwatemalteko]
guest (man/woman) el invitado [eembeetado], la invitada
guesthouse la pensión [pens-yon]
see hotel
guide el/la guía [gee-a]
guidebook la guía
guided tour la visita con guía [beeseeta]
guitar la guitarra [geetarra]
Gulf of Mexico el Golfo
gum (in mouth) la encía [ensee-a]
gun la pistola
gym el gimnasio [Heemnas-yo]

H

hair el pelo
hairbrush el cepillo para el pelo [sepee-yo]
haircut el corte de pelo [korteh deh]
hairdresser's la peluquería [pelookairee-a]
hairdryer el secador de pelo [deh]
hair gel el fijador (para el pelo) [feeHador]
hairgrip la horquilla [orkee-ya]
hair spray la laca
half* la mitad [meeta]
  half an hour media hora [med-ya ora]
  half a litre medio litro [med-yo]
  about half that aproxima-

mente la mitad de eso [aprokseemadamenteh – deh]
half board media pensión [med-ya pens-yon]
half fare el medio boleto [med-yo], el boleto con descuento [deskwento]
half price a mitad del precio [meeta del pres-yo]
ham el jamón [Hamon]
hamburger la hamburguesa [amboorgesa]
hammer el martillo [martee-yo]
hammock la hamaca [amaka]
hand la mano
handbag el bolso
handbrake el freno de mano [deh]
handkerchief el pañuelo [pan-ywaylo]
handle (on door) el mango (on suitcase etc) el asa
hand luggage el equipaje de mano [ekeepaH-eh]
hang-gliding el ala delta
hangover la cruda [krooda]
  I've got a hangover tengo cruda
happen suceder [soosedair]
  what's happening? ¿qué pasa? [keh]
  what has happened? ¿qué pasó?
happy contento
  I'm not happy about this esto no me convence [meh konbenseh]
harbour el puerto [pwairto]

hard duro [**doo**ro]
  (difficult) difícil [dee**fee**seel]
hard-boiled egg el huevo
  duro [**we**bo]
hard lenses las lentillas duras
  [len**tee**-yas]
hardly apenas
  hardly ever casi nunca
hardware shop la ferretería
  [fairretai**ree**-a], la tlapalería
  [tlapalai**ree**-a]
hat el sombrero [som**brai**ro]
hate (verb) odiar [od-**yar**]
have* tener [ten**air**]
  can I have a ...? ¿me da ...?
  [meh]
  do you have ...? ¿tiene ...?
  [t-**ye**neh]
  what'll you have? ¿qué va a
  tomar? [keh ba]
  I have to leave now tengo
  que irme ahora [**eer**meh
  a-**ora**]
  do I have to ...? ¿tengo
  que ...?
  can we have some ...? ¿nos
  pone ...? [**poneh**]
hayfever la fiebre del heno
  [f-**ye**breh del **e**no]
hazelnut la avellana [abeh-
  yana]
he* él
head la cabeza [ka**be**sa]
headache el dolor de cabeza
  [deh], la jaqueca [Ha**ke**ka]
headlights las luces de cruce
  [**loo**s-es de **kroo**seh]
headphones los auriculares
  [owree**koo**lar-es]

health
The lack of sanitation in
Mexico is often
exaggerated, but a degree of caution
is wise. Don't try anything too exotic
in the first few days; avoid food that
has been on display for a while and
is not freshly cooked. You should
also steer clear of salads, and peel
fruit before eating it. Avoid raw
shellfish, and don't eat anywhere
that is obviously dirty (most Mexican
restaurants are scrupulously clean);
street stalls in particular are
suspect. A bout of diarrhoea (or
turista as it's known in Mexico),
caused by the change in food and
routine, affects most people to some
degree, but its symptoms do pass; if
they last for more than a few days,
you should consult a doctor. Malaria
is endemic in many parts of Mexico.
It's a good idea to take malaria
tablets for two weeks before you
leave and continue taking them for
six weeks after you return home.
Two other common problems are
altitude sickness and too much sun.
Allow yourself time to acclimatize by
taking things easy and use a strong
sunscreen, wear a hat or stick to the
shade. As a general rule, drink more
than you would at home, and stay
out of the sun at the hottest times of
day.
see **water** and **mosquito**

health food shop la tienda
  naturista [t-**ye**nda natoo**rees**ta]

healthy sano
hear escuchar [eskoochar]

dialogue

can you hear me? ¿me
escuchas? [meh eskoochas]
I can't hear you, could
you repeat that? no le
escucho, ¿podría repetir-
lo? [leh]

hearing aid el audífono
[owdeefono]
heart el corazón [korason]
heart attack el infarto
heat el calor
heater (in room) la estufa
(in car) la calefacción
[kalefaks-yon]
heating la calefacción
heavy pesado
heel (of foot) el talón
(of shoe) el tacón
could you heel these?
¿podría cambiar los
tacones? [kamb-yar – takon-es]
heelbar el zapatero [sapatairo]
height la altura
helicopter el helicóptero
hello! ¡hola! [ola]
(answer on phone) ¡bueno!
[bweno]
helmet el casco
help la ayuda [ī-yooda]
(verb) ayudar [ī-yoodar]
help! ¡socorro!
can you help me? ¿puede
ayudarme? [pwedeh
ī-yoodarmeh]
thank you very much for your
help muchas gracias por su
ayuda [moochas gras-yas]
helpful amable [amableh]
hepatitis la hepatitis
[epateetees]
her*: I haven't seen her no la
he visto [eh beesto]
to her a ella [eh-ya]
with her con ella
for her para ella
that's her ella es
that's her towel ésa es su
toalla
herbal tea el té de hierbas
[teh deh yairbas]
herbs las hierbas
here aquí [akee]
here is/are ... aquí está/
están ...
here you are (offering) aquí
tiene [t-yeneh]
hers* (el) suyo [soo-yo], (la)
suya
that's hers es de ella [deh eh-
ya], es suyo/suya
hey! ¡oiga! [oyga]
hi! (hello) ¡hola! [ola]
hide (verb) esconder
[eskondair]
high alto
highchair la silla alta para
bebés [see-ya – beh-bes]
highway (US) la autopista
[owtopeesta]
hill el cerro [sairro]
him*: I haven't seen him no lo
he visto [eh beesto]

to him a él
with him con él
for him para él
that's him él es
hip la cadera [kada**ira**]
hire (verb) alquilar [alkee**lar**],
arrendar
  for hire de alquiler [deh
  alkee**lair**]
  where can I hire a bike?
  ¿dónde puedo alquilar una
  bicicleta? [**don**deh **pwe**do]
  see **rent**
his*: it's his car es su carro
  that's his eso es de él [deh],
  eso es suyo [**soo**-yo]
history la historia [eest**or**-ya]
hit (verb) golpear [golpeh-**ar**]
hitch-hike pedir aventón
[a**ben**ton], hacer autostop
[a**sair** owtostop], pedir ráid
[rïd]

Hitching into Mexico from
the US is not
recommended. Quite
apart from the obvious safety risks,
even if you get a through lift, you
will need to walk or take a short bus
ride across the border; otherwise it
will be marked on your tourist card
that you came in by car and
(although it's unlikely) you may have
problems when it's time to leave.
Within Mexico, hitchhiking is also
not recommended. Lifts are scarce,
distances are vast and risks are
high.

hobby el pasatiempo [pasat-
yempo]
hold (verb) tener en la mano
[ten**air**]
hole el agujero [agoo**Hai**ro], el
hoyo [**oy**-o]
holiday las vacaciones [bakas-
yon-es]
  on holiday de vacaciones
  [deh]

New Year (**Año Nuevo**) is
a national holiday in
Mexico, as is Christmas
Day and (unofficially) the Day of the
Virgin of Guadalupe on December
12th. New Year is often the occasion
for family reunions, and people
travel home to their place of origin
to celebrate it – hence the need to
book transport for this period well
ahead of time. **Reyes** (January 6th:
Twelfth Night) is the day when
presents are exchanged, rather than
Christmas Day.
Secular **Independence Day** (Sept
16) is in some ways more solemn
than the religious festivals with their
exuberant fervour.
El Día de los Muertos (Day of the
Dead) is All Souls' Day and its eve
(Nov 1-2) when offerings are made
to ancestors' souls, frequently with
picnics and all-night vigils on their
graves. People build shrines in their
homes to honour their departed
relatives, but it's the cemeteries to
head for if you want to see the really
spectacular stuff. Sweetmeats and

papier mâché statues of dressed up skeletons give the whole proceedings rather a gothic air. The country's biggest holiday, however, is **Semana Santa**, the week leading up to Easter when there are celebrations everywhere. **Viernes Santo** (Good Friday) is the biggest day; Easter Thursday and Saturday are also public holidays (**días feriados**). Many people travel to their home towns over Easter, so public transport is bursting at the seams.

home la casa
 at home (in my house) en casa
 (in my country) en mi país
 [pa-ees]
 we go home tomorrow
 regresamos a casa mañana
honest honrado [onrado]
honey la miel [m-yel]
honeymoon la luna de miel
 [loona deh]
hood (US) el capó, el capote
 [kapoteh], el cofre [kofreh]
hope la esperanza [espairansa]
 I hope so espero que sí
 [espairo keh]
 I hope not espero que no
 hopefully it won't rain no
 lloverá, eso espero [yobaira]
horn (of car) el klaxon
horrible horrible [orreebleh]
horse el caballo [kaba-yo]
horse racing las carreras de
 caballos [karrairas deh kaba-yos]
horse riding la equitación

[ekeetas-yon]
 I like horse riding me gusta
 montar a caballo [meh –
 kaba-yo]
hospital el hospital [ospeetal]
hospitality la hospitalidad
 [ospeetaleeda]
 thank you for your hospitality
 gracias por su hospitalidad
 [gras-yas]
hot caliente [kal-yenteh]
 (spicy) picante [peekanteh],
 picoso
 I'm hot tengo calor
 it's hot today hoy hace calor
 [oy aseh]
hotel el hotel [otel]

Mexican hotels may describe themselves as anything from **posadas** and **casas de huéspedes** to plain **hoteles**. The terms are used almost interchangeably, but the casa de huéspedes will usually be a cheaper guesthouse. Finding a room is rarely difficult; the cheaper hotels will often be concentrated round the main square (**zócalo**), or near the market, train station or bus station. The more modern and expensive hotels will either be in the more expensive districts or on the outskirts of towns, and only accessible by car. **Motel-** or **hotel-garaje** usually indicates hotels where couples go for a few hours (and where you pay by the hour), but they may still be clean and quite

reasonable in price. Hotel prices
have now been deregulated, so you
should shop around if you can: a
little gentle haggling rarely goes
amiss and many places will have
some less expensive rooms, so ask:
¿tiene un cuarto más barato? Air-
conditioning (aire acondicionado)
is a feature that inflates prices.
Unless it is unbearably hot and
humid, a room with a single ceiling
fan is generally fine.

hotel room el cuarto de
  hotel [kwarto deh otel]
hour la hora [ora]
house la casa
house wine el vino de la casa
  [beeno deh]
  see wine
hovercraft el aerodeslizador
  [a-airodesleesador]
how cómo
  how many? ¿cuántos?
  [kwantos]
  how do you do? ¡mucho
  gusto! [moocho goosto]

dialogues

how are you? ¿cómo le
  va? [leh ba]
fine, thanks, and you?
  bien gracias, ¿y Usted?
  [b-yen gras-yas ee oosteh]

how much is it? ¿cuánto
  vale? [kwanto baleh]
1,000 pesos mil pesos

[pesos]
I'll take it me lo quedo
  [meh lo kedo]

humid húmedo [oomedo]
humour el humor [oomor]
hungry hambriento [ambr-
  yento]
  I'm hungry tengo hambre
  [ambreh]
  are you hungry? ¿tiene
  hambre? [t-yeneh]
hurry (verb) apurarse
  [apoorarseh]
  I'm in a hurry tengo prisa
  there's no hurry no hay prisa
  [ī]
  hurry up! ¡apúrese!
  [apooreseh]
hurt doler [dolair]
  it really hurts me duele
  mucho [meh dweleh moocho]
husband el marido
hydrofoil la hidroala [eedro-ala]
hypermarket el
  hipermercado
  [eepairmairkado]

I

I yo
ice el hielo [yelo]
  with ice con hielo
  no ice, thanks sin hielo, por
  favor [seen – fabor]
ice cream el helado [elado]
ice-cream cone el cucurucho
  [kookooroocho]

95

iced coffee el café helado [kafeh elado]

ice lolly la paleta

idea la idea [eedeh-a]

idiot el/la idiota [eed-yota]

if si

ignition el encendido [ensendeedo]

ill enfermo [enfairmo]
I feel ill me encuentro mal [meh enkwentro]

illness la enfermedad [enfairmeda]

imitation (leather etc) de imitación [deh eemeetas-yon]

immediately en seguida [segeeda]

important importante [eemportanteh]
it's very important es muy importante [mwee]
it's not important no tiene importancia [t-yeneh eemportans-ya]

impossible imposible [eemposeebleh]

impressive impresionante [eempres-yonanteh]

improve mejorar [meHorar]
I want to improve my Spanish quiero mejorar mi español [k-yairo – espan-yol]

in: it's in the centre está en el centro
in my car en mi carro
in Xalapa en Xalapa [Halapa]
in two days from now en dos días más
in five minutes dentro de

cinco minutos [deh]

in May en mayo

in English en inglés [eeng-les]

in Spanish en español [espan-yol]

is he in? ¿se encuentra? [seh enkwentra]

inch* la pulgada

include incluir [eenkloo-eer]
does that include meals? ¿están incluídas las comidas? [eenkloo-eedas]
is that included? ¿está incluido en el precio? [eenkloo-eedo en el pres-yo]

inconvenient inoportuno [eenoportoono]

incredible increíble [eenkreh-eebleh]

Indian (adj: from India) indio [eend-yo]
(South American: adj) indígena [eendeeHena]
(man/woman) el/la indígena

indicator el intermitente [eentairmeetenteh]

indigestion la indigestión [eendeeHest-yon]

indoor pool la alberca cubierta [albairka koob-yairta]

indoors dentro de la casa [deh]

inexpensive económico

infection la infección [eenfeks-yon]

infectious contagioso [kontaH-yoso]

inflammation la inflamación [eenflamas-yon]

informal (occasion, meeting)
informal [eenformal]
(dress) de sport [deh]
information la información
[eenformas-yon]
do you have any information
about ...? ¿tiene
información sobre ... ?
[t-yeneh – sobreh]
information desk la información
injection la inyección [een-
yeks-yon]
injured herido [ereedo]
she's been injured está
herida
in-laws la familia política
[fameel-ya]
inner tube (for tyre) la cámara
de aire [deh a-eereh]
innocent inocente
[eenosenteh]
insect el insecto [eensekto]
insect bite la picadura de
insecto [deh]
do you have anything for
insect bites? ¿tiene algo
para la picadura de
insectos? [t-yeneh]
insect repellent el repelente
de insectos [repelenteh deh]
inside dentro de [deh]
inside the hotel dentro del
hotel
let's sit inside vamos a
sentarnos adentro [bamos]
insist insistir [eenseesteer]
I insist insisto
insomnia el insomnio

[eensomn-yo]
instant coffee el café instantáneo [kafeh eenstantaneh-o]
instead: give me that one
instead deme ese otro
[demeh eseh]
instead of ... en lugar de ...
[deh]
intersection el cruce [krooseh]
insulin la insulina
[eensooleena]
insurance el seguro [segooro]
intelligent inteligente
[eenteleeHenteh]
interested: I'm interested in ...
me interesa ... [meh
eentairesa]
interesting interesante
[eenteresanteh]
that's very interesting es
muy interesante [mwee
eenteresanteh]
international internacional
[eentairnas-yonal]
interpret actuar de intérprete
[actoo-ar deh eentairpreteh]
interpreter el/la intérprete
interval (at theatre) el
intermedio [eentairmed-yo]
into en
I'm not into ... no me
gusta ... [meh goosta]
introduce presentar
may I introduce ...? le
presento a ... [leh]
invitation la invitación
[eembeetas-yon]
invite invitar [eembeetar]
Ireland Irlanda [eerlanda]
Irish irlandés [eerland-es]

I'm Irish (man/woman) soy irlandés/irlandesa

iron (for ironing) la plancha (metal) el hierro [**ya**irro]
  can you iron these for me? ¿puede plancharmelos? [**pwe**deh]

is* es, está

island la isla [**ees**la]

it ello, lo [**eh**-yo]
  it is ... es ...; está ...
  is it ...? ¿es ...?; ¿está ...?
  where is it? ¿dónde está? [**don**deh]
  it's him es él
  it was ... era ... [**ai**ra]; estaba ...

Italian (adj) italiano [eetal-**ya**no]

Italy Italia

itch el comezón [kome**son**]
  it itches me pica [meh]

J

jack (for car) el gato

jacket el saco

jam la mermelada [mair**me**lada]

jammed: it's jammed se atoró [seh]

January enero [e**nai**ro]

jar el pote [**po**teh]

jaw la mandíbula

jazz el jazz

jealous celoso [se**lo**so]

jeans los vaqueros [ba**kai**ros]

jellyfish la medusa [me**doo**sa]

jersey el jersey [Hair**seh**]

jetty el muelle [**mwe**h-yeh]

jeweller's shop la joyería [Ho-yairee-a]

jewellery las joyas [**Ho**-yas]

Jewish judío [Hoo**dee**-o]

job el trabajo [tra**ba**Ho], el puesto [**pwes**to]

jogging el footing
  to go jogging hacer footing [a**sair**]

joke el chiste [**chees**teh]

journey el viaje [b-ya**Heh**]
  have a good journey! ¡buen viaje! [bwen]

jug la jarra [**Ha**rra]
  a jug of water una jarra de agua [deh]

juice el jugo [**Hoo**go]

July julio [**Hool**-yo]

jump (verb) brincar

jumper el jersey [Hair**seh**]

jump leads las pinzas (para la batería) [**peen**sas (para la batairee-a)]

junction el cruce [**kroo**seh]

June junio [**Hoon**-yo]

jungle la selva

just (only) solamente [sola**men**teh]
  just two sólo dos
  just for me sólo para mí
  just here aquí mismo [a**kee mees**mo], aquí mero [**mai**ro]
  not just now ahora no [a-**o**ra]
  we've just arrived acabamos de llegar [deh ye**gar**]

K

kayak el kayak

keep quedarse [kedarseh]

keep the change quédese con el cambio [kedeseh – kamb-yo]

can I keep it? ¿puedo quedármelo? [pwedo kedarmelo]

please keep it por favor, quédeselo [fabor kedeselo]

ketchup el catsup [katsoop]

kettle el hervidor [airbeedor]

key la llave [yabeh]

the key for room 201, please la llave del doscientos uno, por favor [fabor]

keyring el llavero [yabairo]

kidneys los riñones [reen-yon-es]

kill matar

kilo* el kilo

kilometre* el kilómetro

how many kilometres is it to ...? ¿cuántos kilómetros hay a ...? [kwantos – ī]

kind (nice) amable [amableh]

that's very kind es muy amable [mwee]

dialogue

which kind do you want? ¿qué tipo quiere? [keh teepo k-yaireh]

I want this/that kind

quiero este/aquel tipo [k-yairo esteh/akel]

king el rey [ray]

kiosk el quiosco [kee-osko]

kiss el beso

(verb) besarse [besarseh]

kitchen la cocina [koseena]

kitchenette la cocina pequeña [pekwen-ya]

Kleenex® el klínex

knee la rodilla [rodee-ya]

knickers los pantis

knife el cuchillo [koochee-yo]

knock (verb: on door) llamar [yamar]

knock down atropellar [atropeh-yar]

he's been knocked down lo atropellaron [atropeh-yaron]

knock over (object) volcar [bolkar]

(pedestrian) atropellar [atropeh-yar]

know (somebody, a place) conocer [konosair]

(something) saber [sabair]

I don't know no sé [seh]

I didn't know that no lo sabía

do you know where I can find ...? ¿sabe dónde puedo encontrar ...? [sabeh dondeh pwedo]

dialogue

do you know how this works? ¿sabe cómo funciona esto? [foons-yona]

sorry, I don't know lo
siento, no sé [s-yento no
seh]

L

label la etiqueta [eteeketa]
ladies' room, ladies' (toilet) el
servicio de señoras [sairbees-
yo deh sen-yoras]
ladies' wear la ropa de señoras
lady la señora [sen-yora]
lager la cerveza clara
[sairbesa]
see beer
lagoon la laguna
lake el lago
lamb (meat) el cordero
[kordairo]
lamp la lámpara
land la tierra [t-yairra]
(verb) aterrizar [aterreesar]
lane (motorway) el carril
(small road) la callejuela [ka-
yeh-Hwela]
language el idioma [eed-
yoma]
language course el curso de
idiomas [koorso deh]
large grande [grandeh]
last último [oolteemo]
last week la semana pasada
last Friday el viernes pasado
last night anoche [anocheh]
what time is the last train to
Veracruz? ¿a qué hora es el
último tren para Veracruz?
[keh ora – bairakroos]

late tarde [tardeh]
sorry I'm late disculpe, me
retrasé [deeskoolpeh meh
retraseh]
the train was late el tren se
demoró
we must go – we'll be late
debemos irnos –
llegaremos tarde [eernos –
yegaremos]
it's getting late se está
haciendo tarde [seh – as-
yendo]
later más tarde [tardeh]
I'll come back later regresaré
más tarde [regresareh]
see you later hasta luego
[asta lwego]
later on más tarde
latest lo último [oolteemo]
by Wednesday at the latest
para el miércoles a más
tardar
Latin America América
[amaireeka]
Latin American (adj)
americano [amaireekano]
(man) el (latino) americano
(woman) la (latino)
americana
laugh (verb) reirse [reh-eerseh]
launderette/laundromat la
lavandería automática
[labandairee-a owtomateeka]
laundry (clothes) la ropa sucia
[soos-ya]
(place) la lavandería
[labandairee-a]
lavatory el baño [ban-yo]

law la ley [lay]
lawn el césped [sesped]
lawyer (man/woman) el abogado, la abogada
laxative el laxante [laksanteh]
lazy flojo [floHo]
lead (electrical) el cable [kableh]
lead (verb) llevar [yevar]
where does this lead to? ¿adónde va esto? [adondeh ba]
leaf la hoja [oHa]
leaflet el folleto [fo-yeto]
leak (in roof) la gotera [gotaira]
(gas, water) el escape [eskapeh]
(verb) filtrar [feeltrar]
the roof leaks el tejado tiene goteras [teHado t-yeneh gotairas]
learn aprender [aprendair]
least: not in the least de ninguna manera [deh – manaira]
at least al menos
leather (fine) la piel [p-yel]
(heavy) el cuero [kwairo]
leave (verb) irse [eerseh]
I am leaving tomorrow me voy mañana [meh]
he left yesterday se fue ayer [seh fweh]
may I leave this here? ¿puedo dejar esto aquí? [pwedo deh-Har esto akee]
I left my coat in the bar dejé el abrigo en el bar [deh-Heh]

dialogue

when does the bus for Taxco leave? ¿cuándo sale el autobús para Taxco? [kwando saleh – tasko]
it leaves at 9 o'clock sale a las nueve

leek el puerro [pwairro]
left izquierda [eesk-yairda]
on the left a la izquierda
to the left hacia la izquierda [as-ya]
turn left dé vuelta a la izquierda [deh bwelta]
there's none left no queda ninguno [keda]
left-handed zurdo [soordo]
left luggage (office) la consigna [konseegna], la paquetería [paketairee-a]
leg la pierna [p-yairna]
lemon el limón
lemonade la limonada
lemon tea el té con limón [teh]
lend prestar
will you lend me your ... ? ¿podría prestarme su ...? [prestarmeh]
lens (of camera) el objetivo [obHeteebo]
lesbian la lesbiana [lesb-yana]
less menos
less expensive menos caro
less than 10 menos de diez [deh]

less than you menos que tú
[keh too]

lesson la lección [leks-yon]

let (allow) dejar [deh-Har]

will you let me know? ¿me
tendrás al corriente? [meh –
korr-yenteh]

I'll let you know le avisaré
[leh abeesareh]

let's go for something to eat
vamos a comer algo [bamos
a komair]

let off: will you let me off
at ...? ¿me deja en...? [meh
deh-Ha]

letter la carta

do you have any letters for
me? ¿tiene cartas para mí?
[t-yeneh]

letterbox el buzón [booson]

Bright red letterboxes
(buzones) in the street
are quite reliable, but to
be absolutely certain of delivery,
post your letters and packets at the
post office.
see post office

lettuce la lechuga [lechooga]

lever la palanca

library la biblioteca [beebl-
yoteka]

licence el permiso

lid la tapa

lie (verb: tell untruth) mentir

lie down acostarse
[akostarseh], echarse
[echarseh]

life la vida [beeda]

lifebelt el salvavidas [sal-
babeedas]

lifeguard el/la socorrista

life jacket el chaleco
salvavidas [salbabeedas]

lift (in building) el ascensor
[asensor]

could you give me a lift?
¿me podría llevar? [meh –
yebar]

would you like a lift? ¿quiere
que lo lleve? [k-yaireh keh lo
yebeh]

light la luz [loos]
(not heavy) ligero [leeHairo]

do you have a light? (for
cigarette) ¿tiene fuego?
[t-yeneh fwego]

light green verde claro
[bairdeh]

light bulb el foco

I need a new light bulb
necesito un foco nuevo
[neseseeto – nwebo]

lighter (cigarette) el
encendedor [ensendedor]

lightning el relámpago

like (verb) gustar [goostar]

I like it me gusta [meh]

I like going for walks me
gusta pasear

I like you me gustas

I don't like it no me gusta

do you like ...? ¿le gusta ...?
[leh]

I'd like a beer quisiera una
cerveza [kees-yaira]

I'd like to go swimming me

gustaría ir a bañarme
would you like a drink?
¿quiere beber algo?
[k-yaireh]
**would you like to go for a
walk?** ¿quieres dar un
paseo? [k-yair-es]
what's it like? ¿cómo es?
I want one like this quiero
uno como éste [k-yairo –
esteh]
lime la lima [leema]
lime cordial el jarabe de lima
[Harabeh deh]
line la línea [leeneh-a]
**could you give me an outside
line?** ¿puede darme línea?
[pwedeh darmeh]
lips los labios [lab-yos]
lip salve la crema de labios
[deh]
lipstick el lápiz de labios
[lapees]
liqueur el licor
listen oir [o-eer]
litre* el litro
a litre of white wine un litro
de vino blanco [deh]
little chico
just a little, thanks un
poquito, gracias [pokeeto
gras-yas]
a little milk un poco de
leche
a little bit more un poquito
más
live (verb) vivir [beebeer]
we live together vivimos
juntos [beebeemos Hoontos]

dialogue

where do you live?
¿dónde vive? [dondeh
beebeh]
I live in London vivo en
Londres [beebo en lond-res]

lively alegre [alegreh],
animado
liver el hígado [eegado]
lizard la lagartija [lagarteeHa]
loaf el pan
lobby (in hotel) el vestíbulo
[besteeboolo]
lobster la langosta
local local
**can you recommend a local
wine/restaurant?** ¿puede
recomendarme un vino/un
restaurante local? [pwedeh
rekomendarmeh]
lock la cerradura [sairradoora]
(verb) cerrar [sairrar]
it's locked está cerrado con
llave [sairrado kon yabeh]
lock in dejar encerrado [deh-
Har ensairrado]
**lock out: I've locked myself
out** he cerrado la puerta
con las llaves dentro [eh
sairrado la pwairta – yab-es]
locker (for luggage etc) la
consigna automática
[konseegna owtomateeka]
lollipop la paleta
London Londres [lond-res]
long largo
how long will it take to fix it?

¿cuánto tiempo tardará en arreglarlo? [kwanto t-yempo]
how long does it take?
¿cuánto tiempo lleva? [yeba]
a long time mucho tiempo [moocho]
one day/two days longer un día/dos días más
long distance call la llamada de larga distancia [yamada deh – deestans-ya]
look: I'm just looking, thanks sólo estoy mirando, gracias [gras-yas]
you don't look well tienes cara de enfermo [t-yen-es kara deh enfairmo]
look out! ¡cuidado! [kweedado]
can I have a look? ¿me deja ver? [meh deh-Ha bair]
look after cuidar [kweedar]
look at mirar
look for buscar
I'm looking for ... estoy buscando ...
look forward to: I'm looking forward to seeing it tengo muchas ganas de verlo [moochas – deh bairlo]
loose (handle etc) suelto [swelto]
lorry el camión [kam-yon], el tráiler [trīlair]
lose perder [pairdair], extraviarse [estrab-yarseh]
I've lost my way me extravié [estrab-yeh]
I'm lost, I want to get to ...

me perdí, quiero ir a ... [k-yairo eer]
I've lost my bag perdí el bolso
lost property (office) (la oficina de) objetos perdidos [(ofeeseena deh) obHetos pairdeedos]
lot: a lot, lots mucho, muchos [moocho]
not a lot no mucho
a lot of people mucha gente
a lot bigger mucho mayor
I like it a lot me gusta mucho [meh goosta]
lotion la loción [los-yon]
loud fuerte [fwairteh]
lounge (in house, hotel) el salón (in airport) la sala de espera [deh espaira]
love el amor
(verb) querer [kairair]
I love Mexico me encanta México [meh – meHeeko]
lovely encantador
low bajo [baHo]
luck la suerte [swairteh]
good luck! ¡buena suerte! [bwena]
luggage el equipaje [ekeepaH-eh]
luggage trolley el carrito portaequipajes [porta-ekeepaH-es]
lump (on body) la hinchazón [eenchason]
lunch el almuerzo [almwairso]
lungs los pulmones [poolmon-es]

luxurious (hotel, furnishings) de
lujo [deh looHo]
luxury el lujo

M

machine la máquina
[makeena]
mad (insane) loco
(angry) furioso [foor-yoso]
magazine la revista [rebeesta]
maid (in hotel) la camarera
[kamaraira]
maiden name el nombre de
soltera [nombreh deh soltaira]
mail el correo [korreh-o]
is there any mail for me?
¿hay correspondencia para
mí? [i korrespondens-ya]
see post office
mailbox el buzón [booson]
see letterbox
main principal [preenseepal]
main course el plato
principal
main post office la oficina
central de correos [ofeeseena
sentral deh korreh-os]
main road (in town) la calle
principal [ka-yeh preenseepal]
(in country) la carretera
principal [karretaira]
mains (for water) la llave de
paso [yabeh deh]
mains switch (for electricity) el
interruptor de la red
eléctrica [eentairrooptor deh la
reh]

make (brand name) la marca
(verb) hacer [asair]
I make it 500 pesos son
quinientos pesos en total
what is it made of? ¿de qué
está hecho? [deh keh esta
echo]
make-up el maquillaje
[makee-yaHeh]
man el hombre [ombreh]
manager el gerente [Hairenteh]
I'd like to speak to the manager quisiera hablar con el
gerente [kees-yaira ablar]
manageress la gerente

mañana
You may never experience
it at all, but Mexico is still a
place where there are days when
everything seems to go wrong –
especially if it involves bureaucrats or
machinery. Getting things done can
be exasperating. Don't even try to
fight it: it will only make things worse.
The only way to survive these days is
to adopt the local attitude that it will
work out in the end, and in the
meantime there's probably something
better to do anyway. The suggestion
that Mexico is in some way inefficient
is, like political criticism, an idea best
kept to yourself.

manual (car with manual gears) el
carro de marchas [deh]
many muchos [moochos]
not many pocos
map (city plan) el plano

(road map, geographical) el mapa

It's always worth stocking up in advance with as many brochures and plans as you can find in **Sectur** tourist offices abroad. Tourist offices in Mexico are frequently closed or have run out.

March marzo [marso]
margarine la margarina
market el mercado [mairkado], el tianguis [t-yangees]

For bargain hunters, the weekly **mercado** (market) or **tianguis** (an Aztec word, still sometimes used) is the place to head for, particularly in smaller provincial towns and villages. By and large, markets are mainly devoted to food and everyday necessities, but most have a section devoted to crafts, and in larger towns you may find a separate crafts bazaar. In larger cities there will be both local markets and larger ones that sell more or less everything. Unless you're hopeless at bargaining, prices will always be lower in the market than in the shops.
see **bargaining**

marmalade la mermelada de naranja [mairmelada deh naranHa]
married: I'm married (said by a man/woman) estoy casado/ casada
are you married? (to a man/woman) ¿está casado/ casada?
mascara el rímel
match (football etc) el partido
matches las cerillas [sairee-yas]
material (fabric) el tejido [teHeedo]
matter: it doesn't matter no importa
what's the matter? ¿qué pasa? [keh]
mattress el colchón
May mayo [mī-yo]
may: may I have another one? ¿me da otro? [meh]
may I come in? ¿se puede? [seh pwedeh]
may I see it? ¿puedo verlo? [pwedo bairlo]
may I sit here? ¿puedo sentarme aquí? [sentarmeh akee]
maybe quizás [keesas]
mayonnaise la mayonesa [mī-yonesa]
me*: that's for me ése es para mí [eseh]
send it to me mándemelo
me too yo también [tamb-yen]
meal la comida

dialogue

did you enjoy your meal? ¿te gustó la comida? [teh goosto]
it was excellent, thank you

estuvo riquísima, gracias
[reek**ee**seema gras-yas]

mean (verb) querer decir
[kair**air** des**ee**r]
what do you mean? ¿qué
quiere decir? [keh k-y**ai**reh]

dialogue

what does this word
mean? ¿qué significa esta
palabra?
it means ... in English
significa ... en inglés
[eeng-l**es**]

measles el sarampión
[saramp-y**on**]
meat la carne [**k**arneh]
mechanic el mecánico
medicine la medicina
[medees**ee**na]
medium (adj: size) medio
[med-yo]
medium-dry semi-seco
medium-rare poco hecho
[**ech**o]
medium-sized de tamaño
medio [taman-yo med-yo]
meet encontrarse
[encontr**a**rseh]
(for the first time) conocerse
[konos**ai**rseh]
nice to meet you encantado
de conocerle [deh konos**ai**rleh]
where shall I meet you?
¿dónde nos vemos? [d**o**ndeh
nos b**e**mos]

meeting la reunión [reh-oon-
y**on**]
meeting place el lugar de
encuentro [loogar deh
enkw**e**ntro]
melon el mel**ó**n
men los hombres [**o**mb-res]
mend (clothes) remendar
could you mend this for me?
¿puede arreglarme esto?
[pw**e**deh arreglarmeh]
men's toilet el servicio de
hombres [sairbee-yos deh **o**mb-
res]
menswear la ropa de
hombre [deh **o**mbreh]
mention (verb) mencionar
[mens-yonar]
don't mention it no hay de
qué [i deh keh]
menu la carta
may I see the menu, please?
¿me deja ver la carta? [meh
d**e**Ha bair]
see menu reader page 248
message: are there any
messages for me? ¿hay
algún recado para mí? [i]
I want to leave a message
for ... quisiera dejar un
recado para ... [kees-y**ai**ra deh-
Har]
metal el metal
metre* el metro
Mexican (adj) mexicano
[meHeek**a**no]
(man) el mexicano
(woman) la mexicana
the Mexicans los mexicanos

Mexico México [meHeeko]

The name of the capital city of Mexico is a source of infinite confusion to travellers. Mexico City is not a place on any Mexican map nor is it ever used by Mexicans – they call it **México** or sometimes **El D.F.** ([el deh efeh]: the **Distrito Federal** is the administrative zone that contains most of the urban areas). The country took its name from the city, and in conversation México almost always means the latter. The nation is **la República** or in speeches **la Patria** – very rarely Mexico.

Mexico City la ciudad de México [s-yooda deh], el Distrito Federal [fedairal], el D.F. [deh efeh]
microwave (oven) el (horno) microondas [(orno) meekro-ondas]
midday el mediodía [med-yodee-a]
  at midday a mediodía
middle: in the middle en el centro [sentro]
  in the middle of the night en las altas horas de la noche [oras deh la nocheh]
  the middle one el de en medio
midnight la medianoche [med-yanocheh]
  at midnight a medianoche

might: I might es posible [poseebleh]
  I might not go puede que no vaya [pwedeh keh no bī-ya]
  I might want to stay another day quizás decida quedarme otro día [keesas deseeda kedarmeh]
migraine la jaqueca [Hakeka]
mild (taste) suave [swabeh]
  (weather) templado
mile* la milla [mee-ya]
milk la leche [lecheh]
milkshake el licuado [leekwa-do]
millimetre* el milímetro
minced meat el picadillo [peekadee-yo]
mind: never mind! ¡no importa!
  I've changed my mind cambié de idea [kamb-yeh deh eedeh-a]

dialogue

do you mind if I open the window? ¿le importa que abra la ventana? [leh eemporta keh – bentana]
no, I don't mind no, no me importa [meh]

mine*: it's mine es mío
mineral water el agua mineral [agwa meenairal], el Tehuacán® [teh-wakan]
mint-flavoured con sabor a menta

mints las pastillas de menta [pastee-yas deh]
minute el minuto [meenooto]
  in a minute ahorita [a-oreeta]
  just a minute un momento
mirror el espejo [espeнo]
Miss Señorita [sen-yoreeta]
miss: I missed the bus perdí el autobús [pairdee]
missing: one of my ... is missing falta uno de mis ... [deh]
  there's a suitcase missing falta una maleta
mist la neblina
mistake el error
  I think there's a mistake me parece que hay una equivocación [meh pareseh keh ī oona ekeebokas-yon]
  sorry, I've made a mistake perdón, me equivoqué [meh ekeebokeh]
misunderstanding el malentendido
mix-up: sorry, there's been a mix-up perdón hubo una confusión [oobo oona konfoos-yon]
modern moderno [modairno]
modern art gallery la galería de arte moderno [galairee-a deh arteh]
moisturizer la crema hidratante [eedratanteh]
moment: I won't be a moment no me tardo [meh]
monastery el monasterio [monastair-yo]
Monday lunes [loon-es]

money el dinero [deenairo]
month el mes
monument el monumento [monoomento]
  (statue) la estatua [estatwa]
moon la luna
moped el ciclomotor [seeklomotor]
more* más
  can I have some more water, please? me da más agua, por favor [meh – fabor]
  more expensive/interesting más caro/interesante
  more than 50 más de cincuenta [deh]
  more than that más que eso [keh]
  a lot more mucho más [moocho]

dialogue

would you like some more? ¿quiere más? [k-yaireh]
no, no more for me, thanks no, para mí no, gracias [gras-yas]
how about you? ¿y Usted? [ee oosteh]
I don't want any more, thanks nada más, gracias

morning la mañana [man-yana]
  this morning esta mañana
  in the morning por la mañana
mosquito el mosquito, el

zancudo [sank**oo**do]

Mosquitos (called **zancudos** more often than **mosquitos**) are active at all times of the day, but are particularly prevalent in the evening. Wear long sleeves, skirts or trousers, avoid dark colours, which attract mosquitos, and put repellent on all exposed skin. Alternatively, use a mosquito coil in your room or sleep under a mosquito net. Other biting insects are bedbugs, sandflies (on beaches), and head or body lice which can be picked up from bedding and people; scorpions and snakes are more serious but rarer hazards; seek medical help if bitten, explaining: **me picó un zancudo/una víbora/un escorpión** [meh peek**o** oon sank**oo**do/**oo**na beebora/oon eskorp-y**o**n] (I've been bitten by a mosquito/snake/ scorpion).

see **health**

mosquito coil el espiral antimosquitos
mosquito net la red antimosquitos
mosquito repellent el repelente de mosquitos [repel**e**nteh deh]
most: I like this one most of all éste es el que más me gusta [**e**steh – keh mas meh g**oo**sta]
most of the time la mayor

parte del tiempo [mī-y**o**r parteh del t-y**e**mpo]
most tourists la mayoría de los turistas [mī-yor**ee**-a deh]
mostly generalmente [нenairalm**e**nteh]
mother la madre [**ma**dreh]
motorbike la m**o**to
motorboat la (lancha) mot**o**ra
motorway la autopista [owtop**ee**sta]
see **driving**
mountain la montaña [mont**a**n-ya]
in the mountains en la sierra [s-y**ai**ra]
mountaineering el montañismo [montan-y**ee**smo]
mountain range la sierra
mouse el rat**ó**n
moustache el bigote [beeg**o**teh]
mouth la b**o**ca
mouth ulcer la llaga [y**a**ga]
move: he's moved to another room se trasladó a **o**tro cuarto [seh – kw**a**rto]
could you move your car? ¿podría cambiar de lug**a**r el carro? [kamb-y**a**r deh]
could you move up a little? ¿puede correrse un p**o**co? [pw**e**deh korr**ai**rseh]
where has it moved to? ¿adónde se trasladó? [ad**o**ndeh seh]
movie la película [pel**ee**koola]
movie theater el cine [s**ee**neh]
Mr Señor [sen-y**o**r]

Mrs Señora [sen-y**o**ra]
Ms Señorita [sen-yor**ee**ta]
much mucho [m**oo**cho]
  much better/worse mucho
  mejor/peor [mi-y**o**r/peh-**o**r]
  much hotter mucho más
  caliente [kal-y**e**nteh]
  not (very) much no mucho
  I don't want very much un
  p**o**co nada más
mud el b**a**rro, el l**o**do
mug (for drinking) la taza [t**a**sa]
  I've been mugged me
  asalt**a**ron
mum la mam**á**
mumps las paperas [pap**ai**ras]
museum el museo [moos**eh**-o]

Most museums and
galleries will be open
from about 9 a.m. to
1 p.m. and again from 3 to 6 p.m.
Many have reduced entry fees or are
free on Sundays, but may open only
in the morning; most are closed on
Monday. Archaeological sites (**zonas
arqueológicas**) are usually open
right through the day.

mushrooms los champiñones
  [champee-y**o**n-es]
music la música [m**oo**seeka]
musician el/la músico
  [m**oo**seeko]
Muslim (adj) musulmán
  [moosool**man**]
mussels los mejillones
  [meHee-y**o**n-es]
must: I must tengo que [keh]

I mustn't drink alcohol no
  debo beber alcohol [beb**air**
  alko-**ol**]
mustard la mostaza [most**a**sa]
my* mi; (pl) mis
myself: I'll do it myself (said by
  man/woman) lo haré yo
  mismo/misma [ar**eh**]
  by myself (said by man/woman)
  yo s**o**lo/s**o**la

N

nail (finger) la uña [**oo**n-ya]
  (metal) el clavo [kl**a**bo]
nailbrush el cepillo para las
  uñas [sep**ee**-yo – **oo**n-yas]
nail varnish el esmalte para
  uñas [esm**a**lteh]
name el nombre [n**o**mbreh]
  my name's John me llamo
  John [meh y**a**mo]
  what's your name? ¿cómo se
  llama? [seh y**a**ma], ¿cuál es su
  nombre? [kwal – n**o**mbreh]
  **what is the name of this
  street?** ¿cómo se llama esta
  calle?

In the Spanish-speaking
world people generally
use two surnames, the
second of which is their mother's. In
Mexico you will come across many
unusual Christian names, some of
them of Aztec origin (**Cuauhtémoc**,
Xóchitl). It is also very common for
people to be addressed by a title:

Licenciado (graduate), **Maestro** (teacher), **Ingeniero** (Engineer) etc.

napkin la servilleta [sairbee-**yeta**]

nappy el pañal [pan-**yal**]

narrow (street) estrecho [estr**echo**]

nasty (person) desagradable [desagrad**ableh**]
(weather, accident) malo

national nacional [nas-yonal]

nationality la nacionalidad [nas-yonaleeda]

natural natural [nat**ooral**]

nausea la náusea [**now**seh-a]

navy (blue) azul marino [as**ool**]

near cerca [**sair**ka]
is it near the city centre?
¿está cerca del centro?
[**sen**tro]
do you go near the Zócalo?
¿pasa Usted cerca del
Zócalo? [oost**eh** – **so**calo]
where is the nearest ...?
¿dónde está el ... más
cercano? [**don**deh – sair**ka**no]

nearby por aquí cerca [ak**ee**]

nearly casi

necessary necesario [nesesar-yo]

neck el cuello [kw**eh**-yo]

necklace el collar [ko-**yar**]

necktie la corbata

need: I need ... necesito
un ... [neses**ee**to]
do I need to pay? ¿necesito
pagar?

needle la aguja [ag**oo**Ha]

negative (film) el negativo [negat**ee**bo]

neither: neither (one) of them
ninguno (de ellos)
[neeng**oo**no (deh **eh**-yos)]
neither ... nor ... ni ... ni ...

nephew el sobrino

net (in sport) la red

Netherlands Los Países Bajos [pa-**ee**s-es ba**Hos**]

network map el mapa

never nunca, jamás [Ham**as**]

dialogue

have you ever been to
Mérida? ¿ha estado alguna
vez en Mérida? [bes]
no, never, I've never been
there no, nunca estuve
[est**oo**beh]

new nuevo [nw**e**bo]

news (radio, TV etc) las noticias [not**ee**s-yas]

newspaper el periódico [pair-yo**dee**ko]

newspaper kiosk el puesto
de periódicos [pw**e**sto deh]

New Year el Año Nuevo [an-yo nw**e**bo]
Happy New Year! ¡Feliz Año
Nuevo! [fel**ees**]
see holiday

New Year's Eve Nochevieja [n**o**cheh-b-ye**Ha**]

New Zealand Nueva Zelanda [nw**e**ba sel**a**nda]

New Zealander: I'm a New Zealander (man/woman) soy neozelandés/neozelandesa [neh-o-seland-es]
next próximo
  the next street on the left la próxima calle a la izquierda [ka-yeh a la eesk-yairda]
  at the next stop en la siguiente parada [seeg-yenteh]
  next week la semana que viene [keh b-yeneh]
  next to al lado de [deh]
Nicaraguan (adj) nicaraguense [neekaragwenseh]
nice (food) bueno [bweno]
  (looks, view etc) lindo
  (person) simpático
niece la sobrina
night la noche [nocheh]
  at night de noche [deh], por la noche
  good night buenas noches [bwenas noch-es]

dialogue

do you have a single room for one night? ¿tiene un cuarto individual para una noche? [t-yeneh oon kwarto eendeebeedwal]
yes, madam sí, señora [sen-yora]
how much is it per night? ¿cuánto es la noche? [kwanto]
it's 3,000 pesos for one night son tres mil pesos

la noche
thank you, I'll take it gracias, me la quedo [gras-yas meh la kedo]

nightclub la discoteca [deeskoteka]
nightdress el camisón
night porter el portero [portairo]
no no
  I've no change no tengo cambio [kamb-yo]
  there's no ... left no queda ... [keda]
  no way! ¡ni hablar! [ablar]
  oh no! (upset, annoyed) ¡Dios mío! [d-yos]
nobody nadie [nad-yeh]
  there's nobody there no hay nadie [ī]
noise el ruido [rweedo]
noisy: it's too noisy hay demasiado ruido [ī demas-yado]
non-alcoholic sin alcohol [seen alko-ol]
none ninguno
non-smoking compartment no fumadores [foomador-es]
noon el mediodía [med-yodee-a]
no-one nadie [nad-yeh]
nor: nor do I yo tampoco
normal normal [nor-mal]
north norte [norteh]
  in the north en el norte
  north of Taxco al norte de Taxco [deh tasko]

North America América del norte [amaireeka del norteh]
North American (man) el norteamericano
(woman) la norteamericana
(adj) norteamericano
northeast nordeste [nordesteh]
northern del norte [norteh]
Northern Ireland Irlanda del Norte [eerlanda del norteh]
northwest noroeste [noro-esteh]
Norway Noruega [norwega]
Norwegian (adj) noruego
nose la nariz [narees]
nosebleed la hemorragia nasal [emorraн-ya]
not* no
no, I'm not hungry no, no tengo hambre [ambreh]
I don't want any, thank you no quiero, gracias [k-yairo gras-yas]
it's not necessary no es necesario [nesesar-yo]
I didn't know that no lo sabía
not that one – this one ése no – éste [eseh – esteh]
note (banknote) el billete [bee-yeteh]
notebook el cuaderno [kwadairno]
notepaper (for letters) el papel de carta [deh]
nothing nada
nothing for me, thanks para mí nada, gracias [gras-yas]
nothing else nada más

novel la novela [nobela]
November noviembre [nob-yembreh]
now ahora [a-ora]
number el número [noomairo]
I've got the wrong number me equivoqué de número [meh ekeebokeh deh]
what is your phone number? ¿cuál es su número de teléfono? [kwal]
number plate la placa
nurse (man/woman) el enfermero [enfairmairo], la enfermera
nursery slope la pista de principiantes [deh preenseep-yant-es]
nut (for bolt) la tuerca [twairka]
nuts las nueces [nwes-es]

O

o'clock: at two o'clock a las dos
occupied (US: toilet etc) ocupado [okoopado]
October octubre [oktoobreh]
odd (strange) extraño [ekstran-yo]
of de [deh]
off (lights) apagado
it's just off calle Corredera está cerca de calle Corredera [sairka deh ka-yeh]
we're off tomorrow nos vamos mañana [bamos]
offensive (language, behaviour)

ofensivo [ofenseebo]

office (place of work) la oficina [ofeeseena]

officer (said to policeman) señor oficial [sen-yor ofee-syal]

often a menudo

not often pocas veces [bes-es]

how often are the buses? ¿cada cuándo pasa el camión? [kwando]

oil el aceite [asayteh]

ointment la pomada

OK bueno [bweno]

are you OK? ¿está bien? [b-yen]

is that OK with you? ¿le parece bien? [leh pareseh]

is it OK to ...? ¿se puede ...? [seh pwedeh]

that's OK thanks (it doesn't matter) está bien, gracias [gras-yas]

I'm OK (nothing for me) para mí nada

(I feel OK) me siento bien [meh s-yento]

is this train OK for ...? ¿este tren va a...? [esteh – ba]

I said I'm sorry, OK? ya pedí disculpas ¿okey? [deeskoolpas okay]

old viejo [b-yeHo]

dialogue

how old are you? ¿cuántos años tiene? [kwantos an-yos t-yeneh]

I'm twenty-five tengo veinticinco años

and you? ¿y Usted? [ee oosteh]

old-fashioned pasado de moda [deh]

old town (old part of town) el barrio antiguo [barr-yo anteegwo]

in the old town en el barrio antiguo

olive la aceituna [asaytoona], la oliva [oleeba]

black/green olives las aceitunas negras/verdes [baird-es]

olive oil el aceite de oliva [asayteh deh oleeba]

omelette la tortilla de huevo [tortee-ya deh webo]

on en

on the street/beach en la calle/playa

is it on this road? ¿está en esta calle?

on the plane en el avión

on Saturday el sábado

on television en la tele

I haven't got it on me no lo traigo [trygo]

this one's on me (drink) ésta me toca a mí [meh]

the light wasn't on la luz no estaba prendida

what's on tonight? ¿qué ponen esta noche? [keh]

once (one time) una vez [bes]

115

at once (immediately) en
seguida [segeeda]
one* uno [oono], una
the white one el blanco, la
blanca
one-way: a one-way ticket
to ... un boleto de ida
para ... [deh eeda]
onion la cebolla [sebo-ya]
only sólo
only one sólo uno
it's only 6 o'clock son sólo
las seis
I've only just got here acabo
de llegar [deh yegar]
on/off switch el interruptor
[eentairrooptor]
open (adj) abierto [ab-yairto]
(verb) abrir [abreer]
when do you open? ¿a qué
hora abre? [keh ora abreh]
I can't get it open no puedo
abrirlo [pwedo]
in the open air al aire libre
[ireh leebreh]
opening times el horario
[orar-yo]
open ticket el boleto abierto
[ab-yairto]
opera la ópera
operation (medical) la
operación [opairas-yon]
operator (telephone: man/woman)
el operador, la operadora

For the international
operator (for collect
calls), dial 09.

opposite: the opposite
direction el sentido
contrario
the bar opposite el bar de
enfrente [deh enfrenteh]
opposite my hotel enfrente
de mi hotel
optician el óptico
or o
orange (fruit) la naranja
[naranHa]
(colour) (color) naranja
orange juice (fresh) el jugo de
naranja [Hoogo deh]
(fizzy, diluted) el refresco de
naranja
orchestra la orquesta [orkesta]
order: can we order now? (in
restaurant) ¿podemos pedir
ya?
I've already ordered, thanks
ya pedí, gracias [gras-yas]
I didn't order this no pedí
esto
out of order averiado [abair-
yado], fuera de servicio
[fwaira deh sairbees-yo]
ordinary corriente [korr-
yenteh]
other otro
the other one el otro
the other day el otro día
I'm waiting for the others
estoy esperando a los demás
do you have any others?
¿tiene otros? [t-yeneh]
otherwise de otra manera
[deh – manaira]
our* nuestro [nwestro],

nuestra; (pl) nuestros, nuestras

ours* (el) nuestro, (la) nuestra

out: he's out no está

three kilometres out of town a tres kilómetros de la ciudad

outdoors fuera de casa [fwaira deh]

outside ... fuera de ...

can we sit outside? ¿podemos sentarnos fuera?

oven el horno [orno]

over: over here por aquí [akee]

over there por allá [a-ya]

over 500 más de quinientos [deh]

it's over se acabó [seh]

overcharge: you've overcharged me me cobró de más [meh – deh]

overcoat el abrigo

overlook: I'd like a room overlooking the courtyard quiero un cuarto que da al patio [k-yairo oon kwarto keh da]

overnight (travel) toda la noche [nocheh]

overtake adelantarse a [adelantarseh]

owe: how much do I owe you? ¿cuánto le debo? [kwanto leh]

own: my own ... mi propio ... [prop-yo]

are you on your own? (to a man/woman) ¿está solo/sola?

I'm on my own (said by man/woman) estoy solo/sola

owner (man/woman) el propietario [prop-yetar-yo], la propietaria

P

Pacific Ocean el Océano Pacífico [oseh-ano]

pack: a pack of ... un paquete de ... [paketeh deh] (verb) hacer las maletas [asair]

a pack of cigarettes una cajetilla de cigarros [kaHetee-ya deh seegarros]

package (parcel) el paquete [paketeh]

package holiday el paquete

packed lunch la bolsa con la comida

packet: a packet of cigarettes una cajetilla de cigarros [kaHetee-ya deh seegarros]

padlock el candado

page (of book) la página [paHeena]

could you page Mr ...? ¿podría llamar al Señor ... (por altavoz)? [yamar – altabos]

pain el dolor

I have a pain here me duele aquí [meh dweleh akee]

painful doloroso

painkillers los analgésicos [analHeseekos]

paint la pintura

painting el cuadro [kwadro]
pair: a pair of ... un par de ...
[deh]
Pakistani (adj) paquistaní
[pakeestanee]
palace el palacio [palas-yo]
pale pálido
pale blue azul claro [asool]
pan la olla [o-ya]
panties (underwear: women's) las
bragas, los pantis
pants (underwear: men's) los
calzones [kalson-es]
(women's) las bragas
(US: trousers) los pantalones
[pantalon-es]
pantyhose las pantimedias
[panteemed-yas]
paper el papel
(newspaper) el periódico [pair-
yodeeko]
a piece of paper un pedazo
de papel [pedaso deh]
paper handkerchiefs los
klínex®
parcel el paquete [paketeh]
pardon (me)? (didn't
understand/hear) ¿mande?
[mandeh]
parents: my parents mis
padres [pad-res]
parents-in-law los suegros
[swegros]
park el parque [parkeh]
(verb) estacionar [estas-
yonar]
can I park here? ¿puedo
estacionarme aquí? [pwedo
estas-yonarmeh akee]

parking
Parking restrictions in
cities are complicated
and foreigners are easy pickings for
traffic police, who usually remove
one or both licence plates in lieu of
giving a ticket (retrieving them can
be an expensive and time-
consuming business). Since theft is
a real threat, it's worth paying extra
for a hotel with secure parking.
There are now increasing numbers
of multi-storey car parks
(**estacionamientos**), often under or
around the central square. Here
your car will be fairly secure,
though it is wise to leave nothing
inside it.

parking lot el
estacionamiento [estas-
yonam-yento]
part la parte [parteh]
partner (boyfriend, girlfriend etc)
el compañero [kompan-yairo],
la compañera
party (group) el grupo
(political) el partido
(celebration) la fiesta
pass (in mountains) el paso
passenger (man/woman) el
pasajero [pasaHairo], la
pasajera
passport el pasaporte
[pasaporteh]

Citizens of most Western
countries (France and
South Africa are

exceptions) do not require a visa to enter Mexico as tourists for less than 90 days. What they do need is a valid passport and a tourist card (or **FMT – Folleto de Migración Turística**). Tourist cards are free and, if flying direct, you should be able to pick one up on the plane, through a travel agent or at a Mexican consulate. It is preferable to obtain a card in advance as it may be difficult to get one from border officials. Don't lose the blue copy of your tourist card, given back to you after immigration inspection. You are legally required to carry it at all times and must hand it in when leaving Mexico.

past*: in the past
antiguamente [anteegwa-menteh]
  just past the information office justo después de la oficina de información [Hoosto despwes deh]
path el camino
pattern el dibujo [deebooHo]
pavement la acera [asaira]
  on the pavement en la acera
pavement café el café terraza [kafeh terrasa]
pay (verb) pagar
  can I pay, please? me pasa la cuenta, por favor [meh – kwenta por fabor]
  it's already paid for ya está pagado

dialogue

who's paying? ¿quién paga? [k-yen]
I'll pay pago yo
no, you paid last time, I'll pay no, Usted pagó la última vez, pago yo [oost-eh – oolteema bes]

pay phone el teléfono público [poobleeko], la caseta telefónica
peaceful tranquilo [trankeelo]
peach el durazno [doorasno]
peanuts los cacahuates [kakawat-es]
pear la pera [paira]
peas los chícharos [cheecharos]
peculiar extraño [ekstran-yo]
pedestrian crossing el paso de peatones [peh-aton-es]
pedestrian precinct la calle peatonal [ka-yeh peh-atonal]
peg (for washing) la pinza [peensa]
  (for tent) la estaca
pen la pluma [plooma]
pencil el lápiz [lapees]
penfriend (male/female) el amigo/la amiga por correspondencia [korrespondens-ya]
penicillin la penicilina [peneeseeleena]
penknife la navaja [nabaHa]
pensioner el jubilado [Hoobeelado], la jubilada

119

people la gente [**H**en**teh**]
  the other people in the hotel
  los **o**tros hu**é**spedes en el
  hotel [**we**sped-es]
  too many people demas**i**ada
  gente [demas-**ya**da]
pepper (spice) la pimi**e**nta
  [peem-**ye**nta]
  (vegetable) el pimi**e**nto
peppermint (sweet) el d**u**lce
  de m**e**nta [**doo**lseh deh]
per: per night por n**o**che
  [**no**cheh]
  how much per day? ¿cu**á**nto
  es por d**í**a? [**kwa**nto]
  per cent por ci**e**nto [s-**ye**nto]
perfect perf**e**cto [pair**fe**kto]
perfume el perf**u**me
  [pair**foo**meh]
perhaps quiz**á**s [**kee**sas]
  perhaps not quiz**á**s no
period (of time) el per**í**odo
  [pair**ee**-odo]
  (menstruation) la r**e**gla
perm la perman**e**nte
  [pairman**e**nteh]
permit el perm**i**so [pair**mee**so]
person la pers**o**na [pair**so**na]
personal stereo el walk-
  man® [**wo**lkman]
Peruvian (adj) peru**a**no [peroo-
  ano]
petrol la gasol**i**na

Petrol can be a problem:
the government oil
company Pemex has a
monopoly and sells two types of
petrol: **nova** (leaded) and **magna**
sin (unleaded) which cost about the
same as regular unleaded north of
the border. Often, however, **nova** is
the only type available; it's very dirty
and is quick to foul up any car with
a highly-tuned engine or anything
designed to run on unleaded petrol.
Two new brands called **nova plus**
and **extra plus** have been
introduced but are not easy to come
by. **Diesel** is also available.

petrol can la l**a**ta de gasol**i**na
  [deh]
petrol station la gasolin**e**ra
  [gasoleen**ai**ra]
pharmacy la farm**a**cia [far-
  mas-ya]

For minor medical
problems, head for the
green cross and the
farmacia signs. Pharmacists are
usually knowledgeable and helpful,
and many also speak some English.
They can sell medicines over the
counter which would only be
available on prescription at home.

phone el tel**é**fono
  (verb) llam**a**r por tel**é**fono
  [yam**a**r]

Local phone calls are
cheap, and most hotels
will let you call locally for
free. Coin-operated phones, even
those that seem to be in a terrible
state, usually work for local calls.

Internal long-distance calls can be made from any reasonably new coin-operated phone, but these are far more expensive. Public phones are blue for long-distance, or orange for local (and operator-connected) calls only. On both, you lift the receiver, insert coins (check for the dialling tone: some have a button to get the tone), then dial. Some take phonecards, available from telephone offices and stores near the phones that use them. Currently there are two types of card, which won't work in the same telephones. Many newer phones say they accept credit cards but in practice they usually don't. Slightly more expensive and reliable are **casetas telefónicas**. They can be simply shops or bars with public phones, indicated by a sign outside, or they can be specialist phone and fax places displaying a blue and white **Larga Distancia** sign. Casetas telefónicas are also found at almost every bus station and airport. You're connected by an operator, who gives you the bill afterwards. Wherever you make them from, international calls are very expensive, particularly from hotels. The least bad rates are from public call boxes using a phonecard. You may prefer to call collect (**por cobrar**), which you can do from any public phone by dialling the international operator (09), or have a calling card that offers service from Mexico.

phone book la guía telefónica [gee-a]
phone box la caseta telefónica
phonecard la tarjeta de teléfono [tarHeta deh]
phone number el número de teléfono [noomairo deh]
photo la foto
  excuse me, could you take a photo of us? ¿le importaría sacarnos una foto? [leh]
phrasebook el libro de frases [deh fras-es]
piano el piano [p-yano]
pickpocket el/la carterista [kartaireesta]
pick up: will you come and pick me up? ¿pasarás a recogerme? [rekoHairmeh]
picnic el picnic
picture el cuadro [kwadro]
pie (meat) la empanada (fruit) la tarta
piece el pedazo [pedaso]
  a piece of ... un pedazo de ... [deh]
pig el chancho, el cerdo [sairdo]
pill la píldora
  I'm on the pill estoy tomando la píldora
pillow la almohada [almo-ada]
pillow case la funda (de almohada) [foonda (deh)]
pin el alfiler [alfeelair]
pineapple la piña [peen-ya]
pineapple juice el jugo de piña [Hoogo deh]

Pi

pink rosa
pipe (for smoking) la pipa [peepa]
(for water) el tubo [toobo]
pipe cleaners los limpiapipas [leemp-yapeepas]
pity: it's a pity! ¡qué pena! [keh]
pizza la pizza
place el lugar [loogar]
at your place en tu casa
at his place en su casa
plain el llano [yano]
(not patterned) liso
plane el avión [ab-yon]
by plane en avión
plant la planta
plaster cast la escayola [eski-yola]
plasters las tiritas
plastic plástico
(credit cards) las tarjetas de crédito [tarHetas deh kredeeto]
plastic bag la bolsa de plástico
plate el plato
platform la vía [bee-a]
which platform is it for Puebla, please? ¿de qué vía sale el tren para Puebla, por favor? [deh keh bee-a saleh – pwebla por fabor]
play (in theatre) la obra
(verb) jugar [Hoogar]
(instrument) tocar
playground el patio de recreo [pat-yo deh rekreh-o]
pleasant agradable [agradableh]

please por favor [fabor]
yes please sí, por favor
could you please ...? ¿podría hacer el favor de ...? [asair – deh]
please don't no, por favor
pleased: pleased to meet you (said by man/woman) encantado/encantada de conocerle [deh konosairleh]
pleasure: my pleasure es un gusto [goosto]
plenty: plenty of ... mucho ... [moocho]
there's plenty of time tenemos mucho tiempo [t-yempo]
that's plenty, thanks es suficiente, gracias [soofees-yenteh gras-yas]
pliers los alicates [aleekat-es]
plug (electrical) el enchufe [enchoofeh]
(for car) la bujía [booHee-a]
(in sink) el tapón
plumber el plomero [plomairo]
p.m. de la tarde [deh la tardeh]
poached egg el huevo escalfado [webo]
pocket el bolsillo [bolsee-yo]
point: two point five dos coma cinco
there's no point no vale la pena [baleh]
points (in car) los platinos
poisonous venenoso [benenoso]
police la policía [poleesee-a]
call the police! ¡llame a la

policía! [yameh]

Mexican police are no better or worse than any others, but they are very badly paid and it is quite usual to have to bribe or tip them. It is common to be accused of some minor traffic violation and be asked to pay an on-the-spot fine. Sometimes these are open to negotiation. These small bribes are known as **mordidas** and they may also be extracted by border officials or bureaucrats. In general, if the amount is small, it's better to pay up and avoid any direct confrontation, particularly with the police. More common than the mordida is the **propina** (tip), a payment that is made on your initiative. There is no need to do this but often it helps to speed bureaucracy. In the event of an emergency, phone 06 for the police.

policeman el (agente de) policía [aHenteh deh]
police station la comisaría de policía
policewoman la policía
polish el betún [betoon]
polite educado [edookado]

politics
There's plenty of political discussion in Mexico, but unless you're sure you know who you're talking to, it's safest to keep your opinions guarded. Praising the bravery of the opposition in the presence of a local PRI bigwig just could land you in trouble. And almost anywhere, ciriticism of the country by a local is fine, but if it's an outsider talking even the most jaded of Mexicans is likely to find a core of outraged patriotism.

polluted contaminado
pony el poney
pool (for swimming) la alberca [albairka]
poor (not rich) pobre [pobreh]
(quality) de baja calidad [deh baHa kaleeda]
pop music la música pop [mooseeka]
pop singer el/la cantante de música pop [kantanteh deh]
population la población [poblas-yon]
pork la carne de chancho [karneh deh chancho]
port (for boats) el puerto [pwairto]
(drink) el Oporto
porter (in hotel) el portero [portairo]
portrait el retrato
posh (restaurant) de lujo [deh looHo]
possible posible [poseebleh]
is it possible to ...? ¿es posible ...?
as ... as possible lo más ... posible
post (mail) el correo [korreh-o]
(verb) echar al correo

could you post this for me?
¿podría echarme esto al
correo? [echarmeh]

postal service
Mexican postal services
are reasonably efficient.
Airmail to Mexico should arrive
within a few days, but may take a
couple of weeks to get anywhere
remote. Post offices are open
Monday to Friday 9 a.m. to 6 p.m.
and Saturday 9 a.m. to noon. Poste
restante letters should be addressed
to **lista de Correos** at the **Correo
Central** (the main post office in any
town). All mail that arrives is
displayed on a list updated daily, but
held for two weeks only. Anything
sent abroad by airmail should have
an airmail stamp (**por avión**) on it or
it is liable to go surface. Sending
packages and parcels out of the
country is difficult and regulations
vary. Take your parcel and its
contents (unsealed) to any post
office and they'll set you on your
way. Many stores will send parcels
for you, which is a great deal easier.

postbox el buzón [booson]
postcard la postal [pos-tal]
postcode el código postal
poster el póster [postair], el
cartel
poste restante la lista de
Correos [leesta deh korreh-os]
post office el correo
[korreh-o]

potato la papa
potato chips (US) las patatas
fritas (de bolsa) [deh]
pots and pans los cacharros
de cocina [deh koseena], las
ollas [o-yas]
pottery (objects) la cerámica
[sairameeka]
pound* (money, weight) la libra
power cut el apagón
power point la toma de
corriente [deh korr-yenteh]
**practise: I want to practise my
Spanish** quiero practicar el
español [k-yairo – espan-yol]
prawns las gambas
prefer: I prefer ... prefiero ...
[pref-yairo]
pregnant embarazada
[embarasada]
prescription (for chemist) la
receta [reseta]
see **pharmacy**
present (gift) el regalo
president (of country) el/la
presidente [preseedenteh]
pretty lindo
it's pretty expensive es
bastante caro [bastanteh]
price el precio [pres-yo]
priest el sacerdote
[sasairdoteh]
prime minister (man/woman) el
primer ministro [preemair],
la primera ministra
printed matter los impresos
priority (in driving) la
preferencia [prefairens-ya]
prison la cárcel [karsel]

private privado [preebado], particular [parteekoolar]
private bathroom el baño privado [ban-yo]
probably probablemente [probableh-menteh]
problem el problema
  no problem! ¡con mucho gusto! [moocho goosto]
program(me) el programa
promise: I promise lo prometo
pronounce: how is this pronounced? ¿cómo se pronuncia esto? [seh pronoons-ya]
properly (repaired, locked etc) bien [b-yen]
protection factor (of suntan lotion) el factor de protección [deh proteks-yon]
Protestant (adj) protestante [protestanteh]
public convenience los servicios públicos [sairbees-yos poobleekos]
public holiday el día feriado [dee-a fer-yado]
pudding (dessert) el postre [postreh]
pull jalar [Halar]
pullover el suéter [swetair]
puncture la ponchadura
purple morado
purse (for money) el monedero [monedairo]
  (US: handbag) el bolso
push empujar [empoo-Har]
pushchair la sillita de ruedas [see-yeeta deh rwedas]

put poner [ponair]
  where can I put ...? ¿dónde pongo ...? [dondeh]
  could you put us up for the night? ¿podría alojarnos esta noche? [aloHarnos – nocheh]
pyjamas el pijama [peeHama]
pyramid la pirámide [peerameedeh]

Q

quality la calidad [kaleeda]
  (personal) la cualidad [kwaleeda]
quarantine la cuarentena [kwarentena]
quarter la cuarta parte [kwarta parteh]
quayside: on the quayside en el muelle [mweh-yeh]
question la pregunta [pregoonta]
queue la cola
quick rápido [rapeedo]
  that was quick sí que ha sido rápido [keh a]
  what's the quickest way there? ¿cuál es el camino más directo? [kwal – deerekto]
  fancy a quick drink? ¿se te antoja una copa? [seh teh antoHa]
quickly rápidamente [rapeedamenteh]
quiet (place, hotel) tranquilo [trankeelo]
  (person) callado [ka-yado]

quiet! ¡cállese! [ka-yeseh]
quite (fairly) bastante
[bastanteh]
(very) muy [mwee]
that's quite right eso es
cierto [s-yairto]
quite a lot bastante

R

rabbit el conejo [koneHo]
race (for runners, cars) la
carrera [karraira]
racket (tennis etc) la raqueta
[raketa]
radiator (of car, in room) el
radiador [rad-yador]
radio la radio [rad-yo]
on the radio por radio
raft la balsa
rail: by rail en tren
railway el ferrocarril
rain la lluvia [yoob-ya]
in the rain bajo la lluvia
[baHo]
it's raining está lloviendo
[yob-yendo]
raincoat el impermeable
[eempairmeh-ableh]
rape la violación [b-yolas-yon]
rare (uncommon) poco común
(steak) (muy) poco hecho
[mwee – echo]
rash (on skin) la erupción
cutánea [airoops-yon kootaneh-a]
raspberry la frambuesa
[frambwesa]
rat la rata

rate (for changing money) el tipo
de cambio [teepo deh kamb-yo]
rather: it's rather good es
bastante bueno [bastanteh
bweno]
I'd rather ... prefiero ... [pref-
yairo]
razor la maquinilla de afeitar
[makeenee-ya deh afaytar]
(electric) la máquina de
afeitar eléctrica [makeena]
razor blades las hojas de
afeitar [oHas]
read leer [leh-air]
ready preparado
are you ready? (to man/woman)
¿estás listo/lista?
I'm not ready yet (said by
man/woman) aún no estoy
listo/lista [a-oon]

dialogue

when will it be ready?
¿cuándo estará listo?
[kwando]
it should be ready in a
couple of days estará listo
en un par de días

real verdadero [bairdadairo],
auténtico [owtenteeko]
really realmente [reh-almenteh]
that's really great eso es
estupendo
really? (doubt) ¿no puede
ser? [pwedeh sair]
(polite interest) ¿de veras? [deh
bairas]

rear lights las calaveras [kalab**ai**ras]

rearview mirror el (espejo) retrovisor [esp**e**Ho retrobee**so**r]

reasonable (prices etc) modesto

receipt el recibo [res**ee**bo]

It is wise to ask for a receipt (**un recibo**) for any goods that you buy, especially mechanical or electrical items, since you may be asked for them by Customs officials. Remember to keep receipts for fairly new items such as cameras that you have brought into the country with you.

recently recientemente [res-yentem**e**nteh], recién [res-y**e**n]

reception la recepción [reseps-y**o**n]

  at reception en la recepción

reception desk la recepción

receptionist el/la recepcionista [reseps-yon**ee**sta]

recognize reconocer [rekono-s**ai**r]

recommend: could you recommend ...? ¿puede Usted recomendar ...? [pw**e**deh oost**eh**]

record (music) el disco [d**ee**sko]

red rojo [r**o**Ho]

  red wine el vino tinto [b**ee**no t**ee**nto]

refund la devolución [deboloos-y**o**n]

  can I have a refund? ¿puede devolverme el dinero? [pw**e**deh debolb**ai**rmeh el deen**ai**ro]

region la zona [s**o**na], la región [reH-y**o**n]

registered: by registered mail por correo certificado [korr**e**H-o sairteefeek**a**do]

registration number el número de placa [n**oo**mairo deh]

relatives los parientes [par-y**e**nt-es]

religion la religión [releeH-y**o**n]

remember: I don't remember no recuerdo [rekw**ai**rdo]

  I remember recuerdo

  do you remember? ¿recuerda?

rent (for apartment etc) la renta, el arriendo [arr-y**e**ndo] (verb) rentar, arrendar, alquilar [alkeel**a**r]

  to/for rent se alquila [seh alk**ee**la]

dialogue

I'd like to rent a car quisiera rentar un carro [kees-y**ai**ra]

for how long? ¿por cuánto tiempo? [kw**a**nto t-y**e**mpo]

two days dos días

this is our range ésta es nuestra selección [nw**e**stra seleks-y**o**n]

I'll take the ... me quedo con el ... [meh **ke**do]

is that with unlimited mileage? ¿es con kilometraje ilimitado? [keelometra**He**h]

it is sí

can I see your licence please? ¿me deja ver su carnet, por favor? [meh deh-**Ha** bair soo kar**neh** por fa**bor**]

and your passport y su pasaporte [ee soo pasa**por**teh]

is insurance included? ¿va incluido el seguro? [ba eenkloo-**ee**do]

yes, but you pay the first 50,000 pesos sí, pero Usted paga los primeros cincuenta mil pesos [**pai**ro oos**teh** paga los pree**mai**ros]

can you leave a deposit of ...? ¿puede dejar un enganche de ...? [**pwe**deh deh-**Har** oon engan**cheh** deh]

rented car el carro rentado

repair (verb) arreglar

  can you repair it? ¿puede arreglarlo? [**pwe**deh]

repeat repetir

  could you repeat that? ¿puede repetir eso? [**pwe**deh]

reservation la reservación [resairbas-**yon**]

  I'd like to make a reservation quisiera hacer reservación

[kees-**yai**ra a**sair**]

dialogue

I have a reservation tengo cuarto reservado [**kwar**to resair**ba**do]

yes sir, what name please? sí, señor, ¿a nombre de quién, por favor? [sen-**yor** a **nom**breh deh k-**yen** por fa**bor**]

reserve reservar [resair**bar**]

dialogue

can I reserve a table for tonight? ¿puedo reservar una mesa para esta noche? [**pwe**do – **no**cheh]

yes madam, for how many people? sí, señora, ¿para cuántos? [sen-**yo**ra – **kwan**tos]

for two para dos

and for what time? ¿y para qué hora? [ee **pa**ra keh **o**ra]

for eight o'clock para las ocho

and could I have your name please? ¿me deja su nombre, por favor? [meh deh-**Ha** soo **nom**breh por fa**bor**]

see alphabet for spelling

rest: I need a rest necesito un descanso [neses**ee**to]

the rest of the group el resto

del grupo [**groo**po]
restaurant el restaurante
[restow**ran**teh]

Basic meals are served at
restaurantes, but you
can get breakfast, snacks
and often full meals at **cafeterías**
too. There are take-out and fast-food
places serving sandwiches, **tortas**
(filled rolls), and **tacos** (soft, rolled
tortillas with a filling) as well as
more international-style food. In
addition you'll find establishments
serving nothing but fruit drinks
(**licuados**) and fruit salads (usually
identified by a sign saying **Jugos y
Licuados**), and street stalls dishing
out everything from tacos to orange
juice to ready-made crisp vegetable
salads sprinkled with chilli, salt and
lime. Just about every market in the
country has a cooked food section
too, and these are invariably the
cheapest places to eat. In the big
cities and resorts, of course, there
are international restaurants too:
pizzas and Chinese food are
ubiquitous.
You can eat a full meal in a
restaurant at any time of day, but
you'd do well to adopt the local habit
of taking your main meal at
lunchtime, since this is when
comidas corridas (set meals,
varied daily) are served, from around
1-5 p.m. You can find these in the
cheaper **cocina económica** or
comedor where it is likely to be all

that is available. In more expensive
places, the same thing may be
known as the **menú del día** or
menú turístico and you may have
to ask for it specifically.

restaurant car el coche-
comedor [**ko**cheh komedor]
rest room el baño [**ban**-yo],
los servicios [sairb**ees**-yos]
see toilet
retired: I'm retired estoy
jubilado/jubilada
[Hoobee**la**do]
return (ticket) el boleto de ida
y vuelta [deh **ee**da ee bwelta]
see ticket
reverse charge call la llamada
por cobrar [ya**ma**da]
reverse gear la marcha atrás
revolting asqueroso [askair**o**so]
rib la costilla [kostee-ya]
rice el arroz [arros]
rich rico [**ree**ko]
ridiculous ridículo
[reedee**koo**lo]
right (correct) correcto
(not left) derecho
you were right tenía razón
[ra**son**]
that's right es cierto [s-**yair**to]
this can't be right esto no
puede ser [**pwe**deh sair]
right! ¡bueno! [**bwe**no]
is this the right road for ...?
¿es éste el camino para ...?
[**es**teh]
on the right a la derecha
turn right dé vuelta a la

129

derecha [deh bwelta]

right-hand drive con el
volante a la derecha
[bolanteh]

ring (on finger) el anillo [anee-yo]

I'll ring you te llamaré [teh
yamareh]

ring back volver a llamar
[bolbair a yamar]

ripe (fruit) maduro

rip-off: it's a rip-off es una
estafa

rip-off prices los precios
exagerados [pres-yos
eksaHairados]

risky arriesgado [arr-yesgado]

river el río

road la carretera [karretaira]

is this the road for ...? ¿es
ésta la carretera para ...?

down the road calle abajo
[ka-yeh abaHo]

road accident el accidente
de tránsito [akseedenteh deh]

road map el mapa de
carreteras

roadsign la señal de tráfico
[sen-yal deh]

rob: I've been robbed! ¡me
robaron! [meh]

rock la roca
(music) el rock

on the rocks (with ice) con
hielo [yelo]

rodeo la charreada [charreh-ada]

roll (bread) el bolillo [bolee-yo]

roof el tejado [teHado]

roof rack la baca

room el cuarto [kwarto]

in my room en mi cuarto

dialogue

do you have any rooms?
¿tiene cuarto? [t-yeneh]
for how many people?
¿para cuántas personas?
[kwantas pairsonas]
for one/for two para uno/
dos
yes, we have rooms free
sí, tenemos cuartos libres
[leeb-res]
for how many nights will it
be? ¿para cuántas
noches? [noch-es]
just for one night para una
noche sólo [nocheh]
how much is it? ¿cuánto
es? [kwanto]
... with bathroom and ...
without bathroom ... con
baño y ... sin baño [ban-
yo ee ... seen]
can I see a room with
bathroom? ¿me enseña
un cuarto con baño?
[meh ensen-ya]
OK, I'll take it me lo
quedo [meh lo kedo]

room service el servicio de
cuarto [sairbees-yo deh]

rope la cuerda [kwairda]

rosé (wine) el vino rosado
[beeno]

roughly (approximately) approximadamente [–menteh]

round: it's my round me toca [meh]

roundabout (for traffic) la glorieta [glor-yeta]

round trip ticket el boleto de ida y vuelta [deh **ee**da ee b**welta**]
see ticket

route la ruta [r**oo**ta]
what's the best route? ¿cuál es la mejor ruta? [kwal es la me**Hor**]

rubber (material) el hule [**oo**leh]
(eraser) la goma de borrar

rubber band la gomita

rubbish (waste) la basura
(poor quality goods) las porquerías [porkair**ee**-as]

rubbish! (nonsense) ¡babosadas!

rucksack la mochila

rude grosero [gros**ai**ro]

rug (mat) la alfombra, el tapete [tap**e**teh]
(blanket) la cobija [kobee**Ha**], la manta, la frazada [fras**a**da]

ruins las ruinas [rw**ee**nas]

rum el ron
rum and Coke® la cubata (de ron)

run (verb: person) correr [korr**air**]
how often do the buses run? ¿cada cuánto pasan los camiones? [kw**a**nto]
I've run out of money se me

acabó el dinero [seh meh – deen**ai**ro]

rush hour la hora pico [**o**ra]

S

sad triste [tr**ee**steh]

saddle (for horse) la silla de montar [**see**-ya deh]
(on bike) el sillín [see-y**ee**n]

safe seguro [seg**oo**ro]

safety pin el seguro

sail la vela [b**e**la]

sailboard el windsurf

sailboarding el windsurf

salad la ensalada

salad dressing el aliño para la ensalada [al**ee**n-yo]

sale: for sale se vende [seh b**e**ndeh]

salmon el salmón [sal-m**on**]

salt la sal

same: the same el mismo, la misma
the same as this igual a éste [eeg**wal** a **e**steh]
the same again, please otro igual, por favor [fab**or**]
it's all the same to me me da igual [meh]

sand la arena [a**reh**-na]

sandals los guaraches [war**a**ch-es]

sandwich el sandwich [s**a**ndweech], la torta

sanitary napkin/towel la compresa

sardines las sardinas

Saturday sábado

sauce la salsa

saucepan la olla [**o**-ya]

saucer el platillo [plat**ee**-yo]

sauna la sauna [**sow**na]

sausage la salchicha

say: how do you say ... in Spanish? ¿cómo se dice ... en español? [seh d**ee**seh en espan-**yol**]

what did he say? ¿qué dijo? [keh d**ee**Ho]

I said ... dije ... [d**ee**Heh]

he said ... dijo ...

could you say that again? ¿podría repetirlo?

scarf (for neck) la bufanda (for head) el pañuelo [pan-y**we**lo]

scenery el paisaje [p**ī**saHeh]

schedule (US) el horario [or**ar**-yo]

scheduled flight el vuelo regular [b**we**lo reg**oo**lar]

school la escuela [esk**we**la]

scissors: a pair of scissors las tijeras [tee**Hai**ras]

scotch el whisky

Scotch tape® el scotch, el Durex®

Scotland Escocia [esk**os**-ya]

Scottish escocés [eskos-**es**]

I'm Scottish (man/woman) soy escocés/escocesa

scrambled eggs los huevos revueltos [**we**bos reb**wel**tos]

scratch el rasguño [rasg**oon**-yo]

scream chillar [chee-**yar**]

screw el tornillo [torn**ee**-yo]

screwdriver el destornillador [destornee-yad**or**]

sea el mar

by the sea junto al mar [**Hoo**nto]

seafood los mariscos

seafood restaurant la marisquería [mareeskair**ee**-a]

seafront el paseo marítimo [pas**eh**-o mar**ee**teemo]

on the seafront en la playa [pl**ī**-ya]

seagull la gaviota [gab-y**ota**]

search for (verb) buscar

seashell la concha marina

seasick: I feel seasick (said by man/woman) est**oy** mareado/ mareada [mareh-**ado**]

I get seasick me mareo [meh mar**eh**-o]

seaside: by the seaside en la playa [pl**ī**-ya]

seat el asiento [as-y**ento**]

is this seat taken? ¿está ocupado este asiento? [est**eh**]

seat belt el cinturón de seguridad [seentoor**on** deh segooreed**a**]

sea urchin el erizo de mar [air**ee**so]

seaweed el alga

secluded apartado

second (adj) segundo (of time) el segundo

just a second! ¡un momentito!

second class (travel) de

segunda clase [seg**oo**nda kl**a**seh]

secondhand usado [oos**a**do]

see ver [bair]

can I see? ¿puedo ver? [pw**e**do]

have you seen ...? ¿ha visto ...? [a b**ee**sto]

I saw him this morning lo vi esta mañana [bee]

see you! ¡hasta luego! [**a**sta lw**e**go]

I see (I understand) entiendo [ent-y**e**ndo]

self-service autoservicio [owtosairb**ee**s-yo]

sell vender [bend**a**ir]

do you sell ...? ¿vende ...? [b**e**ndeh]

Sellotape® el scotch®, el Durex®

send enviar [emb-y**a**r], mandar

I want to send this to England quiero enviar esto a Inglaterra [k-y**a**iro]

senior citizen el jubilado, [Hoobeel**a**do], la jubilada

separate separado

a separate room un cuarto aparte [apart**e**h]

separated: I'm separated (said by man/woman) estoy separado/separada

separately (pay, travel) por separado

September septiembre [set-y**e**mbreh]

septic séptico

serious serio [s**a**ir-yo]

(illness) grave [gr**a**beh]

service charge el servicio [sairb**ee**s-yo]

service station la estación de servicio [estas-y**o**n deh]

serviette la servilleta [sairbee-y**e**ta]

set menu el menú [men**oo**], la comida corrida

several varios [b**a**r-yos]

sew coser [kos**a**ir]

could you sew this back on? ¿podría coserme esto? [kos**a**irmeh]

sex el sexo

sexy sexy

shade: in the shade a la sombra

shallow (water) poco profundo

shame: what a shame! ¡que pena! [keh]

shampoo el champú

a shampoo and set un lavado y marcado [lab**a**do ee]

share (verb) compartir

sharp (knife) afilado

(taste) ácido [**a**seedo]

(pain) agudo

shattered (very tired) agotado

shaver la máquina de afeitar [mak**ee**na deh afayt**a**r]

shaving foam la espuma de afeitar

shaving point el enchufe (para la máquina de afeitar) [ench**oo**feh – mak**ee**na]

shawl el rebozo [reb**o**so]

she* ella [**eh**-ya]
 is she here? ¿está (ella) aquí? [a**kee**]
sheet (for bed) la sábana
shelf la estantería [estantair**ee**-a]
shellfish los mariscos
sherry el jerez [Her-**es**]
ship el barco
 by ship en barco
shirt la camisa
shit! ¡mierda! [m-**yair**da]
shock el susto
 I got an electric shock me dio un choque eléctrico [meh – **cho**keh]
shock-absorber el amortiguador [amorteegwad**or**]
shocking chocante [cho**kan**teh]
shoes los zapatos [sa**pa**tos]
 a pair of shoes un par de zapatos [deh]
shoelaces las agujetas [a-oo**He**tas]
shoe polish el betún
shoe repairer's la zapatería [sapatair**ee**-a]
shop la tienda [t-**yen**da]

It's difficult to generalize about opening hours in Mexico. Shops tend to keep long hours, say from 9 a.m. to 8 p.m., though some places still close for a **siesta**, usually between 1 and 3 p.m., but sometimes longer.

shopping: I'm going shopping
voy de compras [boy deh]
shopping centre el centro comercial [**sen**tro komairs-**yal**]
shop window el escaparate [eskapa**ra**teh]
shore la orilla [o**ree**-ya]
short (time, journey) corto
 (person) bajo [**ba**Ho]
 it's only a short distance queda bastante cerca [**ke**da bas**tan**teh **sair**ka]
shortcut el atajo [ata**Ho**]
shorts los pantalones cortos [pantal**on**-es]
should: what should I do? ¿que hago? [keh **a**go]
 he shouldn't be long no debe tardar [**de**beh]
 you should have told me me lo hubieras dicho [meh oob-**yai**ras]
shoulder el hombro [**om**bro]
shout (verb) gritar
show (in theatre) el espectáculo [espek**ta**koolo]
 could you show me? ¿me lo enseña? [meh lo en**sen**-ya]
shower (in bathroom) la regadera [rega**dai**ra]
 (of rain) el chubasco [choo**ba**sko]
 with shower con baño [**ban**-yo]
shower gel el gel de baño [Hel deh]
shut (verb) cerrar [**sair**rar]
 when do you shut? ¿a qué hora cierran? [keh **o**ra s-**yair**ran]

when do they shut? ¿a qué hora cierran?

they're shut está cerrado [sairrado]

I've shut myself out cerré y dejé la llave dentro [sairreh ee deh-Heh la yabeh]

shut up! ¡cállese! [ka-yeseh]

shutter (on camera) el obturador
(on window) la contraventana [kontrabentana]

shy tímido [teemeedo]

sick (ill) enfermo [enfairmo]

I'm going to be sick (vomit) voy a devolver [boy a debolbair]

side el lado

the other side of town al otro lado de la ciudad [deh la s-yooda]

sidelights los pilotos, las calaveras [kalabairas]

side salad la ensalada aparte [aparteh]

side street la callejuela [ka-yeh-Hwela]

sidewalk la banqueta [banketa]

sight: the sights of ... los lugares de interés de ... [loogar-es deh eentair-es]

sightseeing: we're going sightseeing vamos a hacer un recorrido turístico [bamos a asair oon]

sightseeing tour el recorrido turístico

sign (notice) el letrero [letrairo]

(roadsign) la señal de tráfico [sen-yal deh]

signal: he didn't give a signal no hizo ninguna señal [eeso]

signature la firma [feerma]

signpost el letrero [letrairo]

silence el silencio [seelens-yo]

silk la seda

silly tonto

silver la plata

silver foil el papel de aluminio [aloomeen-yo]

similar parecido [pareseedo]

simple (easy) sencillo [sensee-yo]

since: since yesterday desde ayer [desdeh ī-yair]

since I got here desde que llegamos aquí [keh yegamos akee]

sing cantar

singer el/la cantante [kantanteh]

single: a single to ... un boleto de ida para ... [deh eeda]

I'm single (said by man/woman) soy soltero/soltera [soltairo]

single bed la cama individual [eendeebeedwal]

single room el cuarto individual [kwarto]

single ticket el boleto de ida [deh eeda]

sink (in kitchen) el fregadero [fregadairo]

sister la hermana [airmana]

sister-in-law la cuñada [koon-yada]

sit: can I sit here? ¿puedo sentarme aquí? [pwedo sentarmeh akee]

is anyone sitting here? ¿está ocupado este asiento? [esteh as-yento]

sit down sentarse [sentarseh]
  sit down! ¡siéntese! [s-yenteseh]

size el tamaño [taman-yo]
  (of clothes) la talla [ta-ya]

skin la piel [p-yel]

skin-diving el buceo [booseh-o]

skinny flaco

skirt la falda

sky el cielo [s-yelo]

sleep (verb) dormir
  did you sleep well? ¿dormiste bien? [dormeesteh b-yen]
  I need a good sleep necesito dormir bien [neseseeto]

sleeper (on train) el coche-cama [kocheh kama]

sleeping bag la bolsa de dormir [deh]

sleeping car el coche-cama [kocheh-kama]

sleeping pill la pastilla para dormir [pastee-ya]

sleepy: I'm feeling sleepy tengo sueño [swen-yo]

sleeve la manga

slide (photographic) la diapositiva [d-yaposeeteeba]

slip (under dress) la funda [foonda]

slippery resbaladizo [resbaladeeso]

slow lento
  slow down! ¡cálmese! [kalmeseh]

slowly: could you say it slowly? ¿podría decirlo despacio? [deseerlo despas-yo]
  very slowly muy lento [mwee]

small chico

smell: it smells! (smells bad) ¡apesta!

smile (verb) sonreír [sonreh-eer]

smoke el humo [oomo]
  do you mind if I smoke? ¿le importa que fume? [leh – keh foomeh]
  I don't smoke no fumo
  do you smoke? ¿fuma?

snack la comida ligera [leeHaira]

snake la culebra, la víbora [beebora]

sneeze (verb) estornudar

snorkel el tubo de buceo [toobo deh booseh-o]

snow la nieve [n-yebeh]
  it's snowing está nevando [nebando]

so: it's so good es tan bueno [bweno]
  not so fast no tan de prisa [deh preesa]
  so am I yo también [tamb-yen]
  so do I yo también
  so-so más o menos

soaking solution (for contact lenses) el líquido preservador [leekeedo presairbador]

soap el jabón [Habon]

soap powder el jabón en polvo [em polbo]

sober sobrio [sobr-yo]

sock el calcetín [kalseteen]

socket (electrical) el enchufe [enchoofeh]

soda (water) la soda

sofa el sofá

soft (material etc) suave [swabeh]

soft-boiled egg el huevo pasado por agua [webo – agwa]

soft drink el refresco

soft lenses las lentes blandas [lent-es]

sole (of shoe, of foot) la suela [swela]

could you put new soles on these? ¿podría cambiarles las suelas? [kamb-yarl-es]

some: can I have some water? ¿me da agua? [meh]

can I have some rolls? ¿me da unos bolillos?

can I have some? ¿me da unos?

somebody, someone alguien [alg-yen]

something algo

something to drink algo de beber [deh bebair]

sometimes a veces [bes-es]

somewhere en alguna parte [parteh]

son el hijo [eeHo]

song la canción [kans-yon]

son-in-law el yerno [yairno]

soon dentro de poco [deh]

I'll be back soon no me tardo [meh]

as soon as possible lo antes posible [ant-es poseebleh]

sore: it's sore me duele [meh dweleh]

sore throat el dolor de garganta [deh]

sorry: (I'm) sorry disculpe [deeskoolpeh]

sorry? (didn't understand) ¿mande? [mandeh]

sort: what sort of ...? ¿qué clase de ...? [keh klaseh deh]

soup la sopa

sour (taste) ácido [aseedo]

south el sur [soor]

in the south al sur

South Africa Sudáfrica

South African (adj) sudafricano

I'm South African (man/woman) soy sudafricano/sudafricana

South America América del Sur [amaireeka]

South American (adj) sudamericano

(man/woman) el sudamericano, la sudamericana

southeast el sudeste [sood-esteh]

southwest el sudoeste [soodo-esteh]

souvenir el recuerdo [rekwairdo]

Spain España [espan-ya]

Spaniard (man/woman) el
  español [espan-yol], la
  española
Spanish español
spanner la llave inglesa
  [yabeh]
spare parts los repuestos
  [repwestos], las refacciones
  [refaks-yon-es]
spare tyre la llanta de
  repuesto [yanta deh]
sparkplug la bujía [booнee-a]
speak hablar [ablar]
  do you speak English?
  ¿habla inglés? [abla eeng-les]
  I don't speak ... no hablo ...
  [ablo]

dialogue

  can I speak to Pablo?
  ¿puedo hablar con
  Pablo? [pwedo]
  who's calling? ¿quién le
  llama? [k-yen leh yama]
  it's Patricia soy Patricia
  I'm sorry, he's not in, can I
  take a message? lo
  siento, no está, ¿quiere
  dejar recado? [s-yento –
  k-yaireh deh-нar]
  no thanks, I'll call back
  later no gracias, llamaré
  más tarde [gras-yas yamareh
  mas tardeh]
  please tell him I called
  por favor, dígale que
  llamé [fabor deegaleh keh
  yameh]

speciality la especialidad
  [espes-yaleeda]
spectacles las gafas
speed la velocidad
  [beloseeda]
speed limit el límite de
  velocidad [leemeeteh deh]
speedometer el velocímetro
  [beloseemetro]
spell: how do you spell it?
  ¿cómo se escribe? [seh
  eskreebeh]
  see alphabet
spend gastar
spider la araña [aran-ya]
spin-dryer la secadora
splinter la astilla [astee-ya]
spoke (in wheel) el radio [rad-
  yo]
spoon la cuchara
sport el deporte [deporteh]
sprain: I've sprained my ... me
  torcí el ... [meh torsee]
spring (season) la primavera
  [preemabaira]
  (of car, seat) el resorte
  [resorteh]
square (in town) la plaza
  [plasa]
  main square el zócalo
  [sokalo]
stairs la escalera [eskalaira]
stale (bread) duro
  (food) pasado
stall: the engine keeps stalling
  el motor se para cada rato
  [seh]
stamp la estampilla [estampee-
  ya], el timbre [teembreh]

dialogue

a stamp for England,
please una estampilla
para Inglaterra, por favor
[fabor]
what are you sending?
¿qué es lo que envía?
[keh – embee-a]
this postcard esta postal

Stamps are sold at post
offices (el correo) and in
some shops. If you send
items from post offices you may
have them franked (franqueado)
and you can also send registered
mail (certificado). Parcels should
always be posted from the post
office; letters and postcards can be
mailed at a red post box (buzón).

standby el vuelo standby
[bwelo]
star la estrella [estreh-ya]
(in film) el/la protagonista
start el principio [preenseep-
yo]
(verb) comenzar [komensar]
when does it start? ¿cuándo
comienza? [kwando com-yensa]
the car won't start el carro
no arranca
starter (of car) el motor de
arranque [arrankeh]
(food) la entrada
starving: I'm starving me
muero de hambre [meh
mwairo deh ambreh]

state (country) el estado
the States (USA) los Estados
Unidos [ooneedos]
station la estación de
ferrocarril [estas-yon deh fair-
rokarreel]
statue la estatua [estatwa]
stay: where are you staying?
¿dónde está alojado? [dondeh
– aloнado]
I'm staying at ... (said by
man/woman) estoy alojado/
alojada en ...
I'd like to stay another two
nights me gustaría
quedarme dos noches más
[meh – kedarmeh – noch-es]
steak el filete [feeleteh]
steal robar
my bag has been stolen me
robaron el bolso [meh]
steep (hill) empinado,
escarpado
steering la dirección [deereks-
yon]
step: on the steps en las
escaleras [eskalairas]
stereo el estéreo [estaireh-o]
sterling la libra esterlina
[estairleena]
steward (on plane) el auxiliar
de vuelo [owkseel-yar deh
bwelo]
stewardess la azafata [asafata]
sticking plaster la tirita
still: I'm still waiting sigo
esperando
is he still there? ¿sigue ahí?
[seegeh a-ee]

st

keep still! ¡quédese quieto!
[kedeseh k-yeto]

sting: I've been stung algo
me ha picado [meh a]

stockings las medias [med-
yas]

stomach el estómago

stomach ache el dolor de
estómago [deh]

stone (rock) la piedra [p-yedra]

stop (verb) parar

please, stop here (to taxi driver
etc) pare aquí, por favor
[pareh akee por fabor]

do you stop near ...? ¿para
cerca de ...? [sairka deh]

stop doing that! ¡deje de
hacer eso! [deh-Heh deh asair]

stopover la escala

storm la tormenta

straight: it's straight ahead
todo recto

a straight whisky un whisky
solo

straightaway en seguida
[segeeda]

strange (odd) extraño [estran-
yo]

stranger (man/woman) el
forastero [forastairo], la
forastera

I'm a stranger here no soy
de aquí [deh akee]

strap la correa [korreh-a]

strawberry la fresa, la frutilla
[frootee-ya]

stream el arroyo [arro-yo]

street la calle [ka-yeh]

on the street en la calle

streetmap el plano de la
ciudad [deh la s-yooda]

string la cuerda [kwairda]

strong fuerte [fwairteh]

stuck atascar

the key's stuck la llave se
atascó [yabeh seh]

student el/la estudiante
[estood-yanteh]

stupid
Don't call people
estúpido – it seems a
natural translation from the English
stupid, and travellers tend to use it
unthinkingly, but in Mexico it's a far
stronger word and can cause
serious offence.

subway (US) el metro
see bus

suburb el suburbio [sooboorb-
yo]

suddenly de repente [deh
repenteh]

suede el ante [anteh]

sugar el azúcar [asookar]

suit el traje [traHeh]

it doesn't suit me (jacket etc)
no me queda bien [meh keda
b-yen]

it suits you te queda muy
bien [teh – mwee]

suitcase la maleta

summer el verano [bairano]

in the summer en verano

sun el sol

in the sun al sol

out of the sun a la sombra

sunbathe tomar el sol

sunblock (cream) la crema protectora, el filtro solar

sunburn la quemadura de sol [kemadoora deh]

sunburnt quemado [kemado]

Sunday domingo

sunglasses las gafas de sol [deh]

sun lounger la tumbona

sunny: it's sunny hace sol [aseh]

sunroof (in car) el techo corredizo [korredeeso]

sunset la puesta del sol [pwesta]

sunshade la sombrilla [sombree-ya]

sunshine la luz del sol [loos]

sunstroke la insolación [eensolas-yon]

suntan el bronceado [bronseh-ado]

suntan lotion la loción bronceadora [los-yon bronseh-adora]

suntanned bronceado [bronseh-ado]

suntan oil el aceite bronceador [asayteh]

super fabuloso

supermarket el supermercado [soopairmairkado]

supper la cena [sena]

supplement (extra charge) el suplemento [sooplemento]

sure: are you sure? ¿está seguro?

sure! ¡por supuesto! [soop-westo]

surfboard la tabla de surf [deh soorf]

surfing el surfing

surname el apellido [apeh-yeedo]

swearword la grosería [grosairee-a]

sweater el suéter [swetair]

sweatshirt la sudadera [soodadaira]

Sweden Suecia [swes-ya]

Swedish (adj) sueco [sweko]

sweet (dessert) el postre [postreh]
(adj: taste) dulce [doolseh]

sweetcorn el elote [eloteh]

sweets los dulces [dools-es]

swelling el hinchazón [eenchason]

swim (verb) bañarse [ban-yarseh]

I'm going for a swim voy a bañarme [boy a ban-yarmeh]

let's go for a swim vamos a bañarnos [bamos a ban-yarnos]

swimming costume el traje de baño [traHeh deh ban-yo]

swimming pool la alberca [albairka]

swimming trunks el traje de baño [traHeh deh ban-yo]

switch el interruptor [een-tairrooptor]

switch off apagar

switch on prender [prendair]

swollen hinchado [eenchado]

T

table la mesa
 a table for two una mesa
 para dos
tablecloth el mantel
table tennis el ping-pong
table wine el vino de mesa
 [beeno deh]
tailback (of traffic) la caravana
 de carros [karabana deh]
tailor el sastre [sastreh]
take (lead) tomar
 (accept) aceptar [aseptar]
 can you take me to the
 airport? ¿me lleva al
 aeropuerto? [meh yeba al
 iropwairto]
 do you take credit cards?
 ¿acepta tarjetas de crédito?
 [asepta tarHetas deh kredeeto]
 fine, I'll take it me llevo éste
 [meh yebo esteh]
 can I take this? (leaflet etc)
 ¿puedo llevarme esto?
 [pwedo yebarmeh]
 how long does it take?
 ¿cuánto tarda? [kwanto]
 it takes three hours tarda
 tres horas [oras]
 is this seat taken? ¿está
 ocupado este asiento? [esteh
 as-yento]
 a hamburger to take away
 una hamburguesa para
 llevar [yebar]
 can you take a little off here?
 (to hairdresser) ¿puede

quitarme un poco de aquí?
 [pwedeh keetarmeh – deh akee]
talcum powder el talco
talk (verb) platicar
tall alto
tampons los tampones
 [tampon-es]
tan el bronceado [bronseh-
 ado]
 to get a tan broncearse
 [bronseh-arseh]
tank (in car) el depósito
 [deposeeto]
tap la llave [yabeh]
tape (for cassette) la cinta
 [seenta]
 (sticky) la cinta adhesiva
 [adeseeba]
tape measure la cinta métrica
tape recorder la grabadora
taste el sabor
 can I taste it? ¿puedo
 probarlo? [pwedo]
taxi el taxi, el colectivo
 [kolekteebo]
 will you get me a taxi? ¿me
 consigue un taxi? [meh
 konseegeh]
 where can I find a taxi?
 ¿dónde encuentro un taxi?
 [dondeh enkwentro]

dialogue

to the airport/to the Sol
Hotel please al
aeropuerto/al hotel Sol,
por favor [iropwairto/al otel –
fabor]

how much will it be?
¿cuánto va a ser? [kwanto
ba a sair]
1,000 pesos mil pesos
**that's fine, right here,
thanks** está bien aquí
mismo, gracias [b-yen akee
meesmo gras-yas]

Taxis can be good value,
but beware of rip-offs.
Unless you're confident
that the meter is working, fix a price
before you get in. In the big cities,
there may be tables of fixed prices
posted at prominent spots. At almost
every airport and some of the
biggest bus stations, you'll find a
booth selling vouchers for the
official taxis and even though these
might cost more than a regular cab,
it's worth it for the extra security.
Never accept a ride in any kind of
unofficial or unmarked taxi. In
bigger towns and cities, **combis**,
colectivos or **peseros** offer a faster
and perhaps less crowded
alternative to city buses. These are
minibuses, vans or large saloon cars
that run along a fixed route to set
destinations, and will pick up and
drop off wherever you like along the
way. You pay the driver for the
distance travelled.

taxi-driver el/la taxista
taxi rank la parada de taxis
[deh]
tea (drink) el té [teh]

tea for one/two please un
té/dos tés, por favor [fabor]

Tea is often available, and
you may well be offered a
cup at the end of a meal.
Usually it's some kind of herbal tea
like **manzanilla** (camomile) or
yerbabuena (mint). Non-herbal teas
are not easy to find, though more
expensive restaurants may offer
other specialist teas like Earl Grey.
Tea is always served without milk.

teabags las bolsas de té [deh]
teach: could you teach me?
¿podría enseñarme? [ensen-
yarmeh]
teacher (primary: man/woman) el
maestro [ma-estro], la maestra
(secondary) el profesor, la
profesora
team el equipo [ekeepo]
teaspoon la cucharita
tea towel el trapo de cocina
[deh koseena]
teenager el/la adolescente
[adolesenteh]
telegram el telegrama
telephone el teléfono
see **phone**
television la televisión
[telebees-yon]
tell: could you tell him ...?
¿podría decirle ...?
[deseerleh]
temperature (weather) la
temperatura [tempairatoora]
(fever) la fiebre [f-yebreh]

temple el templo

tennis el tenis

tennis ball la pelota de tenis [deh]

tennis court la cancha de tenis

tennis racket la raqueta de tenis [raketa]

tent la tienda de campaña [t-yenda deh kampan-ya] la carpa

term (at university, school) el trimestre [treemestreh]

terminus (rail) la terminal [tairmeenal]

terrible malísimo

terrific fabuloso [fabooloso]

than* que [keh]

smaller than más pequeño que [peken-yo]

thanks, thank you gracias [gras-yas]

thank you very much muchas gracias [moochas]

thanks for the lift gracias por traerme [tra-airmeh]

no thanks no gracias

dialogue

> thanks gracias
> that's OK, don't mention it no hay de qué [ī deh keh]

that: that man ese hombre [eseh ombreh]

that woman esa mujer [mooнair]

that one ése [eseh]

I hope that ... espero que ...

[espairo keh]

that's nice (clothes, souvenir etc) qué lindo

is that ...? ¿es ése ...?

that's it (that's right) eso es

the* el, la; (pl) los, las

theatre el teatro [teh-atro]

their* su; (pl) sus [soos]

theirs* su, sus; (pl) suyos [soo-yos], suyas; de ellos [deh eh-yos], de ellas

them* (things) los, las (people) les

for them para ellos/ellas [eh-yos/eh-yas]

with them con ellos/ellas

I gave it to them se lo di a ellos/ellas [seh]

who? – them ¿quiénes? – ellos/ellas [k-yen-es]

then luego [lwego]

there allí [a-yee]

over there allá [a-ya]

up there allá arriba

is/are there ...? ¿hay ...? [ī]

there is/are ... hay ...

there you are (giving something) aquí tiene [akee t-yeneh]

thermometer el termómetro [tairmometro]

Thermos® flask el termo [tairmo]

these: these men estos hombres

these women estas mujeres

can I have these? ¿me puedo llevar éstos? [meh pwedo yebar]

they* (male) ellos [eh-yos]

(female) ellas [**eh**-yas]

thick grueso [groo-**eso**]

(stupid) bruto

thief (man/woman) el ladrón, la ladrona

thigh el muslo

thin flaco

thing la cosa

my things mis cosas [mees]

think pensar

(believe) creer [kreh-**air**]

I think so creo que sí [kreh-o keh]

I don't think so no creo

I'll think about it lo pensaré [pensar**eh**]

third party insurance el seguro contra terceros [tairs**air**os]

thirsty: I'm thirsty tengo sed [seh]

this: this man este hombre [**esteh**]

this woman esta mujer

this one éste/ésta [**esteh**]

this is my wife le presento a mi mujer [leh]

is this ...? ¿es éste/ésta ...?

those: those men aquellos hombres [ak**eh**-yos]

those women aquellas mujeres [ak**eh**-yas]

which ones? – those ¿cuáles? – aquéllos/aquéllas [kwal-es]

thread el hilo [**eelo**]

throat la garganta

throat pastilles las pastillas para la garganta [past**ee**-yas]

through a través de [trav-**es**

deh]

does it go through ...? (train, bus) ¿pasa por ...?

throw (verb) echar, aventar [abentar]

throw away (verb) tirar, botar

thumb el pulgar

thunderstorm la tormenta

Thursday jueves [Hw**eb**-es]

ticket el boleto

dialogue

a return to Tijuana un boleto de ida y vuelta a Tijuana [deh **eeda** ee bwelta a teeHwana]

coming back when? ¿cuándo piensa regresar? [kwando p-yensa]

today/next Tuesday hoy/el martes que viene [oy/el mart-es keh b-yeneh]

that will be 2,000 pesos son dos mil pesos

ticket office (bus, rail) la taquilla [tak**ee**-ya], la boletería [boletair**ee**-a]

tide la marea [mar**eh**-a]

tie (necktie) la corbata

tight (clothes etc) ajustado [aHoostado]

it's too tight me viene estrecho [meh b-yeneh]

tights las pantimedias [pan-teemed-yas]

till la caja [ka**Ha**]

time* el tiempo [t-y**empo**]

what's the time? ¿qué hora es? [keh **o**ra]

this time esta vez [bes]

last time la última vez [**oo**lteema]

next time la próxima vez

four times cuatro veces [bes-es]

timetable el horario [or**ar**-yo]

tin (can) la lata, el bote [**bo**teh]

tinfoil el papel de aluminio [aloom**een**-yo]

tin-opener el abrel**a**tas

tiny minúsculo [meen**oo**skoolo]

tip (to waiter etc) la propina

 Tips are hardly ever added to bills, and the amount is entirely up to you: in cheap places it's customary just to leave a small amount of loose change; expensive places tend to expect their full 12 per cent. It is not standard practice to tip cab drivers.

tired cansado

I'm tired (said by a man/woman) est**oy** cansado/cans**a**da

tissues los klínex®

to: to Puebla/London a Puebla/L**o**ndres

to Mexico/England a M**é**xico/Inglat**e**rra

to the post office a la oficina de Correos

toast (bread) la tostada

today hoy [oy]

toe el dedo del pie [p-yeh]

together juntos [H**oo**ntos]

we're together (in shop etc) est**a**mos juntos

can we pay together? ¿podemos pagar todo junto, por favor? [fab**or**]

toilet el baño [**ban**-yo], los servicios [sairb**ee**s-yos]

where is the toilet? ¿dónde están los servicios? [**do**ndeh]

I have to go to the toilet tengo que ir al baño [keh]

Public toilets in Mexico are almost always filthy, and there's never any paper (though someone may sell it outside). They're known usually as **baños** (literally: bathrooms), **excusados**, **sanitarios** or **servicios**. The most common signs are **damas** (ladies) and **caballeros** (gentlemen), though you may find the more confusing **señoras** (women) and **señores** (men).

toilet paper el papel higiénico [eeH-y**e**neeko]

tomato el jitomate [Heeto-m**a**teh]

tomato juice el jugo de jitomate [H**oo**go deh]

tomato ketchup el catsup

tomorrow mañana [man-y**a**na]

tomorrow morning mañana por la mañana

the day after tomorrow pasado mañana

toner (for skin) el tonificador

facial [fas-yal]
tongue la lengua [lengwa]
tonic (water) la tónica
tonight esta noche [nocheh]
tonsillitis las anginas
[anHeenas]
too (excessively) demasiado
[demas-yado]
(also) también [tamb-yen]
too hot demasiado caliente
[kal-yenteh]
too much demasiado
me too yo también
tooth el diente [d-yenteh], la
muela [mwela]
toothache el dolor de muelas
[deh]
toothbrush el cepillo de
dientes [seepee-yo deh d-yent-es]
toothpaste la pasta de
dientes
top: on top of ... encima
de ... [enseema deh], arriba de
at the top en la parte de
arriba [parteh]
at the top of ... en la parte
más alta de ...
top floor el último piso
[oolteemo]
topless topless
torch la linterna [leentairna]
total el total [tot-al]
tour la excursión [eskoors-yon]
is there a tour of ...? ¿hay
recorrido de ...? [i – deh]
tour guide el/la guía turístico
[gee-a]
tourist el/la turista
tourist information office la

oficina de información
turística [ofeeseena deh
eenformas-yon]

The Mexican Government
Ministry of Tourism
(Secretaría de Turismo,
abbreviated to Sectur) has helpful
offices throughout the world. In
Mexico, you'll find tourist offices
(sometimes called turismos) in
virtually every town, some run by
Sectur and others run by state and
municipal authorities.

tour operator la agencia de
viajes [aHens-ya deh b-yaH-es]
towards hacia [as-ya]
towel la toalla [to-a-ya]
town la ciudad [s-yooda]
in town en el centro [sentro]
just out of town a la salida
de la ciudad
town centre el centro de la
ciudad [sentro deh la s-yooda]
town hall el ayuntamiento
[i-yoontam-yento]
toy el juguete [Hoogeteh]
track (US) la vía [bee-a]
tracksuit el chandal
traditional tradicional [tradees-
yonal]
traffic el tránsito, la
circulación [seerkoolas-yon]
traffic jam el
embotellamiento [emboteh-
yam-yento]
traffic lights el semáforo
trailer (for carrying tent etc) el

remolque [remolkeh]
(US: caravan) la caravana
[karabana]
trailer park el camping
train el tren
by train en tren

dialogue

is this the train for ...? ¿es
éste el tren para ...?
[esteh]
sure sí, exacto
no, you want that platform
there no, tiene que ir a
aquella vía [t-yeneh keh eer
a akeh-ya bee-a]

Rail travel is on the whole
cheaper than the bus, but
much slower, infrequent
and rarely on time. In general, trains
are only recommended in Northern
and Central Mexico, though there are
lines to the south. There are two
main classes on Mexican trains; the
standard of first class (**primera**)
may vary, but you will at least be
guaranteed a seat. There is also a
more expensive and more luxurious
primera especial, and the still more
comfortable trains of the **servicio
estrella**. You can also book a
sleeping berth (**camarín**) or a
sleeping compartment (**alcoba**) on
all these trains. The second class
carriages (**segunda**) are much
cheaper, but also very crowded and
often extremely uncomfortable.

Local trains – **locales** (slow trains)
or **autovías** – will usually be second
class, while **rápidos** (faster trains
with limited stops) are often first
class only. Seats must be reserved
for first class and sleepers, as far in
advance as possible; second-class
tickets can only be bought on the
day of departure and seats cannot
be reserved.

trainers (shoes) los tráiner
[trinair]
train station la estación de
ferrocarril [estas-yon deh
fairokareel]
tram el tranvía [trambee-a]
translate traducir [tradooseer]
could you translate that?
¿podría traducir eso?
translation la traducción
[tradooks-yon]
translator (man/woman) el
traductor, la traductora
trashcan el bote de la basura
[boteh deh]
travel (verb) viajar [b-yaHar]
we're travelling around
andamos de paseo [deh
paseh-o]
travel agent's la agencia de
viajes [aHens-ya deh b-yaH-es]
traveller's cheque el cheque
de viajero [chekeh deh
b-yaHairo]
see cheque
tray la bandeja [bandeHa]
tree el árbol
tremendous tremendo

trendy de moda [deh]

trim: just a trim please (to hairdresser) córtemelo sólo un poco, por favor [fabor]

trip (excursion) la excursión [eskoors-yon]

I'd like to go on a trip to ... me gustaría hacer una excursión a ... [meh – asair]

trolley el carrito

trouble problemas [problemas]

I'm having trouble with ... tengo problemas con ...

sorry to trouble you disculpe la molestia [deeskoolpeh]

trousers los pantalones [pantalon-es]

true cierto [s-yairto]

that's not true no es cierto

trunk (US) la cajuela [kaHwela]

trunks (swimming) el traje de baño [traHeh deh ban-yo]

try (verb) intentar

can I try it? ¿puedo intentarlo yo? [pwedo]

try on: can I try it on? ¿puedo probármelo?

T-shirt la camiseta, la playera [plí-yaira]

Tuesday martes [mart-es]

tuna el bonito

tunnel el túnel [toonel]

turn: turn left/right tuerce a la izquierda/derecha [twairseh]

turn off: where do I turn off? ¿dónde doy vuelta? [dondeh doy bwelta]

can you turn the heating off? ¿puede apagar la calefacción? [pwedeh –kale-faks-yon]

turn on: can you turn the heating on? ¿puede poner la calefacción? [ponair]

turning (in road) el desvío [desbee-o]

TV la tele [teleh]

tweezers las pinzas [peensas]

twice dos veces [bes-es]

twice as much el doble [dobleh]

twin beds las camas gemelas [Hemelas]

twin room el cuarto con dos camas [kwarto]

twist: I've twisted my ankle me torcí el tobillo [meh torsee el tobee-yo]

type el tipo [teepo]

a different type of ... otro tipo de ... [deh]

typical típico [teepeeko]

tyre la llanta [yanta]

U

ugly feo [feh-o]

UK el Reino Unido [rayno ooneedo]

ulcer la úlcera [oolsaira]

umbrella el paraguas [paragwas]

uncle el tío

unconscious inconsciente [eenkons-yenteh]

under (in position) debajo de [debaHo deh]

(less than) menos de
underdone (meat) poco hecho [**echo**]
underground (railway) el metro
see **bus**
underpants los calzones [kals**o**n-es]
understand: I understand lo entiendo [ent-y**e**ndo]
I don't understand no entiendo
do you understand? ¿entiende Usted? [ent-y**e**ndeh oost**eh**]
unemployed desempleado [desempleh-**a**do]
unfashionable fuera de moda [fw**a**ira deh]
United States los Estados Unidos [oon**ee**dos]
university la universidad [**oo**neebairseed**a**]
unleaded petrol la gasolina sin plomo [seen]
unlimited mileage sin límite de kilometraje [l**ee**meeteh deh keelometra**H**eh]
unlock abrir [abr**ee**r]
unpack deshacer las maletas [desas**ai**r]
until hasta que [**a**sta keh]
unusual poco común [kom**oo**n]
up arriba
up there allá arriba [a-y**a**]
he's not up yet (not out of bed) todavía no se ha levantado [todab**ee**-a no seh a lebant**a**do]

what's up? (what's wrong?) ¿qué pasa? [keh]
upmarket (restaurant, hotel etc) de lujo [deh l**oo**Ho]
upset stomach el mal del estómago
upside down al revés [reb-**e**s], boca abajo [ab**a**Ho]
upstairs arriba
urgent urgente [oor**H**enteh]
Uruguayan (adj) uruguayo [**oo**roogw**ī**-yo]
us*: with us con nosotros/nosotras
for us para nosotros/nosotras
USA EE.UU., Estados Unidos [oon**ee**dos]
use (verb) emplear [empleh-**a**r]
may I use ...? ¿me permite ...? [meh perm**ee**teh]
useful útil [**oo**teel]
usual de costumbre [deh kost**oo**mbreh]
the usual (drink etc) lo de siempre [s-y**e**mpreh]

V

vacancy: do you have any vacancies? (hotel) ¿tiene cuartos libres? [t-y**e**neh kw**a**rtos l**ee**b-res]
see **room**
vacation las vacaciones [bakas-y**o**n-es]
see **holiday**
vaccination la vacuna

Un

[bak**oo**na]

vacuum cleaner la aspir**a**dora

valid (ticket etc) válido
[bal**ee**do]

how long is it valid for?
¿hasta cuándo tiene
validez? [**a**sta kwando t-y**e**neh
baleed-**es**]

valley el valle [ba-yeh]

valuable (adj) valioso [bal-
y**o**so]

**can I leave my valuables
here?** ¿puedo dejar aquí
mis objetos de valor? [pw**e**do
deh-Har ak**ee** mees obH**e**tos deh
bal**or**]

value el valor

van la camioneta [kam-yon**e**ta]

vanilla vainilla [bin**ee**-ya]

a vanilla ice cream un
helado de vainilla [el**a**do deh]

vary: it varies depende
[dep**e**ndeh]

vase el florero [flor**ai**ro]

veal la ternera [tairn**ai**ra]

vegetables las verduras
[baird**oo**ras]

vegetarian (man/woman) el
vegetariano [beHetar-y**a**no], la
vegetari**a**na

vending machine la máquina
vendedora [m**a**keena
bended**o**ra]

Venezuelan (adj) venezolano
[benesol**a**no]

very muy [mwee]

very little for me muy
poquito para mí [pok**ee**to]

I like it very much me gusta

mucho [meh g**oo**sta m**oo**cho]

vest (under shirt) la camis**e**ta

via por

video el video [beed**eh**-o]

view la vista [b**ee**sta]

villa el chalet [chal**eh**]

village el pueblo [pw**e**blo]

vinegar el vinagre [been**a**greh]

vineyard el viñedo [been-y**e**do]

visa la visa

visit (verb) visitar [beeseet**ar**]

I'd like to visit Guanajuato
me gustaría conocer
Guanajuato [konos**air**
gwanaHw**a**to]

vital: it's vital that ... es
imprescindible que ... [eem-
preseend**ee**bleh keh]

vodka el vodka [b**o**dka]

voice la voz [bos]

volcano el volcán [bolk**an**]

voltage el voltaje [bolt**a**Heh]

The supply is 110 volts
AC, with simple two-flat-
pin rectangular plugs.
Travellers from Europe and
Australasia should bring an adaptor.

vomit vomitar [bome**et**ar]

vulture el zopilote [sopeel**o**teh]

W

waist la cintura [seent**oo**ra]

waistcoat el chaleco

wait esperar [espair**ar**]

wait for me espéreme

[espairemeh]

don't wait for me no me espere [meh espaireh]

can I wait until my wife/ partner gets here? ¿puedo esperar hasta que llegue mi mujer/compañero? [pwedo – asta keh yegeh]

can you do it while I wait? ¿puede hacerlo ahora mismo? [pwedeh asairlo a-ora]

could you wait here for me? ¿puede esperarme aquí? [espairarmeh akee]

waiter el mesero [mesairo]
waiter! ¡señor! [sen-yor]

waitress la mesera [mesaira]
waitress! ¡señorita! [sen-yoreeta]

wake: can you wake me up at 5.30? ¿podría despertarme a las cinco y media? [despair-tarmeh]

wake-up call la llamada para despertar [yamada]

Wales Gales [gal-es]

walk: is it a long walk? ¿se tarda mucho caminando? [seh – moocho]

it's only a short walk está cerca [sairka]

I'll walk iré caminando [eereh]

I'm going for a walk voy a dar una vuelta [boy – bwelta]

Walkman® el walkman® [wolkman]

wall (inside) la pared [pareh]
(outside) el muro

wallet la cartera [kartaira]

wander: I like just wandering around me gusta caminar sin rumbo fijo [meh goosta – seen roombo feeHo]

want: I want a ... quiero un/una ... [k-yairo]

I don't want ... no quiero ninguno/ninguna ...

I want to go home quiero irme a casa [eermeh]

I don't want to no quiero

he wants to ... quiere ... [k-yaireh]

what do you want? ¿qué quiere? [keh]

ward (in hospital) el pabellón [pabeh-yon]

warm caliente [kal-yenteh]
I'm very warm tengo mucho calor [moocho]

was*: it was ... era ... [aira]; estaba ...

wash (verb) lavar [labar]
can you wash these? ¿puede lavar estos? [pwedeh]

washer (for bolt etc) el fregadero [fregadairo]

washhand basin el lavabo [lababo]

washing (clothes) la ropa sucia [soos-ya]

washing machine la lavadora [labadora]

washing powder el detergente [detairHenteh]

washing-up liquid el (detergente) lavavajillas [lababaHee-yas]

152

wasp la avispa [ab**ee**spa]

watch (wristwatch) el reloj [relo**H**]

will you watch my things for me? ¿puede cuidarme mis cosas? [p**we**deh kwee**dar**meh mees]

watch out! ¡cuidado! [kwee**da**do]

watch strap la correa [korr**eh**-a]

water el agua [**a**gwa]

may I have some water? ¿me da un poco de agua? [meh – deh]

> You should stick to bottled or distilled water, which is available everywhere: **Tehuacán** is the most common label, and is used as a general term for mineral water; **con gas** is fizzy and **sin gas** is still. Virtually every hotel will have a supply of drinking water either in the hotel room or in the corridor. Remember that ice may be made of unpurified water and that raw vegetables and salads may also have been washed in it, and this can be risky for visitors. You can buy water purification tablets at most pharmacies.

waterproof (adj) impermeable [eempairmeh-**ab**leh]

waterskiing el esquí acuático [esk**ee** akw**a**teeko]

wave (in sea) la ola [**o**la]

way: **it's this way** es por aquí [ak**ee**]

it's that way es por allí [a-y**ee**]

is it a long way to ...? ¿queda lejos ...? [k**e**da le**h**-Hos]

no way! ¡de ninguna manera! [deh – man**ai**ra]

dialogue

could you tell me the way to ...? podría indicarme el camino a ...? [een-deek**ar**meh]

go straight on until you reach the traffic lights siga recto hasta llegar al semáforo [**a**sta ye**gar**]

turn left tuerce a la izquierda [tw**air**seh]

take the first on the right tome la primera a la derecha [**to**meh]

see **where**

we* nos**o**tros, nos**o**tras

weak d**é**bil

weather el tiempo [t-y**empo**]

dialogue

what's the weather going to be like? ¿qué tiempo va a hacer? [keh – ba a as**air**]

it's going to be fine va a hacer bueno [b**we**no]

it's going to rain va a llover [yob**air**]

it'll brighten up later despejará más tarde

[despeh-Hara mas tardeh]
wedding la boda
wedding ring el anillo de
casado [anee-yo]
Wednesday miércoles
[m-yairkol-es]
week la semana
a week (from) today dentro
de una semana [deh]
a week (from) tomorrow
dentro de una semana a
partir de mañana [man-yana]
weekend el fin de semana
[feen deh]
at the weekend el fin de
semana
weight el peso
weird extraño [ekstran-yo]
weirdo: he's a weirdo es un
tipo raro [teepo]
welcome: welcome to ...
bienvenido a ...
[b-yenbeneedo]
you're welcome (don't mention
it) no hay de qué [ī deh
keh]
well: I don't feel well no me
siento bien [meh s-yento
b-yen]
she's not well no se siente
bien [seh s-yenteh]
you speak English very well
habla inglés muy bien [abla
eeng-les mwee]
well done! ¡bravo! [brabo]
this one as well éste
también [esteh tamb-yen]
well well! (surprise) ¡ándale,
pues! [andaleh pwes]

dialogue

how are you? ¿cómo le
va? [leh ba]
very well, thanks muy
bien, gracias [mwee b-yen
gras-yas]
– and you? – ¿y Usted?
[ee oosteh]

well-done (meat) bien hecho
[b-yen echo]
Welsh galés [gal-es]
I'm Welsh (man/woman) soy
galés/galesa
were*: we were estábamos;
éramos [airamos]
you were estaban; eran
[airan]
they were estaban; eran
west el oeste [o-esteh], el
occidente [okseedenteh]
in the west en el oeste
West Indian (adj) antillano
[antee-yano]
wet mojado [moHado]
what? ¿qué? [keh]
what's that? ¿qué es eso?
what should I do? ¿qué
hago? [a-go]
what a view! ¡qué vista!
what number bus is it? ¿qué
número de camión es ese?
[noomairo deh – eseh]
wheel la rueda [rweda]
wheelchair la silla de ruedas
[see-ya deh rwedas]
when? ¿cuándo? [kwando]
when we get back cuando

regresamos

when's the train/ferry?
¿cuándo es el tren/ferry?

where? ¿dónde? [dondeh]

I don't know where it is no sé dónde está [seh]

dialogue

where is the cathedral?
¿dónde está la catedral?
it's over there está por ahí [a-ee]
could you show me where it is on the map? ¿puede enseñarme en el mapa dónde está? [pwedeh ensen-yarmeh]
it's just here está aquí mero [akee mairo]
see way

which: which bus? ¿qué camión? [keh]

dialogue

which one? ¿cuál? [kwal]
that one ese [eseh]
this one? ¿éste? [esteh]
no, that one no, aquél [akel]

while: while I'm here ya que estoy aquí [keh estoy akee]

whisky el whisky

white blanco

white wine el vino blanco [beeno]

who? ¿quién? [k-yen]

who is it? ¿quién es?

the man who ... el hombre que... [keh]

whole: the whole week toda la semana

the whole lot todo

whose: whose is this? ¿de quién es esto? [deh k-yen]

why? ¿por qué? [keh]

why not? ¿por qué no?

wide ancho

wife la mujer [mooHair], la esposa

will*: will you do it for me?
¿puede hacer esto por mí? [pwedeh asair]

wind el viento [b-yento]

window (of house) la ventana [bentana]
(of ticket office, vehicle) la ventanilla [bentanee-ya]

near the window cerca de la ventana [sairka deh]

in the window (of shop) en el escaparate [eskaparateh]

window seat el asiento junto a la ventana [as-yento Hoonto a la bentana]

windscreen el parabrisas

windscreen wiper el limpiaparabrisas [leemp-ya-parabreesas]

windsurfing el windsurf

windy: it's very windy hace mucho viento [aseh moocho b-yento]

wine el vino [beeno]
can we have some more

Wi

wine? ¿podría traernos más vino? [tra-**air**nos]

 Wine is not seen a great deal, although Mexico does produce a fair number of perfectly good ones. You're safest sticking to the brand names like **Hidalgo** or **Domecq**, or those from Baja California which in many cases have borrowed techniques and winemakers from the US. **El vino de casa** (house wine) would normally be a Mexican wine; make sure you are not given a French wine or a Spanish one, both of which are likely to be very expensive.

wine list la lista de vinos [**lee**sta deh b**ee**nos]
winter el invierno [eemb-**yair**no]
  in the winter en invierno
winter holiday las vacaciones de invierno [bakas-**yon**-es deh]
wire el alambre [al**am**breh] (electric) el cable eléctrico [**kab**leh]
wish: best wishes saludos
with con
  I'm staying with ... est**oy** en casa de ... [deh]
without sin [seen]
witness el/la testigo [test**ee**go]
  will you be a witness for me? ¿acepta ser mi testigo? [as**e**pta sair]

woman la mujer [moo**Hair**]

women
Women travellers, especially blonde ones, can expect to be the almost constant butt of comments from Mexican men. Try to remember that these are rarely meant to be offensive (they are 'compliments') and that, unless your Spanish is good enough to reply with a tirade of abuse, they are best ignored completely. Male companions tempted to intervene in a 'gentlemanly' manner should think twice: this is a direct challenge to the macho male, and likely to raise the stakes considerably.

wonderful estupendo [estoop**en**do]
won't*: it won't start no arranca
wood (material) la madera [mad**air**a]
woods (forest) el bosque [**bos**keh]
wool la lana
word la palabra
work el trabajo [trab**a**Ho]
  it's not working no funciona [foons-**yon**a]
  I work in ... trabajo en ...
world el mundo [**moo**ndo]
worry: I'm worried (said by man/woman) est**oy** preocupado/preocupada [preh-okoop**a**do]

156

worse: it's worse es peor
[peh-or]

worst el peor

worth: is it worth a visit? ¿vale
la pena visitarlo? [baleh –
beeseetarlo]

would: would you give this
to ...? ¿le puede dar esto
a ...? [leh pwedeh]

wrap: could you wrap it up?
¿me lo envuelve? [meh lo
embwelbeh]

wrapping paper el papel de
envolver [deh embolbair]

wrist la muñeca [moon-yeka]

write escribir [eskreebeer]
could you write it down?
¿puede escribírmelo?
[pwedeh]
how do you write it? ¿cómo
se escribe? [seh eskreebeh]

writing paper el papel de
escribir

wrong: it's the wrong key no
es ésa la llave [yabeh]
this is the wrong train éste
no es el tren [esteh]
the bill's wrong la cuenta
está equivocada [kwenta –
ekeebokada]
sorry, wrong number
perdone, me equivoqué de
número [pairdoneh meh
ekeebokeh deh noomairo]
there's something wrong
with ... le pasa algo a ... [leh]
what's wrong? ¿qué pasa?
[keh]

X

X-ray la radiografía [rad-
yografee-a]

Y

yacht el yate [yateh]
yard* (courtyard) el patio
year el año [an-yo]
yellow amarillo [amaree-yo]
yes sí
yesterday ayer [ī-yair]
yesterday morning ayer por
la mañana [man-yana]
the day before yesterday
anteayer [anteh-ī-yair]
yet

dialogue

is it here yet? ¿está aquí
ya? [akee]
no, not yet no, todavía no
[todabee-a]
you'll have to wait a little
longer yet tendrá que
esperar un poquito más
[keh espairar oon pokeeto]

yobbo el hampón [ampon]
yoghurt el yogur [yogoor]
you* (fam, sing) tú [too]
(pol, sing) Usted [oosteh]
(pol, pl) Ustedes [oosted-es]
this is for you esto es para
tí/Usted

with you contigo/con Usted

There are two words for 'you' in Spanish. You use **Usted** if you are talking to someone older, or someone you don't know. You say **tu** when the person you are speaking to is a friend or a family member, or someone younger than yourself. In the plural, Mexicans use **Ustedes**, whoever they are speaking to.

young joven [Hoben]
your* (fam, sing) tu; (pl) tus [toos]
(pol, sing) su; (pl) sus [soos]
yours* (fam, sing) tuyo [**too**-yo], tuya
(pol, sing) suyo [**soo**-yo], suya; de Usted [deh oost**eh**]
youth hostel el albergue juvenil [alb**air**geh Hoobeneel]

Z

zero cero [**sai**ro]
zip el cierre [s-y**ai**rreh]
  could you put a new zip in?
  ¿podría cambiar el cierre? [kamb-y**ar**]
zip code el código postal [pos-tal]
zoo el zoo(lógico) [zo(l**o**Heeko)]

Spanish

→

English

Colloquial Spanish

The following are words you might well hear. Some of them you wouldn't ever want to use and you shouldn't be tempted to use any of the stronger ones unless you are sure of your audience.

¡ándale pues! [andaleh pwes] go on then!, OK!
¡bien! [b-yen] good!
cabrón m bastard
¡carajo! [karaHo] Christ!, shit!
chingar to fuck
¡chinga tu madre! fuck off!
coger [koHair] to fuck
¡Dios mío! [d-yos mee-o] my God!
¿dónde carajos? [dondeh] where in hell?
¡está padre! it's great!
¡hijo de la chingada! [eeHo] son of a bitch!
¡híjole! [eeHoleh] hell!, damn!
joder [Hodair] to screw up
¡lárguese! [largeseh] go away!
¡lo jodiste! [Hodeesteh] you screwed up!
mamón! idiot!
mano pal, buddy
marica m, maricón m queer
mariposa f butterfly; fairy, pansy
me pega la gana I feel like it
me vale (madre) [madreh] I don't give a shit
¡mierda! [m-yairda] shit!
¡ni modo! well, what can you do?
no le hace [leh aseh] don't worry about it
¡oiga! [oyga] listen here!; excuse me!
¡órale! [oraleh] go on then!, get on with it!
pinche [peencheh] bloody, lousy
pocho Americanized (used to refer to Americanized Mexican)
¡qué chingadera! [keh cheengadaira] what a fuck-up!
¡qué desmadre! [keh desmadreh] what a mess!
¿qué húbole? [keh ooboleh] how's it going?
¡qué va! [ba] no way!
un chingo de [deh] loads of

A

a to; at; per; from

abajo [abaHo] downstairs; down below

abarrotes: tienda de abarrotes f [t-yenda deh abarrot-es] grocer's, dry goods store

abierto [ab-yairto] open

abierto de ... a ... open from ... to ...

abierto las 24 horas del día open 24 hours

abogada f, abogado m lawyer

abonos mpl season tickets

aborrezco [aborresko] I hate

ábrase aquí open here

ábrase en caso de emergencia open in case of emergency

abrazo m [abraso] embrace

abrebotellas m [abreboteh-yas] bottle-opener

abrelatas m tin-opener

abrigo m coat

abrigo de pieles [deh p-yel-es] fur coat

abril m April

abrir to open

abróchense los cinturones fasten your seatbelts

abuela f [abwela] grandmother

abuelo m grandfather

abuelos mpl grandparents

aburrido boring, bored

aburrirse [aboorreerseh] to be bored; to get bored

acabar to finish

acabo de ... [deh] I have just ...

acantilado m cliff

acceso a ... access to ...

acceso a la vía to the trains

acceso playa to the beach

accidente m [akseedenteh] accident

tener un accidente [tenair] to have an accident

accidente de carro [deh] car accident

accidente de montaña [montan-ya] mountaineering accident

accidente de tránsito road accident

accidente en cadena [kadena] pile-up

acelerador m [aselairador] accelerator, gas pedal

acelerar [aselairar] to accelerate

acento m [asento] accent

aceptar [aseptar] to accept

acera f [asaira] pavement, sidewalk

acerca de [asairka deh] about, concerning

acero m [asairo] steel

acetona f [asetona] nail polish remover

ácido (m) [aseedo] sour; acid

acompañar [akompan-yar] to accompany

le acompaño en el sentimiento my condolences

acondicionador de pelo m [akondees-yonador deh] hair conditioner

aconsejar [akonseh-Har] to

advise

acordarse [akord**a**rseh] to remember

acostar to put to bed; to lay down

acostarse [akost**a**rseh] to lie down; to go to bed

al acostarse when you go to bed

actriz f [aktr**ees**] actress

acuerdo m [akw**ai**rdo] agreement

estoy de acuerdo [deh] I agree

de acuerdo OK

adaptador m adaptor

adelantado: por adelantado [adelant**a**do] in advance

adelantarse a [–**a**rseh] to overtake

además de [deh] besides, as well as

adentro inside

adolescente m/f [adoles**e**nteh] teenager

aduana f [adw**a**na] Customs

aduanero m [adw**a**nairo] Customs office

aerodeslizador m [a-airo-desleesad**or**] hovercraft

aerolínea f [a-airol**ee**neh-a] airline

aeropuerto m [a-airopw**ai**rto] airport

afeitarse [afayt**a**rseh] to shave

aficionada f [afees-yon**a**da], **aficionado m** fan, enthusiast

afortunadamente [–m**e**nteh] fortunately

afueras fpl [afw**ai**ras] suburbs

agarrar to hold, to grasp; to catch; to take

agencia f [aн**e**ns-ya] agency

agencia de viajes [deh b-ya**н**-es] travel agency

agenda f [aн**e**nda] diary

agítese antes de usar(se) shake before use

agosto m August

agradable [agrad**a**bleh] pleasant

agradar to please

agradecer [agrades**ai**r] to thank

agradecido [agrades**ee**do] grateful

agradezco [agrad**e**sko] I thank

agresivo [agres**ee**bo] aggressive

agricultor m farmer

agua f [**a**gwa] water

agua de colonia [deh kol**o**n-ya] eau de toilette

aguantar: no aguanto ... [agw**a**nto] I can't stand ...

agua potable [pot**a**bleh] drinking water

águila ratonera f [**a**geela] buzzard

aguja f [ag**oo**нa] needle

agujero m [agoo**н**airo] hole

agujetas fpl [a-ooн**e**tas] shoelaces

ahora [a-**o**ra] now

ahorita [a-or**ee**ta] right away; soon; just a moment ago

aire m [**ī**reh] air

aire acondicionado [akondees-yon**a**do] air-conditioning

ajedrez m [aн**e**d-res] chess

ajustado [aн**oo**stado] tight

ala f wing

alambre m [alambreh] wire

alambre de púa [deh poo-a] barbed wire

alarma f alarm

 dar la señal de alarma [sen-yal deh] to raise the alarm

alberca f [albairka] swimming pool

albergue juvenil [albairgeh Hoobeneel] youth hostel

alcoba f bedroom; sleeping compartment

alcohómetro m Breathalyzer®

alegre [alegreh] happy

alegro: me alegro I'm pleased; I'm pleased to hear it

alemán German

Alemania f [aleman-ya] Germany

alérgico a [alairHeeko] allergic to

aletas fpl flippers

alfiler m [alfeelair] pin

alfombra f rug, carpet

algo something

algodón m [algodon] cotton; cotton wool, absorbent cotton

algo más something else

alguien [alg-yen] somebody; anybody

algún some; any

alguno someone; anyone; one; any one

alianza f [al-yansa] wedding ring

alimentos mpl groceries, foodstuffs

allá: más allá [a-ya] further (on)

allí [a-yee] there

almacén m [almasen] department store; warehouse

almohada f [almo-ada] pillow

almuerzo m [almwairso] lunch

alojamiento m [aloHam-yento] accommodation

alojamiento y desayuno [desī-yoono] bed and breakfast

alpinismo m mountaineering

alquilar [alkeelar] to rent; to hire

alquiler m [alkeelair] rental

alquiler de barcos boat hire

alquiler de bicicletas [beeseekletas] cycle hire

alquiler de carros car rental

alquiler de esquís [eskees] water-ski hire

alquiler de tablas surfboard hire

alquileres rentals

alrededor (de) [deh] around

alta costura f haute couture, high fashion

alto (m) stop sign; high; tall

 ¡alto! stop!

 en lo alto at the top

altura f altitude; height

altura máxima maximum headroom

aluminio m aluminium

amable [amableh] kind;

 si fuera tan amable [fwaira] if you wouldn't mind

amamantar to breastfeed

amanecer m [amanesair] sunrise, daybreak

¿cómo amaneciste? how did you sleep?

amargo bitter

amarillo [amaree-yo] yellow

ambos both

ambulancia f [amboolans-ya] ambulance

América f [amaireeka] Latin America

América del Norte [norteh] North America

América del Sur South America

americana (f), americano (m) Latin American

amiga f friend, amigo m friend

amor m love

hacer el amor [asair] to make love

amortiguador m [amorteegwador] shock-absorber

amperio m [ampair-yo] amp

ampliación f [amplee-as-yon] enlargement

amplio broad; loose-fitting

ampolla f [ampo-ya] blister

analgésico m [analHeseeko] painkiller

análisis clínicos mpl clinical tests

anaranjado [anaranHado] orange (colour)

ancho (m) width, breadth; wide; loose

anchura f width, breadth

¡ándale pues! [andaleh pwes] go on then!, OK!

andaluz [andaloos] Andalusian

andar to walk; to move; to work

andinismo m mountaineering

anémico anaemic

anestesia f [anestes-ya] anaesthetic

anfiteatro m [anfeeteh-atro] amphitheatre

Angeles Verdes mpl [angel-es baird-es] breakdown service

angina (de pecho) f [anHeena] angina

anginas fpl tonsillitis

anillo m [anee-yo] ring

anoche [anocheh] last night

anochecer m [anochesair] nightfall, dusk

anochece [anocheseh] it's getting dark

ante m [anteh] suede

anteayer [anteh-ī-yair] the day before yesterday

antepasado m ancestor

antes de [ant-es deh] before

antes de entrar dejen salir let passengers off first

antes de que [keh] before

anticipo m [anteeseepo] advance

anticonceptivo m [anteekonsepteebo] contraceptive

anticongelante m [anteekonHelanteh] antifreeze

anticuado [anteekwado] out of date

anticuario m [anteekwar-yo] antiques dealer

antigüedades: una tienda de antigüedades [t-yenda deh anteegwedad-es] an antique shop

antiguo [anteegwo] old; ancient

antihistamínico m [antee-eestameeneeko] antihistamine

Antillas fpl [antee-yas] the West Indies

antipático unpleasant, nasty

anulado cancelled

anular to cancel

añadir [an-yadeer] to add

año m [an-yo] year

Año Nuevo m [nwebo] New Year

día de Año Nuevo m [dee-a deh] New Year's Day

¡feliz Año Nuevo! [felees] Happy New Year!

apagar to switch off

apagón m power cut

apague el motor switch off your engine

apague las luces switch off your lights

aparato m device

aparatos electrodomésticos electrical appliances

aparecer [aparesair] to appear

aparezco [aparesko] I appear

apasionante [apas-yonanteh] thrilling

apellido m [apeh-yeedo] surname

apenado sorry; embarrassed, shy

apenarse [–arseh] to be ashamed, to be embarrassed

apenas scarcely

apenas ... (cuando) [kwando] hardly ... when

son las seis apenas it's only just six o'clock

apetecer: me apetece [meh apeteseh] I feel like

apetito m appetite

apodo m nickname

apoplejía f [apopleHee-a] stroke; fit

aprender [aprendair] to learn

aprensivo [aprenseebo] fearful, apprehensive

apriete botón para cruzar press button to cross

aprovechar [aprobechar] to take advantage of

¡que aproveche! [keh aprobecheh] enjoy your meal!

aproximadamente [–menteh] about

apto para mayores de 14 años y menores acompañados authorized for those over 14 and young people accompanied by an adult

apto para mayores de 18 años for adults only

apto para todos los públicos suitable for all

apurado in a hurry

apurarse [–arseh] to rush, to hurry

¡apúrate! [apoorateh] hurry up!

aquel [akel] that

aquél that (one)

aquella [akeh-ya] that

aquélla that (one)

aquellas [ak**eh**-yas] those

aqu**éllas** those (ones)

aquellos [ak**eh**-yos] those

aqu**éllos** those (ones)

aquí [ak**ee**] here

aquí tiene [t-y**eneh**] here you are

araña f [aran-ya] spider

arañazo m [aran-y**aso**] scratch

árbol m tree

ardor de estómago m [deh] heartburn

área de servicios m [**a**reh-a deh serb**ees**-yos] service area, motorway services

arena f [**a**reh-na] sand

aretes mpl [ar**et**-es] earrings

argentino (m) [arHent**ee**no] Argentine; Argentinian

armario m cupboard

armería f [armair**ee**-a] gunsmith's

aro m ring

arqueología f [arkeh-oloH**ee**-a] archaeology

arrancar to pull out, to tear out; to start up

arranque m [arr**an**keh] ignition

arreglar to mend; to sort out, to arrange

arrendar [arrend**ar**] to rent; to hire

 se arrienda to rent, for hire

arriba up; upstairs; on top

arroyo m stream

arte m [**ar**teh] art

artesanía f crafts

artículos de artesanía mpl [deh] arts and crafts

artículos de boda wedding presents

artículos de deporte [dep**or**teh] sports goods

artículos de limpieza [leemp-y**esa**] household cleaning products

artículos de piel [p-yel] leather goods

artículos de playa [pl**ī**-ya] beachwear

artículos de viaje [b-ya**Heh**] travel goods

artículos escolares [eskol**ar**-es] schoolwear

artículos para el bebé [beh-b**eh**] babywear

artista m/f artist

artritis f arthritis

ascensor m [asens**or**] lift, elevator

asegurar to insure

aseos mpl [as**eh**-os] toilets, rest rooms

así like this; like that

asiento m [as-y**ento**] seat

así que so (that)

asma m asthma

aspiradora f vacuum cleaner

asqueroso [askair**oso**] disgusting

astigmático long-sighted

asustado afraid

asustar to frighten

atacar to attack

atajo m [ata**Ho**] shortcut

ataque m [at**akeh**] attack

ataque al corazón [koras**on**] heart attack

atención [atens-yon] please note

¡atención! take care!, caution!

atención al tren beware of trains

ateo [ateh-o] atheist

aterrizaje m landing

aterrizaje forzado emergency landing

aterrizar [atairreesar] to land

atletismo m athletics

atorado stuck

atorarse [atorarseh] to get stuck

atracar to assault; to hold up

atracciones turísticas fpl [atraks-yon-es] tourist attractions

atraco a mano armada m armed robbery, hold-up

atractivo [atrakteebo] attractive

atrás at the back; behind

¡atrás! get back!

la parte de atrás [parteh deh] the back

está más atrás it's further back

años atrás [an-yos] years ago

atrasado late

atraso m delay

atravesar [atrabesar] to cross

atravieso [atrab-yeso] I cross

atreverse [atrebairseh] to dare

atropellar [atropeh-yar] to knock down

atroz [atros] dreadful

audífono m [owdeefono] hearing aid

aun [own] even

aún [a-oon] still; yet

aunque [ownkeh] although

auto m [owto] car

autobús m [owtoboos] coach, long-distance bus

auto-estopista m/f [owto-estopeesta] hitch-hiker

automóvil m [owtomobeel] car

autopista f [owtopeesta] motorway, freeway, highway

autopista de cuota [deh kwota] toll motorway/highway

auto-servicio m [owto-sairbees-yo] self-service

autostop: hacer autostop [asair owtostop] to hitchhike

autovía f [owtobee-a] slow, local train

avenida f [abeneeda] avenue

aventar [abentar] to throw

aventón: pedir aventón [abenton] to hitch a lift

avergonzado [abairgonsado] ashamed

avería f [abairee-a] breakdown

averiarse [abair-yarseh] to break down

avión m [ab-yon] aeroplane, airplane

por avión by air

avisar [abeesar] to inform

aviso m [abeeso] advertisement; notice

aviso a los señores pasajeros passenger information

avispa f [abeespa] wasp

ayer [i-yair] yesterday

ayer por la mañana [man-yana] yesterday morning

ayer por la tarde [tardeh] yesterday afternoon

ayuda f [ī-yooda] help

ayudar [ī-yoodar] to help

ayuntamiento m [ī-yoontam-yento] town hall

azotea f [asoteh-a] roof

azteca [asteka] Aztec

azul (m) [asool] blue

azul claro light blue

azul marino navy blue

B

baca f roof rack

bache m [bacheh] hole in the road

bahía f [ba-ee-a] bay

bailar [bīlar] to dance

ir a bailar to go dancing

baile m [bīleh] dance; dancing

¡bajan! [baHan] next stop please!, people getting off!

bajar [baHar] to go down

bajar de [deh] to get off

bajar la velocidad [beloseeda] to slow down

bajarse (de) [baHarseh (deh)] to get off

bajeño [baHen-yo] from/of Baja California

Bajío m [baHee-yo] Baja California

bajo [baHo] low; short; under; underneath

balacera f [balasaira] exchange of fire

balanceo m [balanseh-yo]

wheel-balancing

balcón m balcony

balón m ball

balonmano m handball

balsa f raft

banco m bank; bench

bandeja f [bandeHa] tray

bandera f [bandaira] flag

bandido m bandit

banqueta f [banketa] pavement, sidewalk

bañador m [ban-yador] swimming costume

bañarse [ban-yarseh] to go swimming; to have a bath/shower

bañera f [ban-yaira] bathtub

baño m [ban-yo] bathroom; toilet, rest room; bath

baños mpl toilets, rest room

baraja f [baraHa] pack of cards

barato cheap, inexpensive

barba f chin; beard

barbacoa f barbecue; barbecued meat

barbería f [barbairee-a] barber's shop

barbero m [barbairo] barber

barco m boat

barco de remo [deh] rowing boat

barco de vela [bela] sailing boat

barcos para alquilar boats to rent

barra de labios f [deh lab-yos] lipstick

barrio m [barr-yo] district, area

básquet m [basket] basketball

bastante [bastanteh] enough; quite; very
   bastante más quite a lot more
basura f rubbish, garbage
bata f dressing gown
bate m [bateh] bat
batería f [batairee-a] battery; drum kit
batería de cocina [deh koseena] pots and pans
bautismo m [bowteesmo] christening
bebé m [beh-beh] baby
beber [bebair] to drink
béisbol m [baysbol] baseball
Belice [beleeseh] Belize
bello [beh-yo] beautiful
besar to kiss
beso m kiss
betún m [betoon] shoe polish
biblioteca f [beebl-yoteka] library; bookcase
bicicleta f [beeseekleta] bicycle
bien [b-yen] well
   ¡bien! good!
   bien ... bien ... either ... or ...
   o bien ... o bien ... either ... or ...
bienes mpl [b-yen-es] possessions
¡bienvenido! [b-yenbeneedo] welcome!
bifurcación f [beefoorkas-yon] fork
bigote m [beegoteh] moustache
billete m [bee-yeteh] banknote, (US) bill
blanco (m) white

blusa f blouse
boca f mouth
boda f wedding
bodega f wine cellar
boleador m [boleh-ador] shoeshine boy
boletería f ticket office
boleto m ticket
boleto de ida [deh eeda] single ticket, one-way ticket
boleto de ida y vuelta [ee bwelta] return ticket, round-trip ticket
bolígrafo m ballpoint pen
bolsa f bag; stock exchange
bolsa de dormir [deh] sleeping bag
bolsa de plástico plastic bag
bolsa de viaje [b-yaHeh] travel bag
bolsillo m [bolsee-yo] pocket
bolso m handbag, (US) purse
bomba f bomb
bomba de gas [deh] camping gas cylinder
bomberos mpl [bombairos] fire brigade
bordado embroidered
borracho drunk
bosque m [boskeh] forest
bota f boot
botanas fpl snacks
botar to throw away
botella f [boteh-ya] bottle
botiquín m [boteekeen] first-aid kit
botón m button
botón desatascador coin return button

boxeo m [bokseh-o] boxing

boya f buoy

bracero m [brasairo] migrant labourer from Mexico to the US

bragas fpl pants, panties

brazo m [braso] arm

bricolaje m [breekolaHeh] DIY, do-it-yourself

brillar [bree-yar] to shine

brincar to jump

brisa f breeze

británico British

brocha de afeitar f [deh afaytar] shaving brush

broche m [brocheh] brooch

bronce m [bronseh] bronze

bronceado (m) [bronseh-ado] suntan; suntanned

bronceador m [bronseh-ador] suntan oil/lotion

bronquitis f [bronkeetees] bronchitis

brújula f [brooHoola] compass

bruto stupid

bucear [booseh-ar] to skin-dive

buceo m [booseh-o] skin-diving

buenas noches [bwenas noch-es] good night

buenas tardes [tard-es] good evening

bueno [bweno] good; good-natured; hello

buenos días [dee-as] good morning

bufanda f scarf

bufete m [boofeteh] lawyer's office

bujía f [booHee-a] spark plug

bulto m package; lump, swelling

burro m donkey

buscar to look for

busqué [booskeh] I looked for

butacas fpl stalls

buzón m [booson] letter box, postbox, mailbox

C

c/ street

c/c current account

caballeros mpl [kaba-yairos] gents, men's rest room

caballo m [kaba-yo] horse

cabaña f [kaban-ya] beach hut

cabello m [kabeh-yo] hair

cabeza f [kabesa] head

cabida ... personas capacity ... people

cabina telefónica f telephone booth, phone box

cable m [kableh] wire

cable de extensión m [deh ekstens-yon] extension lead

cabra f goat

cabrón m [kabron] bastard

cachetada f slap in the face

cacto m cactus

cada every

cada vez (que) [bes (keh)] every time (that)

cadena f chain

cadera f [kadaira] hip

caduca ... expires ...

caer [ka-air] to fall

caerse [ka-**air**seh] to fall over, to fall down

café [ka**feh**] coffee; café

cafetera f [kafet**air**a] coffee pot

cafetería f [kafetair**ee**-a] bartype restaurant

caída f [ka-**ee**da] fall

caimán m [k**ai**man] alligator

caja f [k**a**Ha] cash desk, till; cashier

caja de ahorros [deh a-**o**rros] savings bank

caja de cambios [k**a**mb-yos] gearbox

cajera f [ka**Hai**ra], **cajero** m cashier

cajero automático [owtom**a**teeko] cashpoint, automatic teller, ATM

cajeta f [ka**H**eta] fudge

cajetilla f [ka**H**et**ee**-ya] packet, (US) pack

cajuela f [ka**H**wela] boot (of car), (US) trunk

calambre m [kal**a**mbreh] cramp

calcetines mpl [kalset**een**-es] socks

calculadora f calculator

calefacción f [kalefaks-y**on**] heating

calefacción central [s**e**ntral] central heating

calendario m [–**dar**-yo] calendar

calidad f [kal**ee**da] quality

caliente [kal-y**e**nteh] hot

calle f [k**a**-yeh] street

calle comercial [komairs-y**a**l] shopping street

calle de sentido único one-way street

callejón m [ka-yeh-**H**on] lane, alley

callejón sin salida cul-de-sac, dead end

calle peatonal [peh-aton**a**l] pedestrianized street

calle principal [preens**e**epal] main street

callo m [k**a**-yo] corn (on foot)

calmante m [kalm**a**nteh] tranquillizer

calor m heat

hace calor [**a**seh] it's warm/hot

calvo [k**a**lbo] bald

calza: ¿qué número calza? [keh n**oo**mairo k**a**lsa] what is your shoe size?

calzada f [kals**a**da] street

calzada deteriorada poor road surface

calzada irregular uneven surface

calzados shoe shop

calzones mpl [kals**o**n-es] underpants

cama f bed

cama de campaña [deh kamp**a**nya] campbed

cama individual [eendeebeed**wa**l] single bed

cama matrimonial [matreemon-y**a**l] double bed

cámara f camera; inner tube

cámara fotográfica camera

camarín m sleeping berth

camarote m [kamar**o**teh] cabin

cambiar [kamb-y**a**r] to change

cambiarse (de ropa) [kamb-yarseh (deh)] to get changed

cambio m [kamb-yo] change; exchange; exchange rate

cambio de divisas [deh deebeesas] currency exchange

cambio de moneda currency exchange

cambio de sentido take filter lane to exit and cross flow of traffic

camellón m [kameh-yon] central reservation

caminar to walk; to work

camino m path

camino cerrado (al tráfico) road closed to (traffic)

camino privado private road

camión m [kam-yon] bus

camioneta f [kam-yoneta] van

camisa f shirt

camiseta f T-shirt; vest

camisón m nightdress

campana f bell

campechano from/of Campeche

campesino m peasant farmer

camping m camping; campsite; caravan site, trailer park

campo m countryside; pitch; court; field

campo de deportes [deh deportes] sports field

campo de futból football ground

campo de golf golf course

canadiense (m/f) [kanad-yenseh] Canadian

cancelado [kanselado] cancelled; stamped

cancelar [kanselar] to cancel; to stamp

cancha f court; pitch

canción f [kans-yon] song

canguro m/f baby-sitter

canoa f canoe; skiff

canoso greying; grey

cansado tired

cantar to sing

cantina f bar

canto m song; singing

caña f [kan-ya] sugar cane; sugar cane liquor

caña de pescar [deh] fishing rod

cañería f [kan-yairee-a] pipes

cañon m [kan-yon] canyon

capaz: ser capaz (de) [sair kapas (deh)] to be able (to); to be capable (of)

capazo m [kapaso] carry-cot

capilla f [kapee-ya] chapel

capitalina f, capitalino m person who lives in the capital city

capitán m captain

capó(t) m bonnet (of car), (US) hood

cara f face

carácter m [karaktair] character; nature

tiene mal carácter [t-yeneh] he's got a bad temper

¡carajo! [karaHo] Christ!, shit!

¿dónde carajos? [dondeh] where in hell?

caravana f caravan, (US) trailer
carburador m carburettor
cárcel f [karsel] prison
carey m [karay] tortoiseshell
Caribe: el Caribe [kareebeh] the Caribbean
caricaturas fpl cartoons
cariño m [kareen-yo] love; affection
carnet de identidad m [deh eedenteeda] identity card
carnet de chofer m [chofair] driving licence
carnicería f [karneesairee-a] butcher's
caro expensive
carpa f large tent, marquee
carpintería f [karpeentairee-a] joiner's, carpenter's
carrera f [karraira] race; career
carreras de caballos mpl [deh kaba-yos] horse racing
carrete m [karreteh] film (for camera)
carretera f [karretaira] main road
carretera cortada road blocked, road closed
carretera de circunvalación by-pass
carretera de doble carril two-lane road
carril m lane
carrito m trolley; cart; pushchair
carrito de niño [deh neen-yo] pushchair
carrito portaequipajes [porta-ekeepaн-es] baggage trolley

carro m car
carrocería f [karrosairee-a] bodywork
carro-comedor m buffet car, restaurant car
carro rentado m rented car
carta f letter; menu
cartel m poster
cartelera de espectáculos f [kartelaira deh] entertainments guide
cartera f [kartaira] briefcase; wallet
carterista m pickpocket
cartero m postman, mailman
cartón m cardboard; carton
casa f house
  en casa at home
  en casa de Juan [deh] at Juan's
  está en su casa make yourself at home
casa de cambio f [kamb-yo] bureau de change
casa de huéspedes [deh wesped-es] guesthouse
casa de socorro emergency first-aid centre
casado married
casarse [kasarseh] to get married
cascada f waterfall
caseta telefónica phone box, phone booth
casete f [kaset] cassette
casi almost
caso m case
  en caso de que [deh keh] in case

caso urgente [oorHenteh] emergency

caspa f dandruff

castaño (m) [kastan-yo] sweet chestnut; brown

castigar to punish

castigo m punishment

castillo m [kastee-yo] castle

casualidad: de casualidad [deh kaswaleeda] by chance

catarro: tengo catarro I've got a cold

católico (m) Catholic

catorce [katorseh] fourteen

causa f [kowsa] cause

cauteloso [kowteloso] cautious; careful

cayó [ki-yo] he/she fell

caza f [kasa] hunting

cazadora f [kasadora] bomber jacket, blouson jacket

cazar [kasar] to hunt

cazuela f [kaswela] casserole; saucepan

ceda el paso give way

ceja f [seHa] eyebrow

celos: tener celos [tenair selos] to be jealous

celoso [seloso] jealous

cementerio m [sementair-yo] cemetery

cena f [sena] dinner

cenar to have dinner

cenicero m [seneesairo] ashtray

cenote m [senoteh] deep pool used for ceremonial purposes by the Mayas

central camionera f [sentral kam-yonaira] main bus station

central de autobuses [deh owtoboos-es] main bus station

central telefónica telephone exchange

centro m [sentro] centre

centro ciudad [s-yooda] city/town centre

centro comercial [komairs-yal] shopping centre

centro deportivo sports centre

centro de salud [deh saloo] health centre

centro urbano city/town centre

ceñido [sen-yeedo] tight-fitting

cepillo m [sepee-yo] brush

cepillo de dientes [deh d-yent-es] toothbrush

cepillo de pelo hairbrush

cera f [saira] wax

cerámica f [sairameeka] pottery; ceramics

cerca de [sairka deh] near

cerilla f [sairee-ya] match

cero [sairo] zero

cerrada f [sairrada] cul-de-sac

cerrado [sairrado] closed

cerrado por defunción closed due to bereavement

cerrado por descanso del personal closed for staff holidays

cerrado por obras/reforma/vacaciones closed for alterations/renovation/holidays

cerradura f [sairradoora] lock

cerramos los ... we close on ...

cerrar [sairrar] to close

cerrar con llave [yabeh] to lock

cerrojo m [sairroHo] bolt

certificado m [sairteefeekado] certificate; registered letter

cervecería f [sairbesairee-a] bar specializing in beer

césped m [sesped] lawn

cesta f [sesta] basket

cesto de la compra m [sesto deh] shopping basket

chabacano m apricot

chaleco m [chaleko] waistcoat, (US) vest

chaleco salvavidas [salbabeedas] life-jacket

chalet m [chaleh] villa

chalupa f dugout

chamarra f woollen jacket; waistcoat, (US) vest

champú m shampoo

changarro m small store

chapapote m [chapapoteh] tar; pitch

chaparro very small

chaparrón m shower; downpour

chaqueta f [chaketa] cardigan; jacket

charcutería f [charkootairee-a] delicatessen

charlar to chat

charreada f [charreh-ada] horse-riding display, rodeo

charro m horseman

chato snub-nosed

chava f [chaba] girl

chavo m boy

checar to check

cheque de viajero m [chekeh deh b-yaHairo] traveller's cheque

chequera f [chekaira] cheque book

chiapaneco [ch-yapaneko] from/of Chiapas

chica f girl

chicle m [cheekleh] chewing gum

chico m boy

chiflar to whistle

chilango from/of Mexico City

chileno (m) Chilean

chillar [chee-yar] to shout, to scream

chinampa f man-made island

chinche m drawing pin; bug

chingadera: ¡qué chingadera! [keh cheengadaira] what a fuck-up!

chingar to fuck

¡chinga tu madre! [madreh] fuck off!

chingo: un chingo de [deh] loads of

chino (m) Chinese

chiste m [cheesteh] joke

chocar con to run into

chocolate con leche m [chokolateh kon lecheh] milk chocolate

chofer m [chofair] driver

choque m [chokeh] crash; clash

chorros: a chorros loads

chubasco m sudden short shower

chubasquero m [choobaskairo] cagoule

churrasco m roast meat
Cía. company
cicatriz f [seekatrees] scar
ciclismo m [seekleesmo] cycling
ciclista m/f [seekleesta] cyclist
ciego [s-yego] blind
cielo m [s-yelo] sky
cien [s-yen] hundred
ciencia f [s-yens-ya] science
ciento ... [s-yento] a hundred and ...
cierre m [s-yairreh] zip, zipper
cierren las puertas close the doors
cierro [s-yairro] I close
cigarro m [seegarro] cigarette
cinco [seenko] five
cincuenta [seen-kwenta] fifty
cine m [seeneh] cinema, movie theater
cinta f [seenta] tape; ribbon
cintura f [seentoora] waist; waist measurement
cinturón m [seentooron] belt
cinturón de seguridad [deh segooreeda] seat belt
circo m [seerko] circus
circulación f [seerkoolas-yon] traffic; circulation
circule despacio drive slowly
circule por la derecha keep to your right
círculo m [seerkoolo] circle
circunvalación f [seerkoonbalas-yon] ring road
cita f [seeta] appointment
ciudad f [s-yooda] town, city
claro clear; light

¡claro! of course!
clase f [klaseh] class
clausurar [klowsoorar] to close down
clavado de acantilado m [klabado] cliff-diving
clavo m [klabo] nail; clove
claxon m [klakson] horn
clima m climate
climatizado [kleemateesado] air-conditioned
clínica f hospital; clinic
cobija f [kobeeHa] rug, blanket
cobrar to charge; to earn
cobre m [kobreh] copper
cocer [kosair] to boil
coche-cama m sleeper, sleeping car
cochecito m [kocheseeto] pram
coche-comedor m [kocheh komedor] dining car
cocina f [koseena] kitchen
cocinar [koseenar] to cook
cocinera f [koseenaira], cocinero m cook
código de la circulación m highway code
código postal m [pos-tal] postcode, zip code
codo m elbow
coger [koHair] to fuck
cojo m [koHo] person with a limp
cola f tail; queue
hacer cola to queue
colcha f bedspread
colchón m mattress
colchoneta inflable f [eenflableh] air mattress

colección f [koleks-yon]
collection

colectivo m [kolekteebo]
collective taxi

colegio m [koleн-yo] school

collar m [ko-yar] necklace

colocar to place, to put

colonia f [kolon-ya] urban
district

color m colour

columna vertebral f spine

comadre f [komadreh]
godmother

combi m collective taxi,
minibus

combustible m [komboosteebleh]
fuel

comedor m dining room

comenzar [komensar] to begin

comer [komair] to eat

comerciante m [komairs-yanteh]
shopkeeper; dealer

comicios mpl [komees-yos]
elections

comida f lunch; food; meal

comidas para llevar [yevar]
take-away meals, meals to go

comienzo (m) [kom-yenso] I
begin; beginning

comisaría f police station

como as; like

¿cómo está? how are you?

¿cómo le va? [leh ba] how are
things?

como quieras [k-yairas] it's up
to you

compact m compact disc

compadre m [kompadreh]
godfather

compañera f [kompan-yaira]
girlfriend

compañero m mate; boyfriend

compañía f [kompan-yee-a]
company

compañía aérea [a-aireh-a]
airline

comparar to compare

compartir to share

completamente [–menteh]
completely

completo full; no vacancies

complicado complicated

compra: hacer la compra
[asair] to do the shopping

compramos a ... buying
rate ...

comprar to buy

compras: ir de compras [eer
deh] to go shopping

compresa m sanitary towel,
sanitary napkin

comprimido efervescente m
soluble tablet

comprimidos mpl tablets

computadora f computer

comunicando engaged, busy,
occupied

con with

concha f shell

concierto m [kons-yairto]
concert

condenar to sentence

condición: a condición de que
[kondees-yon deh keh] on
condition that

condón m condom

confección f [konfeks-yon]
clothing industry

confecciones fpl [konfeks-yon-es] ready-to-wear clothes

conferencia internacional f [konfairens-ya eentairnas-yonal] international call

conferencia interurbana long-distance call

confesar to admit; to confess

confirmar to confirm

confitería f [konfeetairee-a] sweetshop, candy store

conforme [konformeh] as
estar conforme to agree

congelado [konHelado] frozen

congelador m [konHelador] freezer

congelados mpl [konHelados] frozen foods

conjunto m [konHoonto] group; band

conmigo with me

conmoción cerebral f [konmos-yon sairebral] concussion

conmover [konmobair] to move

conmutadora f switchboard

conocer [konosair] to know

conozco [konosko] I know

conque [konkeh] so, so then

consentido spoiled

consérvese en lugar fresco store in a cool place

consigna f [konseegna] left luggage, baggage check

consigna automática [owtomateeka] left luggage lockers, baggage lockers

consigo with himself; with herself; with yourself; with themselves; with yourselves

constar: me consta I can confirm

consulado m consulate

consulta médica surgery, doctor's office

consúmase antes de ... best before ...

contacto: ponerse en contacto con to contact

contado: pagar al contado to pay cash

contador m, contadora f accountant

contagioso [kontaH-yoso] contagious

contaminado polluted

contar to count; to tell

contener [kontenair] to contain

contenido m contents

contento happy

contestar to reply, to answer

contigo with you

continuación: a continuación [konteenwas-yon] then, next; below

continuar [konteenwar] to continue

contra against

contradecir [kontradeseer] to contradict

contraindicaciones fpl contraindications

contraventanas fpl [kontrabentanas] shutters

control de pasaportes m passport control

convalecencia f [konbalesens-ya] convalescence

convencer [konbensair] to

persuade

copa f wine glass

coquetear [koketeh-**ar**] to flirt

corazón m [koras**on**] heart

corbata f tie, necktie

cordillera f [kordee-y**air**a] mountain range

cordones mpl [kord**on**-es] shoelaces

correa del ventilador f [korr**eh**-a del benteelad**or**] fan belt

correo m [korr**eh**-o] post, mail; post office

correo aéreo [a-**air**eh-o] airmail

correo central [sen-tral] main post office

correo terrestre [tairr**e**streh] surface mail

correo urgente [oorH**en**teh] express (mail)

correr [korr**air**] to run

correspondencia f [–**dens**-ya] transfer, change

  hacer correspondencia en ... to change (trains/buses) at ...

corrida de toros f [deh] bullfight

corriente peligrosa dangerous current

corrimiento de tierras danger: landslides

cortadura f cut

cortar to cut

cortarse [kort**ar**seh] to cut oneself

cortauñas m [korta-**oon**-yas] nail clippers

corte de pelo m [k**or**teh deh] haircut

corte y confección [ee konfeks-y**on**] dressmaking

cortina f curtain

corto short; short of money

cosa f thing

coser [kos**air**] to sew

costa f coast

costar to cost

costilla f [kostee-ya] rib

costumbre f [kost**oo**mbreh] custom

costurera f [kostoor**air**a] seamstress

cráneo m [kr**an**eh-o] skull

crédito m credit; unit(s)

creer [kreh-**air**] to believe

crema f cream

crema base [b**as**eh] foundation cream

crema de belleza [deh beh-y**es**a] cold cream

crema hidratante [eedrat**an**teh] moisturizer

crema limpiadora [leemp-yad**or**a] cleansing cream

creyó [kreh-y**o**] he/she believed

criticar to criticize

cruce m [kr**oo**seh] crossroads; junction, intersection; crossing

cruce de ciclistas danger: cyclists crossing

cruce de ganado danger: cattle crossing

crucero m [kroos**air**o] cruise

cruda f hangover

cruzar [kroos**ar**] to cross

Cruz Roja f [kroos r**o**Ha] Red

Cross
cuaderno m [kwadairno] notebook
cuadra f [kwadra] block
está a dos cuadros it's two blocks away
cuadrado [kwadrado] square
cuadro m [kwadro] painting
de cuadros [deh] checked
cual [kwal] which; who;
¿cuál? which?
¿cuándo? [kwando] when?
¿cuánto? [kwanto] how much?
en cuanto ... as soon as ...
¡cuánto lo lamento! I'm so sorry!
¿cuántos? how many?
cuarenta [kwarenta] forty
cuartel m [kwartel] barracks
cuartilla f [kwartee-ya] writing paper
cuarto (m) [kwarto] quarter; fourth; room
cuarto con dos camas twin room
cuarto de baño [ban-yo] bathroom
cuarto de estar sitting room
cuarto de hora [deh ora] quarter of an hour
cuarto doble [dobleh] double room
cuarto individual [eendeebeedwal] single room
cuarto piso fourth floor, (US) fifth floor
cuate m [kwateh] friend, pal; twin
cuatro [kwatro] four

cuatrocientos [kwatros-yentos] four hundred
cubierta f [koob-yairta] deck
cubierto (m) covered; overcast; menu
cubiertos mpl cutlery
cubo m [koobo] bucket; cube
cubo de la basura [deh] dustbin, trashcan
cucaracha f cockroach
cuchara f spoon
cucharilla f [koocharee-ya] teaspoon
cuchillería f [koochee-yairee-a] cutlery
cuchillo m [koochee-yo] knife
cuelgue, espere y retire la tarjeta hang up, wait and remove card
cuello m [kweh-yo] neck; collar
cuenta f [kwenta] bill, (US) check; account
cuenta corriente [korr-yenteh] current account
cuentas fpl beads
cuento m [kwento] tale
cuerda f [kwairda] rope; string
cuero m [kwairo] leather
cuerpo m [kwairpo] body
cuesta (f) [kwesta] it costs; slope
cuesta abajo/arriba [abaHo] downhill/uphill
cueva f [kweba] cave
cuidado (m) [kweedado] take care; look out; care
cuidado con ... caution ...
cuidado con el escalón mind the step

cuidado con el perro beware of the dog

cuidar [kweedar] to look after; to nurse

culebra f snake

culpa f fault, blame; guilt
es culpa mía it's my fault

culturismo m body building

cumplas: ¡que cumplas muchos más! many happy returns!

cumpleaños m [koompleh-an-yos] birthday

cuna f cot, (US) crib

cuneta f gutter

cuñada f [koon-yada] sister-in-law

cuñado m [koon-yado] brother-in-law

cuota m [kwota] contribution; membership fee; motorway toll

cura m priest

curado cured; drunk; smoked

curar to cure; to heal

curarse [koorarseh] to heal up

curva f [koorba] bend; curve

curva peligrosa dangerous bend

cuyo [koo-yo] whose; of which

D

D. (Don) Mr.

damas fpl draughts, (US) checkers; ladies' toilet, ladies' room

danés [dan-es] Danish

danza f [dansa] dancing; dance

danzón m [danson] popular Mexican dance

dañar [dan-yar] to damage

dañarse la espalda [dan-yarseh] to hurt one's back

daños mpl [dan-yos] damage(s)

dar to give

dar el visto bueno a [bweno] to approve

dcha. (derecha) right

de [deh] of; from
de dos metros de alto two metres high

debajo de [debaHo deh] under

deber (m) [debair] to have to; to owe; duty

deberes mpl [debair-es] homework

débil weak

decepción f [deseps-yon] disappointment

decepcionado [deseps-yonado] disappointed

decidir [deseedeer] to decide

décimo [deseemo] tenth

decir [deseer] to say; to tell

declaración f [deklaras-yon] declaration; statement

declarar to declare, to state

dedo m finger

dedo del pie [p-yeh] toe

defectuoso [defektwoso] faulty

dejar [deh-Har] to leave; to let
dejar de beber [deh bebair] to stop drinking

delante de [delanteh] in front of

delantera f [delantaira] front (part)

delantero front; foward

la parte delantera [parteh] the front (part)

Delegación de Servicios Migratorios f Immigration Department

demás: los demás the others, the rest

demasiado [demas-yado] too much

demasiados too many

democracia f [demokras-ya] democracy

demora f delay

demorar: ¿cuánto demora? [kwanto] how long does it take?

dentadura postiza f [posteesa] dentures

dentista m/f dentist

dentro (de) [deh] inside

dentro de dos semanas in two weeks' time

dentro de poco soon

departamento m apartment

departamento amueblado [amweblado] furnished apartment

departamento sin amueblar [amweblar] unfurnished apartment

depende [dependeh] it depends

dependienta f [–yenta], dependiente m [–yenteh] shop assistant

deporte m [deporteh] sport

deportista m/f sportsman/sportswoman

deportivo [deporteebo] sports

deportivos mpl trainers

depósito m tank; deposit

deprimido depressed

derecha f right

a la derecha (de) on the right (of)

derecho: todo derecho straight ahead

derribar to pull down, to demolish

derrota f defeat

desacuerdo m [desakwairdo] disagreement

desagradable [–dableh] unpleasant

desaparecer [–resair] to disappear

desaparecido m victim of illegal arrest

desarmador m screwdriver

desastre m [desastreh] disaster

desayunar [desī-yoonar] to have breakfast

desayuno m [desī-yoono] breakfast

descansar to rest

descanso m interval

descarado cheeky

descarrilarse to be derailed

descolgar el aparato lift receiver

descomponerse [deskomponairseh] to break down

descompostura breakdown, mechanical problem

descompuesto [deskompwesto] broken; broken down

descubierto [deskoob-yairto] discovered; uncovered

descubrir to discover; to uncover

descuelgue el auricular lift the receiver

descuento [deskwento] discount

descuidado [deskweedado] careless

¡descuide! [deskweedeh] don't worry about it!

desde [desdeh] since

desde luego [lwego] of course

desde que [keh] since

desear [deseh-ar] to want; to wish

¿qué desea? [keh deseh-a] what can I do for you?

desembarcadero m [desembarkadairo] quay

desempleado (m) [desempleh-ado] unemployed person; unemployed

desempleo m [desempleh-o] unemployment

desfile m [desfeeleh] procession

desfile de modas fashion show

desgracia: por desgracia [desgras-ya] unfortunately

desgraciadamente [−damenteh] unfortunately

deshacer las maletas [des-asair] to unpack

desierto m [des-yairto] desert

desinfectante m [−tanteh]

disinfectant

desmadre m [desmadreh] chaos; mess

¡qué desmadre! [keh desmadreh] what a mess!

desmaquillarse [desmakee-yarseh] to remove one's make-up

desmayarse [desmi-yarseh] to faint

desnudo naked

desnutrición f [desnootrees-yon] malnutrition

desobediente [desobed-yenteh] disobedient

desodorante m [−ranteh] deodorant

desordenado untidy

desorientarse [desor-yentarseh] to lose one's way

despachador automático m [owtomateeka] ticket machine

despacho de petróleo m [deh petroleh-o] store selling paraffin and oil for heating

despacio [despas-yo] slowly

despedida f farewell

despedirse [despedeerseh] to say goodbye

despegar to take off

despegue m [despeh-geh] take-off

despejado [despeHado] clear

despertador m [despairtador] alarm clock

despertar to wake

despertarse [−tarseh] to wake up

despierto [desp-yairto] awake

desprendimiento de terreno danger: landslides

despreocupado [despreh-okoo**pa**do] thoughtless

después [desp**we**s] afterwards

después de [deh] after

destinatario m addressee

destino m destination

el avión con destino a ... the plane for ...

destornillador m [destornee-ya**dor**] screwdriver

destruir [destr**weer**] to destroy

desvestirse [desbest**eer**seh] to undress

desviación f [desb-yas-**yon**] diversion

desvío m [desb**ee**-o] detour, diversion

desvío provisional temporary diversion

detener [deten**air**] to arrest; to stop

detergente en polvo m [detairн**en**teh] washing powder

detergente lavavajillas [lababa**нee**-yas] washing-up liquid

detrás (de) [deh] behind

devolver [debolb**air**] to give back; to vomit

D.F. m [deh **e**feh] Mexico City

di I gave; tell me

día m [**dee**-a] day

día de Año Nuevo [deh an-yo n**we**bo] New Year's Day

Día de los Muertos [deh los mw**air**tos] Day of the Dead, All Souls' Day

día feriado [fer-y**a**do] public holiday

diamante m [d-yam**an**teh] diamond

diapositiva f [d-yaposeet**ee**ba] slide

diario (m) [d-y**ar**-yo] diary; daily newspaper; daily

diarrea f [d-yarr**eh**-a] diarrhoea

días feriados public holidays

días laborables [laborab-les] weekdays; working days

dibujar [deeboo**нar**] to draw

dibujos animados mpl [deeboo**нos**] cartoons

diccionario m [deeks-yonar-yo] dictionary

dice [**dee**seh] he/she says; you say

dicho [**dee**cho] said

diciembre m [dees-y**em**breh] December

diecinueve [d-yeseenw**e**beh] nineteen

dieciocho [d-yesee-**o**cho] eighteen

dieciséis [d-yesees**ays**] sixteen

diecisiete [d-yesees-y**e**teh] seventeen

diente m [d-y**en**teh] tooth

dieron [d-y**air**on] they gave; you gave

diesel m [**dee**sel] diesel

dieta f [d-y**e**ta] diet

a dieta on a diet

diez [d-yes] ten

difícil [deef**ee**seel] difficult

dificultad f [deefeek**ool**ta] difficulty

diga tell me

digo I say

dije [dee**H**eh] I said

dijeron [dee**H**airon] they said; you said

dijiste [dee**H**eesteh] you said

dijo [dee**H**o] he/she said; you said

¿qué dijo? what did you say?; what did he/she say?

dilatar to delay; to be late

diminuto tiny

Dinamarca f Denmark

dinero m [dee**n**airo] money

Dios m [d-yos] God

¡Dios mío! [**mee**-o] my God!

dirección f [deereks-**y**on] direction; address; steering; management

director m, directora f manager; director; headteacher

directorio m telephone directory

dirigir [deeree**H**eer] to direct; to lead

disco m record

disconformidad f [deeskonforme**ed**a] disagreement

discoteca f record shop; disco

disculparse [deeskoolp**a**rseh] to apologize

disculpe [deesk**oo**lpeh] excuse me

disculpen las molestias we apologize for any inconvenience

discurso m speech

discusión f [deeskoos-**y**on] discussion; argument

discutir to argue

diseñador de modas m [deesen-**ya**d**or** deh] fashion designer

disimular [deeseemool**a**r] to pretend

disqueta f [deesk**e**ta] diskette

distancia f [deest**a**ns-ya] distance

distinto different

distraído [deestra-**ee**do] absent-minded; distracted

distribuidor m [deestreebwee**d**or] distributor

Distrito Federal m [feda**i**ral] Federal District, Mexico City

distrito postal m postcode, zip code

disuélvase en agua dissolve in water

divertido [deebair**te**edo] entertaining; funny

divertirse [deebair**te**erseh] to have a good time

divisas fpl [deeb**ee**sas] foreign currency

divorciado [deebors-**y**ado] divorced

divorciarse [deebors-**y**arseh] to divorce

divorcio m [deeb**o**rs-yo] divorce

divulgar [deebool**g**ar] to publicize

doble [d**o**bleh] double

doble sentido two-way

doce [d**o**seh] twelve

docena (de) f [dos**e**na] dozen

dólar m dollar

doler [dolair] to hurt

dolor m pain

dolor de garganta [deh] sore throat

dolor de cabeza [kabesa] headache

dolor de muelas [mwelas] toothache

dolor de oídos [o-eedos] earache

doloroso painful

domicilio m [domeeseel-yo] place of residence

domingo m Sunday

domingos y feriados Sundays and public holidays

donativa f donations

donde [dondeh] where

¿dónde? where?

dorado (m) gold, golden; type of fish

dormido asleep

dormir to sleep

dormitorio m [dormeetor-yo] bedroom; dormitory

dos two

doscientos [dos-yentos] two hundred

doy I give

droga f drug

drogadicto m [drogadeekto] drug addict

drogado in debt

drogarse [drogarseh] to take drugs; to get into debt

droguería f [drogairee-a] drugstore

ducha f shower

ducharse [doocharseh] to have a shower

dudar to doubt; to hesitate

duele [dweleh] it hurts

dulce [doolseh] sweet; gentle

dulces mpl [dools-es] sweets, candies

dunas fpl sand dunes

durante [dooranteh] during

Durex® m Sellotape®, Scotch tape®

duro hard

E

E parking

e [eh] and

echar to throw; to throw away

echar a faltar to miss

echo de menos a mi ... [deh] I miss my ...

echar al buzón [booson] to post, to mail

echar al correo [korreh-o] to post, to mail

echar el cerrojo [sairroHo] to bolt

echar sangre [sangreh] to bleed

echarse la siesta [echarseh] to have a nap

ecológico [ekoloHeeko] ecological

ecologista m/f environmentalist, Green

economía f economy

económico cheap,

inexpensive; economic; economical

ecuatoriano (m) [ekwator-yano] Ecuadorean

edad f [eda] age
  ¿qué edad tienes? [keh – t-yen-es] how old are you?

edificio m [edeefees-yo] building

edredón m quilt, eiderdown; duvet

educado polite

EE.UU. (Estados Unidos) USA

efectivo: en efectivo [efekteebo] in cash

eje m [eHeh] axle

eje del cigüeñal [seegwen-yal] crankshaft

ejemplo m [eHemplo] example
  por ejemplo for example

ejidatario m [eHeedatar-yo] member of an agricultural community

ejido m [eHeedo] communal land

el the

él he; him

elástico elastic

elecciones fpl [eleks-yon-es] elections

electricidad f [elektreeseeda] electricity

electricista m [elektreeseesta] electrician

eléctrico electric

electrodomésticos mpl electrical appliances

elegir [eleh-Heer] to choose

ella [eh-ya] she; her

ellas [eh-yas] they; them

ellos [eh-yos] they; them

embajada f [embaHada] embassy

embalse m [embalseh] reservoir

embarazada [embarasada] pregnant

embotellamiento m [emboteh-yam-yento] traffic jam

embrague m [embrageh] clutch

emergencia f [emairHens-ya] emergency

emisión f [emees-yon] programme; emission; distribution date; issue

emocionante [emos-yonanteh] exciting

empacar to pack

empalme m [empalmeh] junction

empaquetado m [empaketado] packing

empaste m [empasteh] filling

empeorar [empeh-orar] to get worse

empezar [empesar] to begin
  empieza a las ocho [emp-yesa] it starts at eight

empinado steep

empleada f [empleh-ada], **empleado** m white collar worker, employee

empresa f firm, enterprise

empresario m businessman

empujar [empooHar] to push

en in; at; on; by

enamorados: día de los enamorados m [dee-a deh] St

Valentine's Day

encantado delighted

¡encantado! pleased to meet you!

encantador lovely

encantar to please

encendedor m [ensendedor] lighter

encerrar [ensairrar] to lock in; to lock up

enchufe m [enchoofeh] plug; socket

encima [enseema] above

encima de [deh] on top of

encontrar to find

encontrarse (con/a) [–trarseh] to meet

encuentra: se encuentra [seh enkwentra] is located

encuentro (m) [enkwentro] meeting, encounter; I find

endrogarse [–garseh] to get into debt

enemigo m enemy

enero m [enairo] January

enfermarse [–marseh] to become ill, to get sick

enfermedad f [enfairmeda] disease

enfermedad venérea [benaireh-a] VD

enfermera f [enfairmaira], **enfermero m** nurse

enfermo [enfairmo] ill, sick

enfrente de [enfrenteh deh] opposite

enganche [engancheh] deposit

engañar [engan-yar] to cheat; to trick

enmicado m [enmeekado] plastic covering (for documents)

enojado [enoHado] angry

enojarse [–Harseh] to get angry

enorme [enormeh] enormous

enseñar [ensen-yar] to teach

entender [entendair] to understand

no entiendo I don't understand

entero [entairo] whole; in one piece

entiendo [ent-yendo] I understand

entierro m [ent-yairro] funeral

entonces [entons-es] then; therefore

entrada f entrance, way in; ticket

entrada gratis admission free

entrada libre [leebreh] admission free

entrar to go in, to enter

entre [entreh] among; between

entretanto meanwhile

entrevista f [entrebeesta] interview

enviar [emb-yar] to send

envolver [embolbair] to wrap up; to involve

equipaje m [ekeepaHeh] luggage, baggage

equipaje de mano [deh] hand luggage

equipajes mpl [ekeepaH-es] left-luggage office, (US) baggage check equipo m [ekeepo] team; equipment, tools

equivocado [ekeebokado] wrong

equivocarse [ekeebokarseh] to make a mistake

equivocarse de número [deh noomairo] to dial the wrong number

era [aira] I/he/she/it was; you were

éramos [airamos] we were

eran [airan] they were; you were

eras [airas] you were

eres [air-es] you are

erupción f [airoops-yon] rash; eruption

es he is; you are

esa that

ésa that (one)

esas those

ésas those (ones)

escala f intermediate stop; scale; ladder

escalera automática f escalator

escaleras fpl stairs

escarcha f frost

escayola f [eskï-yola] plaster cast

escocés [eskos-es] Scottish

Escocia f [eskos-ya] Scotland

escoger [eskoнair] to choose

esconder [eskondair] to hide

escorpión m [eskorp-yon] scorpion

escribir to write

escrito written

por escrito in writing

escritura f deed; document

escuchar to hear

escuela f [eskwela] school

escuela de párvulos [deh parboolos] kindergarten

escuincle m/f [eskweenkleh] kid, nipper; runt

escurrir a mano to wring by hand

ese [eseh] that

ése that (one)

esencial [esens-yal] essential

esfuerzo m [esfwairso] effort

esmalte de uñas m [esmalteh deh oon-yas] nail polish

esmeralda f emerald

eso that

eso es that's it, that's right

esos those

ésos those (ones)

espalda f back

espantoso dreadful; frightening

España f [espan-ya] Spain

español (m) [espan-yol], española (f) Spanish; Spaniard

especialista m/f [espes-yaleesta] specialist

especialmente [espes-yalmenteh] especially

espectáculo m show, spectacle

espejo m [espeнo] mirror

esperar [espairar] to wait; to hope

espere [espaireh] please wait

¡espéreme! [espairemeh] wait for me!

espero que sí I hope so

espeso thick

esponja f [espon**H**a] sponge

esposa f wife

esposo m husband

espuma de afeitar f [deh afaytar] shaving foam

esquí acuático [eskee akw**a**teeko] waterski; waterskiing

esquina f [eskeena] corner

esta this

ésta this one

estación f [estas-y**o**n] station; season

estacionamiento m [estas-yonam-y**e**nto] car park, parking lot

estacionamiento limitado restricted parking

estacionamiento privado private parking

estacionamiento reservado this parking place reserved

estacionamiento subterráneo underground parking

estacionamiento vigilado supervised parking

estacionarse [estas-yonarseh] to park

estación de autobuses [deh owtob**oo**s-es] bus station

estación de ferrocarril train station

estación de servicio [sairb**ee**s-yo] service station

estadio de fútbol m [estad-yo deh] football stadium

Estados Unidos mpl [oon**ee**dos] United States

estallar [esta-yar] to explode

estampilla f [estampee-ya] stamp

estaño m [estan-yo] tin; pewter

estar to be

estas these

éstas these ones

estatua f [estatwa] statue

este m [esteh] east

este this

éste this (one)

esterilizado [estaireeleesado] sterilized

esto this

estómago m stomach

estornudar to sneeze

estos these

éstos these (ones)

estoy I am

estrecho narrow; tight

estrella f [estr**eh**-ya] star

estrellarse contra [estreh-yarseh] to run into; to crash into

estreno m new film/movie release

estreñido [estren-y**ee**do] constipated

estreñimiento m [estren-yeem-y**e**nto] constipation

estropear [estropeh-ar] to damage

estudiante m/f [estood-yanteh] student

estudiar [estood-yar] to study

estupefaciente m [–fas-y**e**nteh] hallucinogenic drug

estupendo wonderful, great

estúpido stupid

etiqueta f [eteeketa] label

... de etiqueta [deh] formal ...

europeo [eh-ooropeh-o]
European

evidente [ebeedenteh] obvious

exactamente [–menteh] exactly

¡exacto! exactly!

excelente [eselenteh] excellent

excepto [esepto] except

excepto domingos y feriados
except Sundays and holidays

excepto sábados except
Saturdays

exceso de equipaje m [eseso
deh ekeepaHeh] excess baggage

exceso de velocidad
[beloseeda] speeding

excursión f [eskoors-yon] trip

excusados mpl [eskoosados]
toilets, rest rooms

expedir [espedeer] to despatch

expendio m [ekspend-yo] stall;
kiosk; shop, store

explicación f [espleekas-yon]
explanation

explicar to explain

exportación f [esportas-yon]
export

exposición f [esposees-yon]
exhibition

exprés m [espres] fast train;
special delivery

exterior (m) [estair-yor]
exterior, outer; foreign;
overseas

**Secretaría de Asuntos
Exteriores** Ministry of
Foreign Affairs

extintor (de incendios) m [deh
eensend-yos] fire extinguisher

extra four-star petrol, (US)
premium gas

extranjera (f) [estranHaira],
extranjero (m) [estranHairo]
foreign; foreigner

en el extranjero abroad,
overseas

extrañar [estranyar] to miss

extraño [estran-yo] strange

F

fábrica f factory

fabricado por ... made by ...

fácil [faseel] easy

facilidad: con facilidades
payment by instalments

factura f bill, (US) check;
invoice

facturación f [faktooras-yon]
check-in

facturar el equipaje [ekeepaHeh]
to check in luggage/
baggage

falda f skirt; hillside

fallar [fa-yar] to fail; to break
down

falso false

falta f lack; mistake; defect;
fault

no hace falta ... [aseh] it's not
necessary to ...

faltaba más don't mention it

falta de visibilidad poor
visibility

faltar to be missing; to be
absent

faltan tres there are three

missing

faltan seis kilómetros para llegar there are six kilometres to go before we get there

¿cuánto falta (para) ...? how much further is it (to) ...?

echar a faltar to miss

familia f [fam**ee**l-ya] family

famoso famous

farmacia f [farm**as**-ya] chemist's, pharmacy

farmacia de turno [deh t**oor**no] emergency chemist's/ pharmacy, duty chemist

faro m light; headlight; lighthouse

faro antiniebla [anteen-y**e**bla] fog lamp

favor: a favor de [fab**or** deh] in favour of

por favor please

si hace favor [**a**seh] if you don't mind

fayuca f [fi-y**oo**ka] contraband goods

fayuquero m [fi-yook**ai**ro] seller of contraband goods

febrero m [febr**ai**ro] February

fecha f date

fecha de caducación, fecha de caducidad expiry date

fecha de nacimiento [deh naseem-y**e**nto] date of birth

fecha límite de venta sell-by date

¡Felices Pascuas y Próspero Año Nuevo! [fel**ee**s-es p**a**skwas ee pr**o**spairo **a**n-yo nw**e**bo] Merry Christmas and a Happy New Year!

felicidad f [feleese**ed**a] happiness

¡felicidades! [feleeseed**a**d-es] happy birthday!; congratulations!

felicitar [feleese**ta**r] to congratulate

feliz [fel**ee**s] happy

¡feliz cumpleaños! [koomple-**an**-yos] happy birthday!

feo [f**eh**-o] ugly

feria f [f**air**-ya] fair; loose change

feriado: días feriados [fair-y**a**dos] public holidays

ferretería f [fairretair**ee**-a] hardware store

ferrocarril m railway, railroad

festividad f [festeeb**ee**da] celebration

festivos bank holidays, public holidays

fibras naturales natural fibres

fiebre f [f-y**e**breh] fever; high temperature

fiebre del heno [**e**no] hay fever

fierro m [f-y**a**iro] iron

fiesta f public holiday; party

fiesta de ... [deh] feast of ...

fila f row

fila india single file

filmar [feel**ma**r] to film

filtro m filter

filtro solar sunblock

fin m [feen] end; purpose

por fin at last, finally

a fin de que [deh keh] so that

final m [feenal] end

final de autopista end of motorway/highway

fin de semana [deh] weekend

fin de serie discontinued articles

fingir [feenHeer] to pretend

fino fine; delicate

firma f signature; company

firmar to sign

flaco thin, skinny

flequillo m [flekee-yo] fringe

flete m [fleteh] carriage, transport cost

flojera: me da flojera [floHaira] I can't be bothered

flojo [floHo] lazy

flor f flower

florería f [florairee-a] florist

florero m [florairo] vase

flotadores mpl lifebelts

flotar to float

FMT [efemeteh] tourist card

foco m light bulb

folleto m [fo-yeto] pamphlet

Folleto de Migración Turística [deh meegras-yon] tourist card

fonda f simple restaurant; boarding house

fondo m bottom; background
  al fondo (de) at the bottom (of)

fondos mpl funds, money

fontanero m [fontanairo] plumber

footing m jogging

forma f form
  en forma fit

fósforo m match

foto f photograph
  sacar fotos to take photographs

fotografía f photograph; photography

fotografiar [fotograf-yar] to photograph

fotógrafo m photographer

fotómetro m light meter

fraccionamiento m [fraks-yonam-yento] housing estate

francamente [–menteh] frankly

francés [frans-es] French

Francia f [frans-ya] France

franqueado [frankeh-ado] franked

franqueo m [frankeh-o] postage

frazada f [frasada] blanket, rug

frecuencia: con frecuencia [frekwens-ya] often

fregadero m [fregadairo] sink

fregar to keep on at; to annoy
  fregarlo to screw up
  fregar los platos to do the washing up

freír [freh-eer] to fry

frenar to brake

freno m brake

freno de mano [deh] handbrake

frente f [frenteh] forehead
  hacer frente a ... [asair] to face up to ...

fresco fresh

frigorífico m fridge

frío [free-o] cold
  hace frío [aseh] it's cold

frontera f [frontaira] border
  la Frontera the Mexican-US

border

frutería f [frootairee-a] fruit shop; greengrocer's

fue [fweh] he/she/it went; he/she/it was; you went; you were

fuego m [fwego] fire
¿**tiene fuego?** have you got a light?

fuegos artificiales [arteefees-yal-es] fireworks

fuente f [fwenteh] fountain; source; font

fuera [fwaira] outside; he/she/it was; he/she/it went; you were; you went
fuera de [deh] apart from

fuera de horas pico off-peak hours

fuera de servicio [deh sairbees-yo] out of order

fuéramos [fwairamos] we were; we went

fueran [fwairan] they were; they went; you were; you went

fueron [fwairon] they were; they went; you were; you went

fuerte [fwairteh] strong; loud

fuerza f [fwairsa] force; strength

fui [fwee] I was; I went

fuimos [fweemos] we were; we went

fuiste [fweesteh] you were; you went

fumadores [foomador-es] smoking

fumar to smoke

funcionar [foons-yonar] to work

funcionario m [foons-yonar-yo] civil servant

función de noche late showing

función de tarde early showing

funeraria f [foonairar-ya] undertaker's

funicular m [fooneekoolar] cable car

furioso [foor-yoso] furious

furúnculo m abscess; boil

fusible m [fooseebleh] fuse

fútbol m football

futuro (m) [footooro] future

G

gachupín m [gachoopeen] Spaniard

gafas fpl glasses, (US) eyeglasses

gafas de bucear [deh booseh-ar] goggles

gafas de sol sunglasses

galería f [galairee-a] gallery; enclosed balcony

galería de arte [deh arteh] art gallery

Gales m [gal-es] Wales

galés [gal-es] Welsh

gama: toda la gama the whole range

gamuza f [gamoosa] suede

ganadería f [–dairee-a] cattle farming

ganadero m [–dairo] (cattle)

rancher
ganado m cattle
ganar to win; to earn
ganga f bargain
ganso m goose
garaje m [garaHeh] garage
garantía f guarantee
garantizar [–teesar] to guarantee
garganta f throat
gasolina f petrol, (US) gas
gasolina normal two-star petrol, (US) regular (gas)
gasolina super [soopair] four-star petrol, (US) premium (gas)
gasolinera f [gasoleenaira] petrol/gas station, filling station
gastar to spend
gato m cat; jack
gemelos mpl [Hemelos] twins; cufflinks
general: por lo general [Henairal] usually
en general generally, in general
genio m [Hen-yo] genius
gente f [Henteh] people
una gente a person
gerente m/f [Hairenteh] manager; manageress
gestionar [Hest-yonar] to negotiate
gimnasia f [Heemnas-ya] gymnastics
gimnasio m gymnasium
ginecólogo m [Heenekologo] gynaecologist

gira f [Heera] tour
girar [Heerar] to turn
gire a la izquierda [Heereh] turn left
giro [Heero] money order
gis m [Hees] chalk
gitano m [Heetano] gypsy
globo m balloon
glorieta f [glor-yeta] roundabout
gobierno m [gob-yairno] government
gol m goal
Golfo (de México) m Gulf of Mexico
golpe m [golpeh] blow
de golpe all of a sudden
golpear [golpeh-ar] to hit; to beat up
golpiza f [golpeesa] beating
goma f glue
gomita f rubber band
gordo fat
gorra f cap
gorro m bonnet, cap
gorro de baño [deh ban-yo] bathing cap
gorro de ducha shower cap
gota f drop
gotera f [gotaira] leak
gozar [gosar] to enjoy
grabadora f tape recorder
gracias [gras-yas] thank you
gracias a Usted [oosteh] thank you (more emphatic)
gracioso [gras-yoso] funny
grado m degree
grafitos mpl graffiti
gramática f grammar

gramo m gramme

Gran Bretaña f [bretan-ya] Great Britain

grande [grandeh] big, large; old

grandes almacenes mpl [grandes almasen-es] large department store

granizo m [graneeso] hail

granja f [granHa] farm

granjero m [granHairo] farmer

grano m grain; spot

grapa f paper clip

grasa f fat

grasiento [gras-yento] greasy

grasoso greasy

gratis free

grave [grabeh] serious; very ill/sick

gravilla loose chippings

Grecia f [gres-ya] Greece

gremio m trade union

grifo m tap, (US) faucet

gripe f [greepeh] flu

gris grey

gritar to shout

Grito: el Grito the Declaration of Independence by Miguel Hidalgo on 16 Sept 1810, repeated by the President every Independence Day

grosería [grosairee-a] swearword, oath

decir groserías [deseer] to swear

grosero [grosairo] rude

grúa f [groo-a] tow truck, breakdown lorry; crane

grueso [grweso] thick

grupo m group

grupo sanguíneo [sangeeneh-o] blood group

guacamayo m [gwakamī-yo] parrot

guajolote m [gwaHoloteh] turkey

guante m [gwanteh] glove

guapo [gwapo] handsome

guardacostas m/f [gwardakostas] coastguard

guardar [gwardar] to keep; to put away

guardarropa m [gwardarropa] cloakroom, (US) checkroom

guardería (infantil) f [gwardairee-a (infanteel)] crèche; nursery school

guárdese en lugar fresco keep in a cool place

guardia m/f [gward-ya] guard

guarura m/f [gwaroora] thug, hood

guata f [gwata] belly

guatemalteco (m) [gwatemalteko] Guatemalan

guayabera f [gwi-yabaira] embroidered shirt

guero [gwairo] blond, light skinned

guerra f [gairra] war

guerra civil civil war

guía m/f [gee-a] guide

guía telefónica f phone book, telephone directory

guía turístico m tourist guide

guisar [geesar] to cook

guitarra f [geetarra] guitar

gusano m worm

gustar to please

me gusta ... [meh] I like ..

(si) gusta pasar would you like to go in?

me gustaría ... I'd like to ...

gusto: mucho gusto [**moo**cho] pleased to meet you

con mucho gusto certainly, with great pleasure

el gusto es mío how do you do; it is a pleasure

¡qué gusto de verte! [keh – deh ba**ir**teh] it's good to see you!

H

h is not pronounced in Spanish

ha he/she/it has; you have

hábil [a**beel**] skilful

días hábiles working days

habitante m/f [abee**tan**teh] inhabitant

habitar to live

hablador talkative

hablar to speak

hable aquí speak here

habrá there will be; he/she/it will have; you will have

habrán they will have; you will have

habrás you will have

habré [a**breh**] I will have

habremos we will have

habría [a**bree**-a] I would have; he/she/it would have; you would have

habríamos [a**bree**-amos] we would have

habrían [a**bree**-an] they would

have; you would have

habrías [a**bree**-as] you would have

hacer [a**sair**] to make; to do

hace tres días [**a**seh] three days ago

hace calor/sol it is hot/sunny

se me hace que ... [seh meh – keh] I believe that ...

no le hace [leh] don't worry about it

¿cuánto se hace de México a Veracruz? how long does it take from Mexico to Veracruz?

hacerse [a**sair**seh] to become

hacia [**a**s-ya] towards

haga: ¡hágalo ahora! do it now!

hago I do; I make

hallar [a-**yar**] to find

hamaca f [a**ma**ka] hammock

hambre: tengo hambre [**am**breh] I'm hungry

han they have; you have

haré [a**reh**] I will do

harto full, stuffed

estar harto (de) [deh] to be fed up (with)

es harto difícil [dee**fee**seel] it's very difficult

has you have

hasta even; until

hasta que [keh] until

hasta luego [lw**e**go] goodbye, cheerio, see you later

¡hasta mañana! [man-**ya**na] see you tomorrow!

h is not pronounced in Spanish

¡hasta pronto! see you soon!
hay [ī] there is; there are
haz [as] do; make
 ¡hazlo tú! you do it!
he [eh] I have
hecho (m) made; done; fact
hecho a la medida made-to-measure
helada f frost
heladería f [eladairee-a] ice-cream parlour
helado m ice cream
helar to freeze
hembra f female
hemos we have
henequén m [eneken] sisal-type fibre from the henequen plant, used for making rope and fabrics
herida f [aireeda] wound
herido injured
hermana f [airmana] sister
hermano m [airmano] brother
hermoso [airmoso] beautiful
herramientas fpl [airram-yentas] tools
hervir [airbeer] to boil
hice [eeseh] I made; I did
hidratante: crema hidratante f [eedratanteh] moisturizer
hielo m [yelo] ice
hierba f [yairba] grass
hierro m [yairro] iron
hija f [eeHa] daughter
hijo m [eeHo] son
¡hijo de la chingada! son of a bitch!

¡híjole! [eeHoleh] hell!, damn!
hilo m thread
hipermercado [eepairmairkado] hypermarket
hipo m hiccups
hipódromo m horse-racing track
historia f [eestor-ya] history; story
hizo [eeso] he/she made; he/she did; you made; you did
hogar m home; household goods
hoja f [oHa] leaf; sheet of paper
hoja de afeitar [deh afaytar] razor blade
hojalata f [oHalata] aluminium
¡hola! hello!, hi!
hombre m [ombreh] man
hombre de negocios [deh negos-yos] businessman
hombro m shoulder
hondo deep
hondureño (m) [ondooren-yo] Honduran
honrado honest
hora f hour
 ¿qué hora es/qué hora tiene/me da su hora? what time is it?
hora local local time
horario m [orar-yo] timetable, (US) schedule
horario de camiones [deh kam-yon-es] bus timetable/schedule
horario de invierno [eemb-yairno] winter timetable/

schedule

horario de recogidas [reko**нee**das] collection times

horario de trenes [tren-es] train timetable/schedule

horario de verano [bairano] summer timetable/schedule

horas de consulta surgery hours, (US) office hours

horas de oficina [ofeesee**na**] opening hours

horas de visita [beesee**ta**] visiting hours

horas pico rush hour

hormiga f ant

horno m oven

horquilla m [or**kee**-ya] hairslide, hairpin

hospedarse [ospe**dar**seh] to stay

hotel-garaje m [–gara**неh**] hotel where rooms are rented by the hour

hoy [oy] today

hoyo m [o-yo] hole

huaraches mpl [warach-es] leather sandals

hube [**oo**beh] I had

hubieron [oob-**yair**on] they had; you had

hubimos [oobee**mos**] we had

hubiste [oobee**steh**] you had

hubo [**oo**bo] he/she/it had; you had; there was/were

húbole: ¿qué húbole? [keh **oo**boleh] how's it going?

huele: huele a ... [**we**leh] it smells of ...

huelga f [**wel**ga] strike

huella f [**we**ya] print; trace

huellas digitales [dee**нee**tal-es] fingerprints

hueso m [**we**so] bone; stone (of fruit etc)

huésped m/f [**wes**ped] guest

huipil m [**wee**pil] short, embroidered blouse

hule m [**oo**leh] rubber

humedad f [oome**da**] humidity, dampness

húmedo damp

humo m smoke

humor m humour

hundirse [oond**eer**seh] to sink

huracán m hurricane

I
■

idéntico (a/que) [keh] identical (to)

idioma m [eed-**yo**ma] language

idiota m/f [eed-**yo**ta] idiot

iglesia f [eegles-ya] church

ignorar: ignoro si ... I don't know whether ...

igual [eeg**wal**] equal; like
me da igual [meh] it's all the same to me

imbécil (m) [embe**seel**] idiot; stupid

impaciente [eempas-**yen**teh] impatient

impactante [eempakt**an**teh] striking; shocking

impermeable (m) [eempairmeh-**ab**leh] waterproof; raincoat

importación f [eemportas-**yon**]

import; importing
artículos de importación
imported goods
importante [eemportanteh]
important
importar: no importa it doesn't
matter
¿le importa si ...? [leh] do you
mind if ...?
importe m [eemporteh] amount,
sum
importe total total due
imposible [eemposeebleh]
impossible
impreso m [eempreso] form
impuesto m [eempwesto] tax
incendiar [eensend-yar] to set
fire to
incendio m [eensend-yo] fire
(blaze)
incluido [eenkloo-eedo]
included
incluso even
inconsciente [eenkons-yenteh]
unconscious; unaware
increíble [eenkreh-eebleh]
incredible
indemnizar [eendemneesar] to
compensate
independiente [eendepend-
yenteh] independent
indicaciones fpl [eendeekas-yon-
es] instructions
indicador m indicator
indicador de nivel [deh neebel]
gauge
indicar to indicate
indígena (m/f) [eendeeHena]
Indian; native inhabitant

indignado indignant
indispuesto [eendeespwesto]
unwell
industria f industry; factory
infantil children's
infarto m heart attack
infección f [eenfeks-yon]
infection
infectarse [eenfektarseh] to
become infected
inflamado swollen
inflamarse [eenflamarseh] to
swell
influenciar [eenflwens-yar] to
influence
información f [eenformas-yon]
information
información de vuelos flight
information
información turística tourist
information
información y turismo tourist
information office
informar to inform
informarse (de/sobre) [–marseh
(deh/sobreh)] to get
information (on/about)
informe m [informeh] report
infracción f [eenfraks-yon]
offence
ingeniero m [eenHen-yairo]
engineer
Inglaterra f [eenglatairra]
England
inglés (m) [eeng-les] English;
Englishman
inglesa f Englishwoman
ingresar to enter
ingreso m [eengreso] income;

entry

ingresos mpl income; deposits

iniciales fpl [eenees-yal-es] initials

inmediatamente [eenmed-yatamenteh] immediately

inocente [eenosenteh] innocent

inscribirse [–beerseh] to register, to enrol

insistir to insist

insolación f [eensolas-yon] sunstroke

instrucciones fpl [eenstrooks-yon-es] instructions

instrucciones de lavado washing instructions

íntegro [eentegro] complete; intact

inteligente [eenteleeHenteh] intelligent

intentar to try

interés m [eentair-es] interest

interesante [eentairesanteh] interesting

intereses mpl [eentaires-es] interest

interino: en el interino [eentaireeno] meanwhile

interior (m) [eentairee-or] interior, inner; domestic, home

intermedio (m) [eentairmed-yo] intermission, interval; intermediate

intermitente m [eentairmeetenteh] indicator

intérprete m/f [eentairpreteh] interpreter

interruptor m [eentairrooptor]

switch

interurbano long-distance

intoxicación alimenticia f [eentokseekas-yon aleementees-ya] food poisoning

introduzca el dinero exacto insert exact amount

introduzca la tarjeta y marque insert card and dial

introduzca moneda insert coin

inundación f [eenoondas-yon] flood

inundar to flood

inútil useless, pointless

inversión f [eenbairs-yon] investment

invierno m [eemb-yairno] winter

invitada f [eembeetada], **invitado m** guest

invitar [eenbeetar] to invite

inyección f [een-yeks-yon] injection

ir [eer] to go

ir de paseo [deh paseh-o] to go for a walk

Irlanda f [eerlanda] Ireland

Irlanda del Norte [norteh] Northern Ireland

irlandés (m) [eerland-es] Irish; Irishman

irlandesa f Irishwoman

irse [eerseh] to leave, to go away

isla f [eesla] island

itinerario m [eeteenairair-yo] itinerary

IVA (impuesto sobre el valor añadido) [eeba] VAT

izq. (izquierda) left

izquierda f [eesk-ya**i**rda] left
  a la izquierda (de) [deh] on
  the left (of)

J

jabón m [Hab**o**n] soap
jabón de afeitar [deh afaytar]
  shaving soap
jacal m [Hakal] straw hut;
  shack
jaiba f [H**i**ba] crab
jalar [Halar] to pull
jaliscense [Halees**e**nseh]
  from/of Jalisco
jamás [Hamas] ever; never
jardín m [Hard**ee**n] garden
jardín de niños [deh neen-yos]
  kindergarten
jardines públicos mpl [Hard**ee**n-
  es] park, public gardens
jarocho [Har**o**cho] from/of
  Veracruz
jarra f [Harra] jug
jarrón m [Harr**o**n] vase
jefe m [H**e**feh] boss; chief
jefe de tren [deh] guard
jícara f [H**ee**kara] gourd
joder [Hod**ai**r] to irritate, to
  annoy; to mess about; to
  screw up
  ¡lo jodiste! [Hod**ee**steh] you
  screwed up!
jodido [Hod**ee**do] annoying, a
  nuisance; knackered
jornada f [Horn**a**da] working
  day
jorocho [Hor**o**cho] from/of
  Veracruz

jorongo m [Hor**o**ngo] poncho
joropo m [Hor**o**po] dance from
  Veracruz
joven (m/f) [H**o**ben] young;
  young man; young woman
joyas fpl [H**o**yas] jewellery
joyería f [Hoyair**ee**-a] jewellery;
  jeweller's
jubilación f [Hoobeelas-y**o**n]
  pension
jubilada f [Hoobeel**a**da], **jubilado**
  m retired person, pensioner
jubilarse [Hoobeel**a**rseh] to retire
judío [Hood**ee**-o] Jewish
juego (m) [H**we**go] game; I play
  el juego gambling
jueves m [H**we**b-es] Thursday
jugar [Hoo**ga**r] to play
jugos y licuados juices and
  milkshakes
juguete m [H**o**o**ge**teh] toy
juguetería f [Hoogetair**ee**-a]
  toyshop
juicio m [H**wee**s-yo] judgement;
  opinion; trial
  llevar una persona al juicio to
  take someone to court
julio m [H**oo**l-yo] July
junio m [H**oo**n-yo] June
juntar [Hoontar] to collect, to
  gather
junto (a) [H**oo**nto] next (to)
juntos together
justo [H**oo**sto] just; exact,
  precise
juventud f [Hooben**too**] youth;
  the young
juzgar [Hoos**ga**r] to judge

K

kínder m [keendair] kindergarten

klaxon m [klakson] horn

L

la the; her; it

labios mpl [lab-yos] lips

laborables weekdays, working days

laca f hair spray

LADA national telephone system

Ladatel long-distance phone

lado m side
 al lado de [deh] beside, next to

ladrar to bark

ladridos mpl barking

ladrillo m [ladree-yo] tile

ladrón m thief

lagartija f [lagarteeHa] lizard

lagarto m alligator

lago m lake

lágrimas fpl tears

lámpara f lamp

lana f wool; money

lana pura pure wool

lanzar [lansar] to throw

lápiz m [lapees] pencil

lápiz de ojos [deh oHos] eyeliner

lapizlabios m [lapees-lab-yos] lipstick

larga distancia [deestans-ya] long-distance

largo (m) length; long
 a lo largo de [deh] along

¡lárguese! [largeseh] go away!

las the; them; you
 las que ... the ones that ...

lata f tin; can
 dar lata to be a nuisance

latinoamericana (f), latinoamericano (m) Latin American

latón m brass

lavabo m [lababo] washbasin

lavado m [labado] washing

lavado de carros [deh] carwash

lavadora f [labadora] washing machine

lavandería f [labandairee-a] laundry

lavandería automática [owtomateeka] launderette, laundromat

lavar [labar] to wash

lavar a mano wash by hand

lavar en seco dry clean

lavar la ropa to do the washing

lavarse [labarseh] to wash
 lavarse la cara to wash one's face

lavar separado wash separately

lavavajillas m [lababaHee-yas] dishwasher

laxante m [laksanteh] laxative

le [leh] him; her; you

lección f [leks-yon] lesson

leche limpiadora f [leemp-yadora] skin cleanser

lechería f [lechairee-a] dairy; dairy shop

lectura f [lektoora] reading

leer [leh-air] to read

lejano [leh-Hano] distant, faraway

lejía f [leHee-a] bleach

lejos [leHos] far away

lejos de [deh] far from

lengua f [lengwa] tongue; language

lenguaje m [lengwaHeh] language

lentes de contacto fpl [lent-es deh] contact lenses

lentillas fpl [lentee-yas] contact lenses

lentillas blandas soft lenses

lentillas duras hard lenses

lentillas porosas gas permeable lenses

lento slow

les them; you

letra f letter; banker's draft

levantar [lebantar] to raise, to lift

levantarse [lebantarseh] to get up

ley f [lay] law

libra f pound

libre [leebreh] free; vacant

libre de impuestos [deh eempwestos] duty-free

librería f [leebrairee-a] bookshop, bookstore

librero m [leebrairo] bookshelves

libreta de ahorros f [deh a-orros] savings account book

libreta de direcciones [deereks-yon-es] address book

libro m [leebro] book

libro de bolsillo [deh bolsee-yo] paperback

libro de frases [fras-es] phrasebook

licenciado m [leesens-yado] graduate

líder m [leedair] leader

liga f elastic band; suspender

ligero [leeHairo] light

lima de uñas f [deh oon-yas] nailfile

límite f [leemeeteh] limit

límite de altura maximum height

límite de peso weight limit

límite de velocidad [deh beloseedad] speed limit

limpiaparabrisas m [–breesas] windscreen wiper

limpiar [leemp-yar] to clean

limpieza f [leemp-yesa] cleanliness; cleaning

limpieza en seco dry-cleaning

limpio [leemp-yo] clean

lindo [leendo] beautiful, lovely

línea f [leeneh-a] line

linterna f [leentairna] torch

lío m [lee-o] mess

liquidación f [leekeedas-yon] sale; redundancy pay

liquidación total clearance sale

liso flat; plain; straight

lista f list

lista de correos [deh korreh-os] poste restante, (US) general delivery

lista de espera [espaira] standby; waiting list
listo clever; ready
litera f [leetaira] couchette
litro m litre
llamada f [yamada] call
llamada por cobrar reverse charge call
llamar [yamar] to call; to name
llamar por teléfono to call, to phone
llamarse [yamarseh] to be called
¿cómo te llamas? [teh yamas] what's your name?
llame a la puerta please knock
llame al timbre please ring
llame antes de entrar knock before entering
llamo: me llamo ... [meh yamo] my name is ...
llanos mpl [yanos] plains
llanta f [yanta] tyre, (US) tire
llantero m [yantairo] tyre repairs
llave f [yabeh] key; spanner, (US) wrench; tap, (US) faucet
llave inglesa [eenglesa] spanner, (US) wrench
llegada f [yegada] arrival
llegadas internacionales [eentairnas-yonal-es] international arrivals
llegadas nacionales [nas-yonal-es] domestic arrivals
llegar [yegar] to arrive; to get to
llegué [yegeh] I arrived
llenar [yenar] to fill

llenar el depósito to fill up
lleno [yeno] full
llevar [yebar] to carry; to take; to bring
llevo dos años trabajando aquí I've been working here for two years
llevar a juicio [Hwees-yo] to take to court
llevarse [yebarseh] to take away; to remove
llorar [yorar] to cry
llover [yobair] to rain
lloviendo: está lloviendo [yob-yendo] it's raining
llovizna f [yobeesna] drizzle
llueve [yweh-beh] it is raining
lluvia f [yoob-ya] rain
lo it; the
localidad f [lokaleeda] place; seat
localidades fpl [lokaleedad-es] ticket office
loción antimosquitos f [los-yon anteemoskeetos] insect repellent
loción bronceadora [bronseh-adora] suntan lotion
loción para después del afeitado [despwes del afaytado] aftershave
loco (m) mad; madman
locomotora f engine
locutor m [lokootor], **locutora** f television presenter
lodo m mud
loma f hill
lonchería f lunch counter
Londres [lond-res] London

longitud f [lonHeet**oo**] length
los the
  los que ... the ones that ...
loza f [l**o**sa] crockery
luces de cruce [l**oo**s-es deh kr**oo**seh] dipped headlights
luces de posición fpl [posees-**yon**] sidelights
luces traseras [tras**ai**ras] rear lights
lucha f [l**oo**cha] fight, struggle
lucha libre [l**ee**breh] all-in wrestling
luchar to fight
luego [l**we**go] then; afterwards; soon
  luego luego right away, immediately
lugar m place
  en lugar de [deh] instead of
lugar de veraneo [bairan**eh**-o] summer resort
lugares de interés [l**oo**gar-es deh eentair-**es**] places of interest
lujo m [l**oo**Ho] luxury
lujoso [looH**o**so] luxurious
luna f moon
lunes m [l**oo**n-es] Monday
luto m mourning
luz f [l**oo**s] light
luz de carretera full beam

M

machista m male chauvinist, sexist
macho m male; large banana
machete m [mach**e**teh] long, broad knife
madera f [mad**ai**ra] wood
madrazo m [madr**a**so] beating
madre f [m**a**dreh] mother
  dar en la madre a uno to give someone a good beating
  ¡me vale madre! [meh b**a**leh] I don't give a shit!
madrina f [madr**ee**na] godmother
madrugada f small hours
  las cuatro de la madrugada four o'clock in the morning
madrugador m someone who stays up very late/gets up very early, early riser
madrugar to stay up very late; to get up very early
madurar to mature, to ripen; to come to term
maduro ripe
maestra f [ma-**e**stra], **maestro** m teacher; primary school teacher
magna sin [seen] unleaded
maguey m [mag**ay**] agave cactus
maíz m [ma**ee**s] maize, (US) corn
mal (m) wrong; evil; bad; badly
maleducado rude
malentendido m misunderstanding
maleta f suitcase
  hacer las maletas to pack
maletero m [malet**ai**ro] boot (of car), (US) trunk
mal genio m [**H**en-yo] bad

LO

temper

mal humor m [oomor] bad mood; bad temper; anger

Malinche f [maleencheh] Cortés' interpreter who later became his lover

malinchismo m betrayal of one's country

malo bad; sick, ill, unwell

mamá f mum

mamón! idiot!

manantial m [manant-yal] spring

mancha f stain

manchar to stain, to dirty

mandar to send; to order

mandatario: el primer mandatario [mandator-yo] leader; President; Prime Minister

mandato m period in government

¿mande? [mandeh] sorry?, pardon (me)?

mandíbula f jaw

manejar [maneHar] to drive

maneje con cuidado drive with care

manejo [maneHo] I drive

manera: de esta manera [deh – manaira] in this way

de manera que so (that)

manga f sleeve

sin manga sleeveless

manglar m mangrove swamp

mango m handle; mango

manifestación f [maneefestas-yon] demonstration; manifestation

mano f hand; pal, mate, buddy

manoplas fpl mittens

manta f blanket, rug

mantel m tablecloth

mantelerías fpl [mantelairee-as] table linen

mantenga limpia la ciudad keep our city tidy

manténgase en lugar fresco store in a cool place

manténgase fuera del alcance de los niños keep out of the reach of children

mantenimiento m [manteneem-yento] maintenance

manzana f [mansana] apple; city block

mañana (f) [man-yana] morning; tomorrow

por la mañana/de mañana in the morning

¡hasta mañana! see you tomorrow!

pasado mañana the day after tomorrow

mañana por la mañana tomorrow morning

mañana por la tarde [tardeh] tomorrow afternoon; tomorrow evening

mañanitas: cantar las mañanitas [man-yaneetas] to serenade someone for their birthday

mapa m map

mapa de carreteras [deh karretairas] road map

mapa de recorrido network map

maquiladora f [makeeladora] foreign-owned assembly plant located in Mexico

maquillaje m [makee-yaнeh] make-up

maquillarse [makee-yarseh] to put one's make-up on

máquina de afeitar eléctrica f [makeena deh afaytar] electric shaver

máquina de escribir typewriter

máquina de fotos camera

maquinaria f [makeenar-ya] machinery

máquina tragaperras slot machine

maquinilla de afeitar f [makeenee-ya deh afaytar] electric shaver

mar m sea

maravilloso [marabee-yoso] marvellous

marcar to dial; to mark

marca registrada f [reнeestrada] registered trade mark

marcar el número dial the number

marcha f [marcha] gear

marcha atrás reverse gear

marcharse [marcharseh] to go away

marea f [mareh-a] tide

mareado [mareh-ado] dizzy; sick; drunk

mareo m [mareh-o] sickness; faintness

marica m, maricón m queer

marido m husband

marina f navy

mariposa f butterfly; fairy, pansy

marisquería f [mareeskairee-a] shellfish restaurant

marque ... dial ...

martes m [mart-es] Tuesday

martes de carnaval [deh karnabal] Shrove Tuesday

martillo m [martee-yo] hammer

marzo m [marso] March

más more

más de/que [deh/keh] more than

más pequeño smaller

el más caro the most expensive

ya no más that's enough

más o menos more or less

matar to kill

matrícula f licence plate; registration; registration fees

máximo personas maximum number of people

maya (m/f) [mī-ya] Maya; Mayan

mayo m [mī-yo] May

mayor [mī-yor] adult; bigger; older; biggest; oldest

la mayor parte (de) [parteh (deh)] most (of)

mayor de edad of age (18), adult

mayoría: la mayoría [mī-yoree-a] most; the majority

me me; myself

me duele aquí [dweleh] I have a pain here

mecánico m mechanic

mecate m [mekateh] string; rope; cord

media docena (de) f [med-ya dosena (deh)] half a dozen

media hora f [ora] half an hour

mediano [med-yano] medium; average

medianoche f [med-yanocheh] midnight

media pensión f [pens-yon] half board

medias fpl [med-yas] stockings; tights, pantyhose

ir/pagar a medias to go Dutch, to share the costs

medicina f [medeeseena] medicine

médico m [medeeko] doctor

médico general [Henairal] GP

medida f size; measure

medida del cuello f [kweh-yo] collar size

medio m [med-yo] middle

por medio de [deh] by (means of)

de tamaño medio [taman-yo] medium-sized

medio boleto m half fare

mediodía m [med-yodee-a] midday

medio litro m half a litre

medir to measure

medusa f jellyfish

mejor [meHor] better; best

mejorar [meHorar] to improve

se está mejorando [seh] he's getting better

mencionar [mens-yonar] to mention

menor smaller; younger; smallest; youngest

menor de edad minor, under-age

menos less; least; fewer; fewest

a menos que [keh] unless

mensual [menswal] monthly

mentar: mentarle la madre a uno [mentarleh la madreh] to insult someone, to swear at someone

menú turístico m set menu

menudo tiny, minute

a menudo often

mercado m [mairkado] market

mercado cubierto [koob-yairto] indoor market

mercado de divisas [deh deebeesas] exchange rates

mercería f [mairsairee-a] haberdashery

merendar to have an afternoon snack

merendero m [mairendairo] open-air café

merienda f [mair-yenda] tea, afternoon snack

mero [mairo] exact; almost, nearly

ya mero any minute now, right away

el mero mero the big cheese

está aquí mero it's just near here

mes m month

mesa f table

mesera f [mesaira] waitress; chambermaid

mesero m waiter

mesón m restaurant specializing in regional dishes

mestizo [mesteeso] mixed race, interracial

meta f goal

metate m [metateh] mortar and pestle

metro m metre; underground, (US) subway

mexicana (f), [meHeekana] mexicano (m) Mexican

México m [meHeeko] Mexico; Mexico City

mezquita f [meskeeta] mosque

mi my

mí me

mía [mee-a] mine

microondas: horno microondas [orno meekro-ondas] microwave oven

miedo m [m-yedo] fear

tengo miedo (de/a) [deh] I'm afraid (of)

miel f [m-yel] honey

mientras [m-yentras] while

mientras que [keh] whereas

mientras tanto meanwhile

miércoles m [m-yairkol-es] Wednesday

miércoles de ceniza [deh seneesa] Ash Wednesday

¡mierda! [m-yairda] shit!

mil [meel] thousand

militar m soldier, serviceman

millón m [mee-yon] million

un millón de ... [deh] a million ...

milpa f maize field

mina f mine

minifalda f mini-skirt

minúsculo tiny

minusválido (m) [meenoosbaleedo] disabled; disabled person

minuto m minute

mío [mee-o] mine

miope [m-yopeh] short-sighted

mirador m scenic view; vantage point

mirar to look (at); to see

mis my

misa f mass

mismo same

mitad f [meeta] half

mitad de precio [deh pres-yo] half price

mixteca (f) [meesteka] from/of the Mixtec region; indigenous language of Southern Mexico

M.N. (moneda nacional) f national currency

mochila f rucksack

moda f fashion

de moda fashionable

moda juvenil [Hoobeneel] young fashions

modas caballeros fpl [kaba-yairos] men's fashions

modas niños/niñas [neen-yos] children's fashions

modas pre-mamá maternity fashions

modas señora [sen-yora] ladies' fashions

modelo m model; design; style

moderno [modairno] modern

modista f dressmaker; fashion designer

modisto m fashion designer

modo: de modo que [deh – keh] so (that)

ni modo that's how it is, what can you do?

modo de empleo instructions for use

mojado [moHado] wet

molcajete m [molkaHeteh] mortar and pestle

moldeado con secador de mano [moldeh-ado – deh] blow-dry

molestar to disturb; to bother

molesto annoying

monasterio m [monastair-yo] monastery

moneda nacional f [nas-yonal] national currency

monedas fpl coins

monedero m [monedairo] purse

montacargas m service lift, service elevator

montaje m [montaHeh] assembly

montaña f [montan-ya] mountain

montaña rusa f big dipper, roller coaster

montañismo m [montan-yeesmo] climbing

montar to get in; to ride; to assemble

montar a caballo [kaba-yo] to go horse-riding

montar en bicicleta [beeseekleta] to cycle

morado purple

morbo m morbid interest

mordedura f bite

morder [mordair] to bite

mordida f bribe

moreno dark-haired; dark-skinned

moretón m bruise

morir to die

mosca f fly

mostrador m counter

mostrar to show

motel-garaje m [garaHeh] hotel where rooms are rented by the hour

moto f motorbike

motora f motorboat

mover [mobair] to move

mucha [moocha] much; a lot; a lot of

muchacha f girl

muchacho m boy

muchas a lot; a lot of; many

muchas gracias [gras-yas] thank you very much

muchísimas gracias thank you very much indeed

muchísimo enormously, a great deal

mucho [moochos] much; a lot; a lot of

mucho más a lot more

mucho menos a lot less

mucho gusto a pleasure to meet you

muchos a lot; a lot of; many

muebles mpl [mwebl-es] furniture

muela f [mwela] tooth

sacarse una muela [sak**ar**seh] to have a tooth taken out

muela del juicio [Hw**ee**s-yo] wisdom tooth

muelle m [mw**eh**-yeh] spring; quay

muerte f [mw**air**teh] death

muerto (m) [mw**air**to] dead; dead person

mugriento [moogr-y**en**to] filthy

mujer f [mooH**air**] woman; wife

muletas fpl crutches

multa f fine; parking ticket

multa por uso indebido penalty for misuse

mundo m world

muñeca f [moon-y**eka**] wrist; doll

muro m wall

músculo m muscle

museo m [moos**eh**-o] museum

museo de arte [deh **arte**h] art gallery

música f music

muslo m thigh

musulmán Muslim

muy [mwee] very

muy bien [b-yen] very well

N

N$ m new peso

nácar m mother-of-pearl

nacer [nas**air**] to be born

nacido [nas**ee**do] born

nacimiento m [naseem-y**en**to] birth; Nativity

nacional [nas-yon**al**] domestic

el turismo nacional Mexican tourism, local tourism

nacionalidad f [nas-yonaleed**a**] nationality

nacionalismo m [nas-yonal**ee**smo] nationalism

nacionalización f [nas-yonaleesas-y**on**] nationalization

nada nothing

de nada [deh] you're welcome, don't mention it

antes que nada [**ant**-es keh] first of all

nada que declarar nothing to declare

nadar to swim

nadie [**nad**-yeh] nobody

náhuatl (m) [**na**watl] Aztec; language of the Aztecs

narcotraficante m/f [–k**ant**eh] drug trafficker

narcotráfico m drug trade, drug traffic

nariz f [nar**ees**] nose

natación f [natas-y**on**] swimming

natural [nat**oor**al] natural

al natural at room temperature

naturaleza f [natooral**esa**] nature

naturalmente [–m**en**teh] naturally; of course

náusea: siento náuseas [s-y**en**to n**ow**seh-as] I feel sick

navaja f [nab**a**Ha] penknife; flick knife

Navidad f [nabeed**a**] Christmas

¡feliz Navidad! [fel**ees**] merry Christmas!

nayarita [nī-yareeta] from/of
 Nayarit
neblina f mist
necesario [nesesar-yo]
 necessary
necesitar [neseseetar] to need
negar to deny
negativa f [negateeba] denial;
 refusal
negativo m negative
negocio m [negos-yo] business
negro (m) black; furious; black
 man
nena f baby girl; little girl
nene m [neneh] baby boy; little
 boy
nervioso [nairb-yoso] nervous
 me pone nervioso [meh poneh]
 it makes me nervous
neurótico [neh-ooroteeko]
 neurotic
nevar [nebar] to snow
nevería f [neberee-a] ice cream
 parlour
ni neither; nor
 ¡ni modo! what can you do!
 ni ... ni ... neither ... nor ...
nica m/f Nigaraguan
nicaraguense (m/f)
 [neekaragwenseh] Nicaraguan
niebla f [n-yebla] fog
nieta f [n-yeta] granddaughter
nieto m [n-yeto] grandson
nieva [n-yeba] it is snowing
nieve f [n-yebeh] snow; ice
 cream; sorbet
ningún none; not one; no ...
 en ningún sitio [seet-yo]
 nowhere

ninguno nobody; none; not
 one
niña f [neen-ya] child
niñera f [neen-yaira] nanny
niño m [neen-yo] child
nivel del aceite m [neebel del
 asayteh] oil level
no no; not
noche f [nocheh] night
 de noche at night
 buenas noches [bwenas noch-
 es] good night
 esta noche tonight
 por la noche at night
 pasar la noche to spend the
 night
Nochebuena f [nocheh-bwena]
 Christmas Eve
Nochevieja f [nocheh-b-yeнa]
 New Year's Eve
no contiene alcohol does not
 contain alcohol
nocturno [noktoorno] night
no estacionarse no parking
no estacionarse, se usa grúa
 illegally parked vehicles will
 be towed away
no exceda la dosis indicada do
 not exceed the stated dose
no fumadores [foomador-es] no
 smoking
no fumar no smoking
no funciona [foons-yona] out of
 order
no hay de qué [ī deh keh] you
 are welcome
no hay localidades sold out
no le hace [leh aseh] don't
 worry about it

nomás just, only
  díselo nomás [deeselo] just
  tell him/her
nombre m [nombreh] name
nombre de pila [deh] first
  name
nombre de soltera [soltaira]
  maiden name
no molestar do not disturb
nopal m cactus leaf
no para en ... does not stop
  in ...
no pisar el pasto keep off the
  grass
nordeste m [nordesteh] northeast
no rebasar no overtaking, no
  passing
no recomendada para menores
  de 18 años not
  recommended for those
  under (18 years of age
normal (m) [nor-mal] normal;
  lower grade petrol, (US)
  regular (gas)
normalmente [–menteh] usually
noroeste m [noro-esteh] northwest
norte m [norteh] north
  al norte de la ciudad [deh la
  s-yooda] north of the city
norteamericana (f) [norteh-
  amaireekana], norteamericano
  (m) North American
norteño [norten-yo] from the
  north of Mexico
Noruega f [norwega] Norway
nos us; ourselves
no se admiten devoluciones

no refunds given
no se admiten perros no dogs
  allowed
no ... sino ... not ... but ...
nosotras, nosotros we; us
nota f note
nota de consumo [deh] receipt
noticias fpl [notees-yas] news
noticiero m [notees-yairo] news
  bulletin
no tocar please do not touch
no utilizar lejía do not bleach
nova f [noba] two-star petrol,
  (US) regular gas
nova plus four-star petrol, (US)
  premium gas
novecientos [nobes-yentos] nine
  hundred
novecito [nobeseeto] very new
novela f [nobela] novel
noveno [nobeno] ninth
noventa [nobenta] ninety
novia f [nob-ya] girlfriend;
  fiancée; bride
noviembre m [nob-yembreh]
  November
novillada f [nobee-yada]
  bullfight featuring young
  bulls
novio m [nob-yo] boyfriend;
  fiancé; groom
Nte. north
nube f [noobeh] cloud
nublado cloudy
nuboso cloudy
nuera f [nwaira] daughter-in-
  law
nuestra [nwestra], nuestras,
  nuestro, nuestros our

Nueva York [nweba] New York

nueve [nwebeh] nine

nuevo [nwebo] new

nuevoleonés [nweboleh-on-es] from/of Nuevo Leon

nuevo peso m new peso

número m [noomairo] number; size

número de calzado [deh kalsado] shoe size

número de teléfono phone number

nunca never

nutritivo [nootreeteebo] nutritious

O

o or

o ... o ... either ... or ...

oaxaqueño [waHaken-yo] from/of Oaxaca

obispo m [obeespo] bishop

objeción f [obHes-yon] objection

objetar [obHetar] to object

objetivo m [obHeteebo] lens; objective

objetos de escritorio [obHetos deh eskreetor-yo] office supplies

objetos perdidos lost property, lost and found

obra f work; play

obras fpl roadworks

obrero m [obrairo] worker

obsequio m [obsek-yo] gift

obstruido [obstroo-eedo] blocked

obturador m shutter

ocasión f [okas-yon] occasion; opportunity; bargain

de ocasión [deh] second hand

occidental [okseedental] Western

occidente m [okseedenteh] West

Océano Pacífico m [oseh-ano] Pacific Ocean

ochenta eighty

ocho eight

ochocientos [ochos-yentos] eight hundred

ocho días mpl [dee-as] week

ocote m [okoteh] resinous pine used for burning

octavo [oktabo] eighth

octubre m [oktoobreh] October

oculista m/f optician

ocultar to hide

oculto hidden

ocupado engaged; occupied; busy

ocupar to occupy

ocurrir [okooreer] to occur, happen

ocurre que [okoorreh keh] it so happens that

odiar [od-yar] to hate

odio (m) [od-yo] hate, hatred; I hate

odioso odious, revolting; horrible

oeste m [o-esteh] west

al oeste de la ciudad [deh la s-yooda] west of the city

ofender [ofendair] to offend

oferta f [ofairta] special offer

oficial (m/f) [ofees-yal] officer; official

oficina f [ofeeseena] office

oficina de correos [deh korrehos] post office

oficina de correos y telégrafos post office and telegrams

oficina de información y turismo [eenformas-yon] tourist information office

oficina de objetos perdidos [obHetos] lost property office, lost and found

oficina de reclamaciones [reklamas-yon-es] complaints department

oficina de registros [reHeestros] registrar's office

oficina de turismo tourist information office

oficinista m/f [ofeeseeneeesta] office worker

oficio m [ofees-yo] job; trade

ofrecer [ofresair] to offer

oído (m) [o-eedo] ear; hearing; heard

¡oiga! [oyga] listen here!; excuse me!

oigo I am listening

oír [o-eer] to listen

ojo m [oHo] eye

¡ojo! watch out!

ola f wave

ola de calor [deh] heatwave

oler [olair] to smell

olfato m sense of smell

olmeca from/of ancient Olmec culture

olor m smell

olvidar [olbeedar] to forget

once [onseh] eleven

ONU f [o eneh oo] UN

operación f [opairas-yon] operation

operadora f operator

operarse [opairarseh] to have an operation

oportunidad f [oportoonida] chance, opportunity

oposición f [oposees-yon] opposition

óptica f optician's

óptico m optician

optimista optimistic

¡órale! [oraleh] go on then!, get on with it!

orden f order, instruction

a sus órdenes at your service

orden m order

en orden in order

organización f [organeesas-yon] organization

organizar [organeesar] to organize

orgulloso [orgoo-yoso] proud

oriental east, eastern

orientar to direct, to guide

oriente m [or-yenteh] east

orilla f [oree-ya] shore; side

oro m gold

orquesta f [orkesta] orchestra

oscuro dark

Ote. east

otoño m [oton-yo] autumn, (US) fall

otorrinolaringólogo m ear, nose and throat specialist

otra vez [bes] again

otro another (one); other
oveja f [obeHa] sheep
overol m [obairol] overall
oye [o-yeh] he/she listens; you
 listen; he/she hears; you hear

P

pabellón m [pabeh-yon]
 (hospital) ward
pachanga f party; partying
paciente m/f [pas-yenteh]
 patient
padecer [padesair] to suffer
 padecer del corazón [korason]
 to have a heart condition
padre m [padreh] father
 ¡está padre! it's great!
padres mpl [pad-res] parents
padrino m [padreeno] godfather
pagadero [pagadairo] payable
pagar to pay
página f [paHeena] page
páginas amarillas [amaree-yas]
 yellow pages
pago m payment
país m [pa-ees] country
paisaje m [pīsaHeh] landscape;
 scenery
pájaro m [paHaro] bird
pala f spade
palabra f word
palacio m [palas-yo] palace
Palacio de Justicia [deh
 HoostEEs-ya] Law Courts
palanca de velocidades f
 [beloseedad-es] gear lever
palco m box (at theatre)

paleta f ice lolly
paliacate m [pal-yakateh]
 headscarf
palmera f [palmaira] palm tree
palo m stick; tree
palomitas fpl popcorn
palos de golf mpl [deh] golf
 clubs
paludismo m [paloodeesmo]
 malaria
PAN (Partido de Acción
 Nacional) m National Action
 Party (centre-right party)
panadería f [panadairee-a]
 baker's
panal m honeycomb
panameño (m) [panamen-yo]
 Panamanian
pantalla f [panta-ya] screen
pantalón corto m shorts
pantalones mpl [pantalon-es]
 trousers, (US) pants
panteón m [panteh-on]
 cemetery
pantimedias fpl tights,
 pantyhose
panza f [pansa] belly
pañal m [pan-yal] nappy, diaper
pañuelo m [panwelo]
 handkerchief; scarf
papa f [papa] potato
papá m dad
papalote m [–loteh] kite
papel m [papel] paper; rôle
papel de envolver [deh
 embolbair] wrapping paper
papel de escribir writing
 paper
papel de plata silver foil

papelera f [papelaira] litter; litter bin

papelería f [papelairee-a] stationery, stationer's

papel sanitario [saneetar-yo] toilet paper

papel tapiz [tapees] wallpaper

paquete m [paketeh] packet; package holiday

paquetería f [paketairee-a] left luggage office, baggage check

par m pair

para for; in order to

cuarto para las tres quarter to three

parabrisas m windscreen

paracaidismo m [parakīdeesmo] parachuting; squatting

paracaidista m/f parachutist; squatter

parachoques m [parachok-es] bumper, (US) fender

parada f stop

parada de camión [deh] bus stop

paradero f [paradairo] stop

paraguas m [paragwas] umbrella

para que [keh] in order that

parar to stop

pararse to stand (up)

para uso del personal staff only

para uso externo not to be taken internally

parcela f [parsela] plot (of land)

parecer [paresair] to seem; to resemble

parece que sí/no it seems so/not

me parece (que) ... I think (that) ...

parecido [pareseedo] similar

pared f [pareh] wall

pareja f [pareHa] pair; couple; partner

parezco [paresko] I am like

pariente m/f [par-yenteh] relative

parir to give birth

parque m [parkeh] park

parque de atracciones [deh atraks-yon-es] amusement park

parque de bomberos [bombairos] fire station

parque de recreo [rekreh-o] amusement park

parque infantil [eenfanteel] children's park

parrilla f [parree-ya] grill

párroco m parish priest

parte m [parteh] report

parte f [parteh] part

en todas partes [part-es] everywhere

en otra parte elsewhere

en alguna parte somewhere

¿de parte de quién? [deh – k-yen] who's calling?

participar [parteeseepar] to take part; to inform

particular [parteekoolar] private

un particular a private individual

partida f game

partido m match, game, bout; (political) party
partir to cut (into pieces); to leave, to go
 a partir de mañana from tomorrow onwards
parto m birth
parvulario m [parboolaree-o] nursery school
pasado last
 la semana pasada last week
 pasado mañana [man-yana] the day after tomorrow
 pasado de moda [deh] out of fashion
pasaje m [pasaнeh] ticket; fare
pasajero m [pasaнairo] passenger
 pasajeros de tránsito transit passengers
pasaporte m [pasaporteh] passport
 pasaportes passport control
pasar to pass; to overtake; to happen
 pasar la aduana [adwana] to go through Customs
 pasarlo bien [b-yen] to enjoy oneself
pasatiempo m [pasat-yempo] hobby
Pascua [paskwa] Easter
pase [paseh] come in
pasear [paseh-ar] to go for a walk; to take for a walk
paseo m [paseh-o] walk; drive; ride
 paseo de ... ... avenue
pasillo m [pasee-yo] corridor

paso m passage; pass; step
 estar de paso [deh] to be passing through
pasó: ¿qué pasó? how's it going?, what's happening?
paso a desnivel underpass
paso a nivel level crossing, (US) grade crossing
paso de contador [deh] (metered) unit
paso de peatones [peh-aton-es] pedestrian crossing
paso prohibido no admittance, no entry
paso subterráneo pedestrian underpass
pasta de dientes f [deh d-yent-es] toothpaste
pastelería f [pastelairee-a] cake shop
pastilla f [pastee-ya] pill, tablet
 pastillas para la garganta throat pastilles
patatas fritas crisps, (US) potato chips
patinaje m [pateenaнeh] skating
patinar to skid; to skate
patria f [patree-a] motherland, home country
 las fiestas patrias celebration of national independence
paz f [pas] peace
PB ground floor, (US) first floor
peatón m [peh-aton] pedestrian
peatonal pedestrian
 peatón, circula por tu izquierda pedestrians keep to the left
peatones [peh-aton-es]

pedestrians

pecado m sin

pecho m chest; breast

pedazo m [pedaso] piece

pediatra m/f [pedee-atra] pediatrician

pedir to order; to ask for
 pedir hora [ora] to ask the time

pedir disculpas to apologize

pegar to hit; to stick
 no me pega la gana I don't feel like it

peinar [paynar] to comb

peinarse [paynarseh] to comb one's hair

peine m [payneh] comb

pelado cropped; bare, barren; skint, penniless

pelea f [peleh-a] fight

peletería f [peletairee-a] furs, furrier

película f film, movie

película de color [deh] colour film

película en versión original [bairs-yon oreeHeenal] film/ movie in the original language

peligro m danger

peligro de incendio danger: fire hazard

peligro deslizamientos slippery road surface

peligroso dangerous
 es peligroso bañarse danger: no swimming
 es peligroso asomarse do not lean out

pelirrojo [peleerroHo] redheaded

pelo m hair

pelón bald

pelota f ball

peluca f wig

peluquera f [pelookaira], **peluquero** m hairdresser

peluquería f [pelookairee-a] hairdresser's

peluquería de caballeros [deh kaba-yairos] gents' hairdresser's

peluquería de señoras [sen-yoras] ladies' salon

Pemex State-owned oil company

pena f sadness, sorrow
 ¡qué pena! [keh] what a pity!
 me da mucha pena [meh] I'm very sorry
 tener pena [tenair] to be shy, embarrassed

penca f cactus leaf

pendejada f [pendeHada] (piece of) stupidity

pendejo m [pendeHo] bloody idiot, (US) jerk

pendiente m [pend-yenteh] slope
 estar pendiente de [deh] to be waiting for
 estar al pendiente de to watch out for

pene m [peneh] penis

penetrar [penetrar] to enter

penicilina f [peneeseeleena] penicillin

pensamiento m [pensam-yento] thought

pensar to think

pensión f [pens-yon]

guesthouse, boarding house; pension

pensión completa [kompleta] full board

pensionista m [pens-yoneeesta] old-age pensioner

peña f [pen-ya] rock, boulder; singing club

peón m [peh-on] labourer; pawn

peor [peh-or] worse; worst

pepenar to scavenge, to scour rubbish tips

pequeño (m) [peken-yo] small; child

perder [pairdair] to lose
 echar a perder to miss

perderse [pairdairseh] to get lost

pérdida f [pairdeeda] loss

perdón [pairdon] sorry, excuse me; pardon, pardon me

perfecto [pairfekto] perfect

perfumería f [pairfoomairee-a] perfume shop

periódico m [pair-yodeeko] newspaper

periodista m/f [pair-yodeeesta] journalist

período m [pairee-odo] period

perla f [pairla] pearl

permiso m [pairmeeeso] licence; permit
 con permiso excuse me, may I pass

permitir [pairmeeteer] to allow

pero [pairo] but

perro m [pairro] dog

perro caliente m [kal-yenteh]

hot dog

persona f [pairsona] person

persona mayor [mɪ-yor] elderly person, senior citizen

pesadilla f [pesadee-ya] nightmare

pesado heavy; boring, tedious

pésame: dar el pésame [pesameh] to offer one's condolences

pesar: a pesar de que [deh keh] despite the fact that
 a pesar de in spite of

pesca f fishing
 ir a pescar to go fishing

pescadería f [peskadairee-a] fishmonger's

pescar to fish; to catch out

pesero m [pesairo] collective taxi

peso m weight; Mexican national currency

peso máximo maximum weight

peso neto net weight

pestañas fpl [pestan-yas] eyelashes

petate m [petateh] straw mat

petróleo para lámparas m [petroleh-o] paraffin oil, kerosene oil

pez m [pes] fish

picadura f bite

picante [peekanteh] hot, spicy

picar to sting; to itch

pico: horas pico fpl rush hour

picor m itch

picoso [peekoso] hot

pidió [peed-yo] he/she asked

for; you asked for
pie m [p-yeh] foot
 a pie on foot
piedra f [p-yedra] stone
piedra preciosa [pres-yosa] precious stone
piel f [p-yel] skin
pienso [p-yenso] I think
pierna f [p-yairna] leg
pijama m [peeHama] pyjamas
pila f battery
píldora f pill
piloto m pilot
pilotos mpl rear lights
pincel m [peensel] paint brush
pinchazo m [peenchaso] puncture
pinche [peencheh] bloody, lousy
pintada f graffiti
pintar to paint
pintura f painting; paint
pinzas fpl [peensas] tweezers
piña f [peen-ya] pineapple
pipa f pipe
piragua f [peeragwa] canoe
piragüismo m [peeragweesmo] canoeing
pirámide f [peerameedeh] pyramid
piscina f [peeseena] swimming pool
piscina cubierta [koob-yairta] indoor swimming pool
piso m floor
pista f track; clue
pista de baile [deh bīleh] dance floor
pista de tenis tennis court

pistola f gun
placa f [plaka] number plate, licence plate
plancha f iron
planchar to iron
planear [planeh-ar], **planificar** [planeefeekar] to plan
plano (m) flat; map
planta f plant; floor
planta baja [baHa] ground floor, (US) first floor
plástico (m) plastic
plata f silver; money, (US) dough
plateado [pleteh-ado] silver
plática [plateeka] conversation; talk
platicar [plateekar] to talk, to converse
platillo m [platee-yo] saucer
plato m plate; dish, course
playa f [plī-ya] beach
playera f [plī-yaira] T-shirt
playeras fpl [plī-yairas] trainers
plaza f [plasa] square; seat
plaza de toros [deh] bullring
plazas libres [leeb-res] seats available
plomero m [plomairo] plumber
pluma f pen; feather
plumón m [ploomon] felt-tip pen
población f [poblas-yon] village; town; population
poblano from/of Puebla
pobre [pobreh] poor
pobreza f [pobresa] poverty
pocho Americanized (used to refer to Americanized Mexican)

poco little; rarely
poco profundo shallow
pocos few
 unos pocos a few
poder (m) [podair] to be able
 to; power
podrido rotten
policía f [poleesee-a] police
policía m/f policeman;
 policewoman
política f politics
político (m) politician;
 political
póliza de seguros f [poleesa
 deh] insurance policy
polvo m [polbo] powder; dust
pólvora f [polbora] gunpowder
pomada f ointment
pon put
poner [ponair] to put
ponerse de pie [ponairseh deh
 p-yeh] to stand up
ponerse en marcha to set off
pongo I put
poniente m [pon-yenteh] west
popote m [popoteh] (drinking)
 straw
poquito: un poquito [pokeeto] a
 little bit
por by; through; for
 por allí [a-yee] over there
 por fin [feen] at last
 por lo menos at least
 por qué [keh] why
 por semana per week
por avión [ab-yon] airmail
porcentaje m [porsentaHeh]
 percentage
por ciento [s-yento] per cent

por correo terrestre [korreh-o
 tairrestreh]
por favor [fabor] please
porfiriato m [porfeer-yato]
 period under rule of
 Porfirio Diaz 1876-1911
por qué [keh] why
porque [porkeh] because
portada f cover
portaequipajes m [porta-
 ekeepaH-es] luggage rack
portátil [portateel] portable
portero m [portairo] porter;
 doorman; goalkeeper
portugués [portoog-es]
 Portuguese
posada f hotel
posible [poseebleh] possible
postal f [pos-tal] postcard
potosino from/of San Luis
 Potosí
PRD (Partido Revolucionario
 Democrático) m Democratic
 Revolutionary Party (left-
 wing party)
precaución f [prekows-yon]
 caution
precio m [pres-yo] price
precios fijos [feeHos] fixed
 prices
precioso [pres-yoso] beautiful;
 precious
precio unidad [ooneeda] price
 per unit, price per item
preferencia f [prefairens-ya]
 right of way; preference
preferir [prefaireer] to prefer
prefijo m [prefeeHo] dialling
 code, area code

pregunta f question

preguntar to ask

premio m [prem-yo] prize

prenda las luces switch on your lights

prendas fpl clothing

prender [prendair] to light; to switch on

prender luces de cruce switch headlights on

prensa f press; newspapers

preocupado [preh-okoopado] worried

preocuparse [preh-okooparseh] to worry (about)

¡no te preocupes! [teh preh-okoop-es] don't worry!

preparar to prepare

prepararse [prepararseh] to get ready

prepa(ratoria) f pre-university level school

prepotente [prepotenteh] arrogant

presentar to introduce

preservativo m [presairbateebo] condom

presidencia f [preseedens-ya] presidency

presión f [pres-yon] pressure

presión de las llantas [deh las yantas] tyre pressure

prestado: pedir prestado to borrow

prestar to lend

PRI (Partido Revolucionario Institucional) m Institutional Revolutionary Party (party of government since 1920)

prieto [pree-yeto] dark-skinned; black

prima f cousin

primavera f [preemabaira] spring

primera (clase) f [klaseh] first class

primera especial [espes-yal] deluxe first-class

primero first

primeros auxilios [owk-seel-yos] first-aid post

primer piso first floor, (US) second floor

primer plato m first course

primo m cousin

principal [preenseepal] main

principiante m/f [preenseep-yanteh] beginner

principio m [preenseep-yo] beginning

prioridad a la derecha give way/yield to vehicles coming from the right

prisa: tener prisa to be in a hurry

privado (m) [preebado] private; cul-de-sac

privatización f [preebateesas-yon] privatization

probablemente [probableh-menteh] probably

probador m fitting room

probarse [probarseh] to try on

problema m problem

producto preparado con ingredientes naturales product prepared using natural ingredients

productos alimenticios
[prod**oo**ktos aleement**ee**s-yos]
foodstuffs

productos de belleza [deh beh-
y**e**sa] beauty products

profesor m, **profesora** f
teacher; lecturer

profundidad f [profoond**ee**da]
depth

profundo deep

prohibida la entrada no entry,
no admission

**prohibida la entrada a menores
de ...** no admission for those
under ... years of age

prohibida la vuelta en U no U-
turns

prohibida su reproducción
copyright reserved

prohibida su venta not for sale

prohibido [pro-eeb**ee**do]
prohibited, forbidden; no

prohibido asomarse do not
lean out of the window

prohibido bañarse no
swimming

prohibido cantar no singing

prohibido echar basura no
litter

prohibido el paso no entry; no
trespassing

prohibido escupir no spitting

prohibido estacionarse no
parking

**prohibido estacionarse
excepto carga y descarga** no
parking except for loading
and unloading

prohibido fijar carteles stick no

bills

prohibido fumar no smoking

prohibido girar a la izquierda
no left turn

prohibido hablar con el chofer
do not speak to the driver

prohibido hacer auto-stop no
hitch-hiking

prohibido pescar no fishing

prohibido pisar el pasto keep
off the grass

prohibido prender fuego no
campfires

prohibido sacar fotografías no
photographs

prohibido tocar el claxon do
not sound your horn

prometer [promet**air**] to
promise

prometida f fiancée

prometido (m) engaged; fiancé

pronóstico del tiempo m
[t-y**e**mpo] weather forecast

pronto early; soon

de pronto suddenly

¡hasta pronto! [**a**sta] see you
soon!

llegar pronto [yeg**ar**] to be
early

pronunciar [pronoons-y**ar**] to
pronounce

propaganda f advertising;
publicity; propaganda

propiedad privada [prop-yed**a**
preeb**a**da] private property

propietario m [prop-yet**ar**-yo]
owner

propina f tip

propósito: a propósito

deliberately

proteger [proteHair] to protect

provecho: ¡buen provecho!
[bwen probecho] enjoy your
meal!

provincia f [probeens-ya]
province

en provincia in the country,
in the provinces

provocar [probokar] to cause

¿te provoca un café? [teh] do
you feel like a coffee?

próximo next

la semana próxima next week

prudente [proodenteh] careful

prueba de alcoholemia f
[prweba deh alko-olem-ya] breath
test

prueba de embarazo
[embaraso] pregnancy test

Pte. west

público (m) public; audience

pueblo m [pweblo] village;
people; nation; ordinary
people

puede [pwedeh] he/she can;
you can

puede ser [sair] maybe

puedo [pwedo] I can

puente m [pwenteh] bridge

puente aéreo [a-aireh-o] shuttle
flight

puente colgante [kolganteh]
rope bridge

puente de cuota [kwota] toll
bridge

puerta f [pwairta] door; gate

por la otra puerta use other
door

puerta de embarque [embarkeh]
gate

puerta nº. gate no.

puerto m [pwairto] harbour,
port

puerto de montaña [deh montan-
ya] mountain pass

puerto deportivo marina

pues [pwes] since; so

puesta de sol f [pwesta deh]
sunset

puesto de periódicos m [pair-
yodeekos] newspaper kiosk

puesto de socorro first-aid
post

puesto que [keh] since

pulga f flea

pullman m luxury bus

pulmones mpl [poolmon-es]
lungs

pulmonía f [poolmonee-a]
pneumonia

pulque m [poolkeh] drink
made from fermented agave
cactus sap

pulquería f [poolkairee-a] bar
specializing in pulque

pulsera f [poolsaira] bracelet

pulso m pulse

punto m dot; spot; point

hacer punto [asair] to knit

punto de vista [deh beesta]
point of view

puntual: llegar puntual [yegar
poontwal] to arrive on time

pura lana virgen pure new
wool

puro (m) [pooro] cigar; pure

es la pura verdad [vairda] it's

the absolute truth
puse [pooseh] I put

Q

que [keh] who; that; which; than

¿qué? what?; which?

quedar [kedar] to stay; to remain

  quédate con él [kedateh] keep it

  no me queda otra [meh keda] I've no choice

  ¿dónde queda? [dondeh] where is it?

  queda muy cerca it's very near

quedarse [kedarseh] to stay

quedarse con to keep

quedarse sin gasolina to run out of petrol/gas

¿qué hubo? [oobo] what's happening?; how's things?

quejarse [keh-Harseh] to complain

quemadura f [kemadoora] burn

quemadura de sol [deh] sunburn

quemar [kemar] to burn

quemarse [kemarseh] to burn oneself

querer [kerair] to love; to want

querido [kaireedo] dear

queso m [keso] cheese

¿qué tal? how do you do?

¡qué va! [ba] no way!

¿quién? [k-yen] who?

quiero [k-yairo] I want; I love

  no quiero I don't want to

¿quihubo? [k-yoobo] how's it going?

quince [keenseh] fifteen

quince días [dee-as] fortnight

quinientos [keen-yentos] five hundred

quinto [keento] fifth

quiosco m [k-yosko] kiosk

quisiera [kees-yaira] I would like; he/she would like; you would like

quiso [keeso] he/she wanted; you wanted

quitaesmalte m [keeta-esmalteh] nail polish remover

quitar [keetar] to remove

quizá(s) [keesa(s)] maybe

R

rabia f [rab-ya] rage; rabies

  me da rabia it makes me mad

rabioso [rab-yoso] furious

ración f [ras-yon] portion

radiador m [rad-yador] radiator

radio m [rad-yo] spoke

radio f radio

radiografía f [rad-yografee-a] X-ray

rajarse [raHarseh] to back down, to run away

ranchero m [ranchairo] small farmer

rancho m small farm, smallholding

rápidamente [–menteh] quickly

rápido fast

raro rare; strange

rascar to scratch

rasgar to tear

rasgo m feature

rasuradora f shaver

rasurarse [rasoorarseh] to shave

rata f rat

rato: espera un rato wait a minute, wait a bit

pasar buen/mal rato to have a good/bad time

cada rato every now and then

ratón m mouse

rayas: de rayas [deh rī-yas] striped

razón f [rason] reason; rate

tiene razón [t-yeneh] you're right

con razón ... so that's why ...

razonable [rasonableh] reasonable

realizar [reh-aleesar] to carry out

realmente [reh-almenteh] really; in fact

rebajado [rebaHado] reduced

rebajas fpl [rebaHas] reductions, sale

rebajas de verano [deh bairano] summer sale

rebasar to overtake, to pass

rebozo m [reboso] shawl

recado m message

¿quiere dejar recado? would you like to leave a message?

recámara f bedroom

recepción f [reseps-yon] reception

recepcionista m/f [reseps-yoneesta] receptionist

receta f [reseta] recipe; prescription

con receta médica only available on prescription

recetar [resetar] to prescribe

recibir [reseebeer] to receive

recibo m [reseebo] receipt

recién [res-yen] recently

recién salía de casa cuando ... I'd just left home when ...

recién pintado wet paint

reclamación de equipajes f [reklamas-yon deh ekeepaH-es] baggage claim

reclamaciones fpl [reklamas-yon-es] complaints

recoger [rekoHair] to collect; to pick up

recogida de equipajes f [rekoHeeda deh ekeepaH-es] baggage claim

recoja su boleto take your ticket

recomendar to recommend

reconocer [rekonosair] to recognize; to examine

reconocimiento m [rekonoseem-yento] examination

reconocimiento médico medical examination

recordar to remember

recorrer [rekorair] to travel; to travel through; to move along

recorrido m journey

recreo m [recr**eh**-o] playtime, break

recto straight

todo recto straight ahead

recuerdo (m) [rekw**ai**rdo] memory; souvenir; I remember

red f [reh] network; net

redondo round

reduzca la velocidad reduce speed now

reembolsar [reh-embolsar] to refund

reembolsos refunds

reestreno m [reh-estr**e**no] re-release (of a classic movie)

refacciones fpl [refaks-y**o**n-es] spare parts, spares

regadera f [regad**ai**ra] shower

regalo m present

regalón spoiled

regatear [regateh-**a**r] to haggle

regenta f [reH**e**nta], **regente** m [reH**e**nteh] mayor

régimen m [reH**e**emen] diet; regime

regiomontano [reH-yomont**a**no] from/of Monterrey

registrar [reH**e**estr**a**r] to search; to register, to certify

registro de equipajes m [reH**ee**stro deh ekeep**a**H-es] check-in

regla f rule; period

reglamento m rule

regresar to return

regresar a casa to go home

regreso m return

reina f [r**ay**na] queen

Reino Unido m United Kingdom

reír [ray-**eer**] to laugh

relajarse [relaH**a**rseh] to relax

relajo m [rel**a**Ho] disorder; noise, hubbub

rellenar [reh-yenar] to fill in; to fill

reloj m [rel**o**H] watch; clock

reloj de pulsera [deh pools**ai**ra] watch, wristwatch

relojería f [reloHair**ee**-a] watches and clocks; watchmaker's shop

remar to row

remate m [rem**a**teh] sale, auction sale; the final detail

remitente m/f [remeet**e**nteh] sender

remo m oar

remolque m [rem**o**lkeh] trailer

renta f rent; rental

rentado rented

rentar to rent; to hire

se renta to rent, for hire

renunciar [renoons-y**a**r] to resign

reparación f [reparas-y**o**n] repair(s)

reparación de calzado [deh kals**a**do] shoe repairs

reparaciones [reparas-y**o**n-es] faults service

reparar to repair

repelente de mosquitos m [repel**e**nteh deh] mosquito repellent

repente: de repente [deh rep**e**nteh] suddenly

repetir to repeat; to have a second helping

reponerse [reponairseh] to recover

representante m/f [representanteh] representative, agent

repuestos mpl [repwestos] spare parts

repugnante [repoognanteh] disgusting

requisito m [rekeeseeto] requirement, condition

res m cow, bull

resbaladizo [resbaladeeso] slippery

resbalar to slip

rescatar to rescue

reserva f [resairba] reservation

reserva de asientos [deh as-yentos] seat reservation

reservado [resairbado] reserved

reservado el derecho de admisión the management reserve the right to refuse admission

reservar [resairbar] to reserve; to book

reservas fpl reservations

resfriado m [resfree-ado] cold

respeto m respect

respirar to breathe

responder [respondair] to answer, to reply

responsable (m/f) [responsableh] the person in charge; responsible

respuesta f [respwesta] answer

restaurante m [restowranteh]

restaurant

resto m rest

retar to challenge

rete: está rete lindo [reteh] it's really beautiful

reumatismo m [reh-oomateesmo] rheumatism

reunión f [reh-oon-yon] meeting

revelado m [rebelado] film processing

revelar [rebelar] to develop; to reveal

revisar [rebeesar] to check

revisor m [rebeesor] conductor; guard

revista f [rebeesta] magazine

revolución f [reboloos-yon] revolution

la Revolución Mexicana the Mexican Revolution 1910–17

rey m [ray] king

Reyes: día de los Reyes m [dee-a deh los ray-es] 6th of January, Epiphany

rico rich

ridículo ridiculous

riego: tierras de riego fpl irrigated land

rímel m mascara

rincón m corner

riñón m [reen-yon] kidney

río m [ree-o] river

risa f laughter

me da risa [meh] it makes me laugh

rizado [reesado] curly

robar to steal

robo m theft

roca **f** rock

rodilla **f** [rod**ee**-ya] knee

rogar to beg

rojo [ro**H**o] red

rómpase en caso de emergencia break in case of emergency

romper to break

ropa **f** clothes

ropa de caballeros [deh kaba-**yai**ros] men's clothes

ropa de cama bed linen

ropa de señoras [sen-**yo**ras] ladies' clothes

ropa infantil [eenfant**eel**] children's clothes

ropa interior [eentair-**yor**] underwear

ropa sucia [s**oo**s-ya] laundry

rosa **(f)** pink; rose

roto broken

rubeola **f** [roob**eh**-ola] German measles

rubí **m** [roob**ee**] ruby

rubio [r**oo**b-yo] blond

rueda **f** [r**we**da] wheel

rueda de repuesto **f** [deh repw**e**sto] spare wheel

ruega: se ruega ... [seh rw**e**ga] please ...

ruego I request

ruido **m** [r**wee**do] noise

ruidoso [rweed**o**so] noisy

ruinas **fpl** [r**wee**nas] ruins

rural [r**oo**ral] rural, country

ruta **f** route

S

S.A. (Sociedad Anónima) PLC, Inc

sábado **m** Saturday

sábana **f** sheet

saber [sab**air**] to know

  saber a to taste of

sabor **m** taste

sabroso tasty, delicious

sacacorchos **m** corkscrew

sacar to take out; to get out

sacar una foto to take a photo

sacar un boleto to buy a ticket

saco **m** jacket

sal **(f)** salt; leave

sala **f** room; lounge; hall

sala climatizada [kleematis**a**da] air-conditioned

sala de belleza [beh-y**e**sa] beauty salon

sala de cine [deh s**ee**neh] cinema, movie theater

sala de conciertos [kons-y**ai**rtos] concert hall

sala de embarque [embark**eh**] departure lounge

sala de espera [esp**ai**ra] waiting room

sala de exposiciones [esposees-y**o**n-es] exhibition hall

sala de tránsito transit lounge

salado salty

sala X X-rated cinema, adult movie theater

saldar to sell at a reduced price

saldo m clearance; balance
sales de baño fpl [sal-es deh ban-yo] bath salts
salgo I'm leaving, I'm going out
salida f exit; departure
salida ciudad take this direction to leave the city
salida de ambulancias ambulance exit
salida de autopista end of motorway/highway; motorway/highway exit
salida de camiones heavy goods vehicle exit, works exit
salida de emergencia [deh emairHens-ya] emergency exit
salida de incendios [eensend-yos] fire exit
salida de socorro f emergency exit
salidas fpl departures
salidas internacionales [eentairnas-yonal-es] international departures
salidas nacionales [nas-yonal-es] domestic departures
salir to go out; to leave
salón de baile m [deh bīleh] dance hall
salón de belleza [beh-yesa] beauty salon
salón de demostraciones [demostras-yon-es] exhibition hall
salón de peluquería [pelookairee-a] hairdressing salon

salpicadera f [salpeekadaira] mudguard
saltar to jump
Salubridad f Ministry of Health
salud f [saloo] health
saludar to greet
saludos best wishes
salvadoreño (m) [salbadoren-yo] Salvadorean
salvo que [keh] except that
sangrar to bleed
sangre f [sangreh] blood
sanitarios mpl [saneetar-yos] toilets, rest rooms
sano healthy
sarampión m [saramp-yon] measles
sarape m [sarapeh] woven blanket
sartén f frying pan
sastre m [sastreh] tailor
scotch® m Sellotape®, Scotch tape®
se [seh] himself; herself; itself; yourself; themselves; yourselves; oneself
sé I know
no sé I don't know
se aceptan tarjetas de crédito we accept credit cards
secador de pelo m [deh] hair dryer
secar to dry
secarse el pelo [sekarseh] to dry one's hair, to have a blow-dry
sección f [seks-yon] department

seco dry

secretaria f, secretario m secretary

secretaría f Ministry

Secretaría de Turismo Ministry of Tourism

secreto secret

Sectur tourist office

sed: tengo sed [seh] I'm thirsty

seda f silk

seda natural pure silk

sede f [**se**deh] head office, headquarters

seguida: en seguida [seg**ee**da] immediately, right away

seguido [seg**ee**do] often

seguir [seg**eer**] to follow

según according to

segunda (clase) f [**kla**seh] second class

segundo (m) second

de segunda mano second-hand

segundo piso m second floor, (US) third floor

seguridad f [segooreed**a**] safety; security

seguro (m) safe; sure; insurance; safety pin

seguro de viaje m [deh b-ya**Heh**] travel insurance

se habla inglés English spoken

se hacen fotocopias photocopying service

seis [says] six

seiscientos [says-**yen**tos] six hundred

selva f [**sel**ba] jungle; rain forest

semáforo m traffic lights

semana f week

semanal weekly

Semana Santa Holy Week

senador m Senator

sencillo [sens**ee**-yo] simple

se necesita ... ... needed, required

sensible [sens**ee**bleh] sensitive

sentar: sentar bien (a) [b-yen] to suit

sentarse [sent**ar**seh] to sit down

sentido m direction; sense; meaning

sentir to feel; to hear

señas fpl [sen-yas] address

señor [sen-**yor**] gentleman, man; sir

  el señor López Mr López

señora f [sen-**yo**ra] lady, woman; madam

  la señora López Mrs López

señoras fpl ladies; ladies' toilet, ladies' room; ladies' department

señores mpl [sen-**yor**-es] men; gents' toilet, men's room

señorita f [sen-yor**ee**ta] young lady, young woman; miss

  la señorita López Miss López

separado separate; separated

  por separado separately

se precisa ... ... needed

se prohibe ... ... forbidden

se prohibe echar basura no litter

se prohibe fumar no smoking
se prohibe hablar con el chofer do not speak to the driver
se prohibe la entrada no entry, no admittance
se prohibe la entrada a mujeres, uniformados e integrantes de la fuerzas armadas no admittance to women, members of the armed forces and anyone in uniform
septiembre m [set-y**e**mbreh] September
séptimo [s**e**pteemo] seventh
sequía f [sek**ee**-a] drought
ser [sair] to be
  a no ser que [keh] unless
se renta for hire, to rent
se renta departamento flat to let, apartment for rent
se rentan cuartos rooms to rent
serio [s**air**-yo] serious
  en serio seriously
serpiente f [sairp-y**e**nteh] snake
serranía f mountains
se ruega please ...
se ruega desalojen su cuarto antes de las doce please vacate your room by twelve noon
se ruega no ... please do not ...
se ruega no estacionarse no parking please
se ruega no molestar please do not disturb
se ruega pagar en caja please

pay at the desk
se vende for sale
servicio a través de operadora operator-connected calls
servicio automático direct dialling
servicio de cuarto [sairb**ee**s-yo deh kw**a**rto] room service
servicio de fotocopias photocopying service
servicio estrella [estr**eh**-ya] first class (coach) service
servicios mpl [sairb**ee**s-yos] toilets, rest rooms
servicios de rescate [deh resk**a**teh] mountain rescue
servicios de socorro emergency services
servilleta f [sairbee-y**e**ta] serviette, napkin
servir [sairb**ee**r] to serve
sesenta [ses**e**nta] sixty
sesión continua continuous showing
setecientos [setes-y**e**ntos] seven hundred
setenta seventy
sexenio m six year Presidential term
sexo m sex
sexto [s**e**sto] sixth
si [see] if
sí yes; oneself; herself; itself; yourself; themselves; yourselves; each other
SIDA m [s**ee**da] AIDS
sido been
siempre [s-y**e**mpreh] always
siempre que [keh] whenever;

as long as

siento [s-**ye**nto] I sit down; I
feel; I regret

sierra f [s-**ya**irra] mountain
range

siesta f siesta, nap

siete [s-**ye**teh] seven

siga recto straight ahead

siglo m century

significado m meaning

significar to mean

siguiente [seeg-**ye**nteh] next
 al día siguiente [**dee**-a] the
 day after

silencio m [see**le**ns-yo] silence

silla f [**see**-ya] chair

silla de ruedas [deh r**we**das]
 wheelchair

sillita de ruedas [see-**yee**ta]
 pushchair, buggy

sillón m [see-**yon**] armchair

simpático nice

sin [seen] without

sinagoga f synagogue

sincero [seen**sai**ro] sincere

sindicalista m/f trade unionist

sindicato m trade union, labor
 union

sin duda undoubtedly

sin embargo however,
 neverthless

sino: no ... sino ... not ... but ...

si no otherwise

sino que [keh] but

sin plomo unleaded

siquiera [seek-**ya**ira] even if; at
 least

sírvase [**seer**baseh] please

sírvase frío serve cold

sírvase Usted mismo help
 yourself

sitio m [**seet**-yo] place
 en ningún sitio [neen-**goon**]
 nowhere

smoking m [**smo**keen] dinner
 jacket

sobrar to be left over; to be
 too many

sobre (m) [**so**breh] envelope;
 on; above

sobrecarga [sobre**kar**ga] excess
 weight; extra charge

sobrevivir [sobrebee**beer**] to
 survive

sobrina f niece

sobrino m nephew

sobrio [**sobr**-yo] sober

sociedad f [sos-**ye**da] society;
 company

socio m [**sos**-yo] associate;
 member

socorrer [soko**rair**] to help

socorrista m/f lifeguard

¡socorro! help!

sois [soys] you are

sol m sun
 al sol in the sun

solamente [sola**men**teh] only

soleado [soleh-**a**do] sunny

solo lonely

sólo only
 no sólo ... sino también ...
 [tamb-**yen**] not only ... but
 also ...

sólo camiones buses only

sólo carga y descarga loading
 and unloading only

sólo laborables weekdays only

sólo motos motorcycles only
sólo para residentes (del hotel) hotel patrons only
soltera (f) [sol**tai**ra] single; single woman
soltero (m) [sol**tai**ro] single; bachelor
solterón m [soltai**ron**] bachelor
solterona f [soltai**ro**na] spinster
sombra f shade; shadow
sombra de ojos [deh **o**Hos] eyeshadow
sombrero m [sombr**ai**ro] hat
sombrilla f [sombr**ee**-ya] parasol
somnífero m [som**nee**fairo] sleeping pill
somos we are
son they are; you are
sonreír [sonreh-**eer**] to smile
sonrisa f smile
sordo deaf
sorprendente [sorprend**en**teh] surprising
sorpresa f surprise
sótano m lower floor; basement
soy I am
sport: de sport [deh] casual
Sr (Señor) Mr
Sra (Señora) Mrs
Sres (Señores) Messrs
Srta (Señorita) Miss
su [soo] his; her; its; their; your
suave [sw**a**beh] soft; quiet
subir to go up; to get on; to get in; to take up
subtitulado sub-titled

subtítulos mpl subtitles
suburbios mpl [soob**oor**b-yos] suburbs; poor quarters
suceder [soosed**air**] to happen
sucio [**soo**s-yo] dirty
sucursal f branch
sudamericana (f) [soodamaireek**a**na], **sudamericano** (m) South American
sudar to sweat
Suecia f [sw**e**s-ya] Sweden
sueco [sw**e**ko] Swedish
suegra f [sw**e**gra] mother-in-law
suegro m [sw**e**gro] father-in-law
suela f [sw**e**la] sole
suelo (m) floor; I am used to
suelto [sw**el**to] small change
sueño (m) [sw**en**-yo] dream; I dream
tener sueño [ten**air**] to be tired/sleepy
suerte f [sw**air**teh] luck
por suerte luckily, fortunately
¡buena suerte! [bw**e**na] good luck!
suéter m [sw**e**tair] sweater
suficiente: es suficiente [soofees-y**en**teh] that's enough
sufragio efectivo, no reelección effective suffrage, no re-election (slogan on many official documents)
suicidarse [sweeseed**ar**seh] to commit suicide
Suiza f [sw**ee**sa] Switzerland
sumar to add; to add up to

supe [**soo**peh] I knew
súper [**soo**pair] four-star
  petrol, (US) premium (gas);
  supermarket
supermercado m
  [soopairmair**ka**do] supermarket
supuesto: por supuesto
  [soop**wes**to] of course
sur m south
  al sur de [deh] south of
sureste m [soor**es**teh] southeast
suroeste m [sooro-**es**teh] southwest
surtido m assortment
sus [soos] his; her; its; their;
  your
susto m shock
susurrar to whisper
sutil subtle
suya [**soo**-ya], **suyas, suyo,**
  suyos his; hers; its; theirs;
  yours

T

tabaco m tobacco; cigarettes
tabasqueño [tabas**ken**-yo]
  from/of Tabasco
tabique m [ta**bee**keh] brick
tabla de surf f [deh soorf]
  surfboard
tabla de windsurf f sailboard
tablero de instrumentos m
  [tab**lai**ro deh eenstroo**men**tos]
  dashboard
tablón de anuncios m [anoons-
  yos] notice board, bulletin

board
tablón de información [deh
  eenformas-**yon**] indicator board
tacón m heel
tacones altos [tak**on**-es] high
  heels
tacones planos flat heels
tal such
  con tal (de) que provided that
talco m talcum powder
talla f [**ta**-ya] size
  ¿qué número talla? what size
  are you?
tallas grandes [**grand**-es] large
  sizes
tallas sueltas [**swel**tas] odd
  sizes
taller mecánico m [ta-**yair**
  mek**anee**ko] garage
talón m heel
talonario (de cheques) m
  [talonar-yo (deh chek-es)] cheque
  book, checkbook
talón de equipajes [ekeepaн-es]
  baggage slip
tal vez [bes] maybe
tamaño m [tam**an**-yo] size
tamaulipeco [tamowlee**pe**ko]
  from/of Tamaulipas
también [tamb-**yen**] also
  yo también me too
tampoco neither, nor
  yo tampoco me neither, nor
  me
tan: tan bonito so beautiful
  tan pronto como as soon as
tanque m [**tan**keh] tank
tantito: espere tantito wait a
  moment

tanto (m) so much; point

tanto ... como ... both ...
and ...

tantos so many

tapa f lid

tapar to cover

tapas fpl savoury snacks, tapas

tapatío from/of Guadalajara

tapete m [tapeteh] rug, carpet

tapón m plug

taquería f [takairee-a] taco
restaurant, taco stall

taquilla f [takee-ya] ticket
office

tarahumara m/f [tara-oomara]
indigenous person from
northern Mexico

tarasco (m) indigenous
person from Michoacan;
from/of Tarascan culture

tardar: ¿cuánto tarda? [kwanto]
how long does it take?

no tarda he/she won't be
long

no tardes [tard-es] don't be
long

tarde (f) [tardeh] afternoon;
evening; late

a las tres de la tarde [deh] at 3
p.m.

esta tarde this afternoon, this
evening

por la tarde in the evening

llegar tarde [yegar] to be late

tarifa f charge, charges

tarifa especial estudiante
[espes-yal estood-yanteh]
student reduced rate

tarifa normal standard rate

tarifa reducida [redooseeda]
reduced rate

tarjeta f [tarHeta] card

tarjeta verde Green Card
(tourist permit in Mexico)

tarjeta bancaria [bankar-ya]
cheque card

tarjeta de crédito [deh kredeeto]
credit card

tarjeta de embarque [embarkeh]
boarding pass

tarjeta postal postcard

tarjeta telefónica phonecard

tauromaquia f [towromak-ya]
bullfighting

taxista m/f taxi driver

taza f [tasa] cup

te [teh] you; yourself

té m tea

teatro m [teh-atro] theatre

techo m ceiling

teclado m keyboard

técnica f technique;
technology

técnico technical

tecnología f [teknoloHee-a]
technology

tecolote m [–loteh] owl

tejado m [teHado] roof

tejanos mpl [teHanos] jeans

tejidos mpl [teHeedos]
materials, fabrics

tela f material

teleférico m cable car

teléfono m telephone

teléfono interurbano long-
distance phone

teléfonos de emergencia
emergency telephone

numbers

telesilla m [telese**e**-ya] chairlift

Televisa largest Mexican
television corporation

televisión f [telebees-yon]
television

televisor m television (set)

temblor m earthquake

temer [tem**air**] to fear

temor m fear

tempestad f [tempest**a**] storm

templo m temple; church

temporada f season

ten hold

tenedor m fork

tener [ten**air**] to have

 tener derecho to have the
 right

 tener prisa to be in a hurry

 tener prioridad [pree-oree**da**] to
 have right of way

 tener que [keh] to have to

 ¡tenga cuidado! [kweed**a**do] be
 careful!

tengo I have

 tengo que I have to, I must

tensión f [tens-yon] blood
pressure

teñirse el pelo [ten-y**ee**rseh to
dye one's hair, to have one's
hair dyed

tepetate m [tepet**a**teh] type of
soft stone used for building

tercera edad f [ed**a**] old age

tercero third

tercer piso m [tairs**air**] third
floor, (US) fourth floor

tercio m [t**ai**rs-yo] third

terciopelo m [tairs-yop**e**lo]

velvet

terco [t**ai**rko] stubborn

terminal f [tairmeen**a**l]
terminus; terminal

terminar to finish

termo m Thermos® flask

termómetro m thermometer

terrateniente m/f [tairra-ten-
y**e**nteh] large landowner

terreno m [tairr**e**no] piece/plot
of land

testigo m witness

testimonio m [testeem**o**n-yo]
evidence; statement

tetera f [tet**ai**ra] teapot

tezontle m [tes**o**ntleh] volcanic
marble-like rock

ti [tee] you

tía f [t**ee**-a] aunt

tianguis m [t-y**a**ngees] market

tibio [t**ee**b-yo] lukewarm

tiburón m shark

tiempo m [t-y**e**mpo] time;
weather

 a tiempo on time

 al tiempo at room
 temperature

 tiempo de recreo [deh rekr**eh**-o]
 leisure

tiempo libre [l**ee**breh] free time

tienda f [t-y**e**nda] shop, store;
tent

 esta tienda se traslada a ...
 this business is transferred
 to ...

tienda de abarrotes f [deh
abarr**o**t-es] grocer's, dry goods
store

tienda de artículos de piel

Ti

[p-yel] leather goods shop

tienda de campaña tent

tienda de comestibles [komesteebl-es] grocer's

tienda de deportes [deport-es] sports shop

tienda de electrodomésticos electrical goods shop

tienda de muebles [mwebl-es] furniture shop

tienda de regalos gift shop

tienda de ultramarinos grocer's

tienda de vinos y licores [beenos ee leekor-es] off-licence, liquor store

tienda libre de impuestos [leebreh deh eempwestos] duty-free shop

tiene: ¿tiene ...? [t-yeneh] have you got ...?, do you have ...?; do you sell ...?

tiene que [keh] he/she must; you must

tierra f [t-yairra] earth; land

tifo m typhus

tijeras fpl [teeHairas] scissors

tiliches mpl [teeleech-es] bits and pieces

timbre m [teembreh] bell; stamp

timbre de alarma [deh] alarm bell

tímido shy

tina f bath(tub)

tintorería f [teentorairee-a] dry-cleaner's

tío m [tee-o] uncle

tipo de cambio m [deh kamb-yo] exchange rate

tirita f Elastoplast®,

Bandaid®

tiro m shot

tlapalería f [tlapalairee-a] hardware store

toalla f [to-a-ya] towel

toalla de baño [deh ban-yo] bath towel

tobillo m [tobee-yo] ankle

tocadiscos m record player

tocar to touch; to play

tocayo m [tokī-yo] namesake

todavía [todabee-a] still; yet

todavía no not yet

todo all, every; everything

todos los días every day

todo derecho straight on

todo recto straight ahead

todos everyone

tolteca from/of Toltec culture

tomado drunk

tomar to take; to drink

tomar el sol to sunbathe

tomavistas m cine-camera

tómese antes de las comidas to be taken before meals

tómese después de las comidas to be taken after meals

tómese ... veces al día to be taken ... times per day

tome Usted [tomeh oosteh] take

tonelada f tonne

tono m dialling tone; shade

tonto silly

topes mpl speed bumps, 'sleeping policemen'

torcer [torsair] to twist; to sprain; to turn

torcerse el tobillo [tobee-yo] to

twist one's ankle

torero m [torairo] bullfighter

tormenta f storm

tormentoso stormy

tornillo m [tornee-yo] screw

toro m bull

toros mpl bullfighting

torpe [torpeh] clumsy

torre f [torreh] tower

tos f cough

toser [tosair] to cough

tosferina f [tosfaireena] whooping cough

total: en total [tot-al] altogether

totalmente [tot-almenteh] absolutely

tóxico [tokseeko] poisonous

toxicómano m [tokseekomano] drug addict

trabajador (m) [trabaHador], **trabajadora** (f) worker; industrious

trabajar [trabajar] to work

trabajo m [trabaHo] work; job

traducir [tradooseer] to translate

traer [tra-air] to bring

tráfico: tráfico de drogas drug traffic; drug-trafficking

tragar to swallow

traigo [trīgo] I bring

tráiler m [trīlair] large truck; caravan, (US) trailer

tráiners mpl [trīnairs] trainers

traje (m) [traHeh] I brought; suit; clothes

traje de baño [deh ban-yo] swimming costume

traje de noche [nocheh]

evening dress

traje de señora [sen-yora] lady's suit

traje típico traditional regional costume

trámites mpl [tra-meet-es] bureaucracy, paperwork

tranquilizante [trankeeleesanteh] tranquillizer

tranquilizarse [trankeeleesarseh] to calm down

tranquilo [trankeelo] quiet

transar to sell out, to compromise

tránsito m traffic

tras after

trasbordo m transfer; change **hacer trasbordo en ...** change at ...

trasero (m) [trasairo] bottom; back; rear

trasladar to move **se traslada** under new management

trasnochar to spend the night

tratamiento m [–m-yento] treatment

tratar to treat; to try

trato m way of treating people

través: a través de [trav-es deh] across, through

travieso [trab-yeso] mischievous

trece [treseh] thirteen

treinta [traynta] thirty

tren m train

tren de carga [deh] goods train

tren de lavado automático [labado owtomateeko] carwash

tren de pasajeros [pasaнairos] passenger train

tren directo through train

tren tranvía [tranbee-a] stopping train

tres three

trescientos [tres-yentos] three hundred

tres cuartos de hora mpl [kwartos deh ora] three quarters of an hour

tribunal m [treeboonal] court; tribunal

tripulación f [treepoolas-yon] crew

triste [treesteh] sad

tristeza f [treestesa] sadness

tronco m [tronko] body; buddy

tropezar [tropesar] to trip

trueno m [trweno] thunder

tu [too] your

tú you

tubo de escape m [deh eskapeh] exhaust

tubo de respirar snorkel

tuerce a la izquierda turn left

tuerza [twairsa] turn

tú mismo yourself

túnel m [too-nel] tunnel

turismo m tourism; luxury bus; tourist office

turista m/f tourist

turístico [tooreesteeko] tourist

turno m [toorno] turn; round; shift

es mi turno it's my turn/round

tus [toos] your

tuya [too-ya], tuyas, tuyo,

tuyos yours

U

u [oo] or

ubicarse [oobeekarseh] to be located

¿lo ubicas? do you know the one I mean?

Ud (Usted) [oosteh] you

Uds (Ustedes) [oostedes] you

úlcera (de estómago) f [oolsaira] (stomach) ulcer

últimamente [oolteemamenteh] recently, lately

último last; latest

últimos días [dee-as] last days; last few days

ultramarinos m grocer's

un [oon] a

una [oona] a

unas some

universidad f [ooneebairseeda] university

uno one; someone

unos some; a few

uña f [oon-ya] fingernail

urbanización f [oorbaneesas-yon] housing estate

urbano urban, city

urgencias [oorнens-yas] casualty (department); emergencies

uruguayo [ooroogwī-yo] Uruguayan

usado used; secondhand

usar to use

no se usa [seh] it isn't done

uso use

  el uso del tabaco es perjudicial para su salud smoking can damage your health

uso externo not to be taken internally

uso obligatorio cinturón de seguridad seatbelts must be worn

Usted [oosteh] you

Ustedes [oosted-es] you

útil useful

V
—

v is pronounced more like a **b** than an English **v**

va he/she/it goes; you go

vaca f cow

vacaciones fpl [bakas-yon-es] holiday, vacation

vacilar [baseelar] to party, to have a good time

vacilón [baseelon] fun-loving

vacío [basee-o] empty

vacuna f vaccination

vacunarse [bakoonarseh] to be vaccinated

vagón m carriage, coach

vagón de literas [deh leetairas] sleeping car

vagón restaurante [restowranteh] restaurant car

vajilla f [baHee-ya] dinner service, set of crockery

vale: ¿cuánto vale? [kwanto baleh] how much is it?

me vale (madre) [madreh] I don't give a shit

valer [balair] to be worth

valiente [bal-yenteh] brave

valla f [ba-ya] fence

valle m [ba-yeh] valley

valores mpl [balor-es] securities

válvula f valve

vamos we go

van they go; you go

vapor m steam

vaquero m [bakairo] cowboy

vaqueros mpl jeans

variar [bar-yar] to vary

  para variar for a change

varicela f [bareesela] chickenpox

varios [bar-yos] several; different

varón m male

varonil manly

vas you go

vasco Basque

vaso m glass

vatio m [bat-yo] watt

vaya [bī-ya] go; I/he/she/you should go; I/he/she/you might go

Vd (Usted) you

Vds (Ustedes) you

ve [beh] go; he/she sees; you see

veces: a veces [bes-es] sometimes

vecindad f [beseenda] inner city slum

vehículos pesados heavy vehicles

v is pronounced more like a **b** than an English **v**

veinte [**bay**nteh] twenty

vejez f [beH-**es**] old age

vela f candle; sail

velero m [be**lai**ro] sailing boat

velocidad f [belo**seeda**] speed

velocidad controlada por radar radar speed checks

velocidades fpl [beloseed**ad**-es] gears

velocidad limitada speed limits apply

velocímetro m [belos**ee**metro] speedometer

ven [ben] come; they see; you see

vena f vein

venda f bandage

vendar to dress (wound)

vendemos a ... selling rate

vender [ben**dair**] to sell

veneno m poison

venezolano [bene**so**lano] Venezuelan

vengo I come

venir to come

venta f sale

de venta aquí on sale here

venta de estampillas stamps sold here

venta de localidades tickets (on sale)

ventana f window

ventanilla f [benta**nee**-ya] window; ticket office

ventas a crédito credit terms available

ventas al contado cash sales

ventas a plazos hire purchase, (US) installment plan

ventilador m fan

ver [bair] to see; to watch

veraneante m/f [bairaneh-**anteh**] holiday-maker, vacationer

veranear [bairaneh-**ar**] to holiday, to take a vacation

veraneo: centro de veraneo [**sen**tro deh bairaneh-o] holiday resort

verano m [bair**ano**] summer

veras: de veras [deh **bai**ras] really, honestly

verdad f [bair**da**] truth

¿verdad? don't you?; do you?; isn't it?; isn't he?; is he? etc

verdadero [bairdad**ai**ro] true

verde (m) [**bair**deh] green

verguenza f [bair**gwen**sa] shame

versión f [bairs-**yon**] version

en versión original [oree**geen**al] in the original language

vestido m dress

vestir to dress

vestirse [best**eer**seh] to get dressed; to dress

vestuarios mpl [best**war**-yos] fitting rooms; changing rooms

vez f [bes] time

una vez once

en vez de [deh] instead of

vi [bee] I saw

vía f [**bee**-a] platform, (US) track

vía aérea: por vía aérea [a-**air**-eh-a] by air mail

viajar [b-yaHar] to travel

viaje m [b-yaHeh] journey

¡buen viaje! [bwen] have a good trip!

viaje de negocios [deh negos-yos] business trip

viaje de novios [nob-yos] honeymoon

viaje organizado [organeesado] package tour

viajero m [b-yaHairo] traveller

vía oral orally

vía rectal per rectum

víbora f [beebora] snake

vida f life

vidrio m [beedr-yo] glass; window

viejo (m) [b-yeHo] old; mate, buddy

mi viejo my old man, my father

mis viejos my parents

viene: la semana que viene [keh b-yeneh] next week

viento m [b-yento] wind

vientre m [b-yentreh] stomach

viernes m [b-yairn-es] Friday

Viernes Santo Good Friday

vine [beeneh] I came

vinos y licores wines and spirits

viñedo [been-yedo] vineyard

violación f [b-yolas-yon] rape

violar [b-yolar] to rape

violencia f [b-yolensee-a] violence

violento [b-yolento] violent

visita f visit

visita con guía [gee-a] guided tour

visitante m/f [beeseetanteh] visitor

visitar to visit

visor m viewfinder

víspera f [beespaira] the day before

vista f view

visto seen

viuda f [b-yooda] widow

viudo m widower

vivir to live

vivo alive; I live

VO (versión original) original language

voceador m [boseador] newspaper seller

vocero m [bosairo] spokesman

volante m [bolanteh] steering wheel

volar to fly

volcán m [bolkan] volcano

volibol m [boleebol] volleyball

voltaje m [boltaHeh] voltage

voltear [bolteh-ar] to turn over; to knock over

volver [bolbair] to come back

volver a hacer algo to do something again

vomitar to vomit

v.o. subtitulada version in the original language with subtitles

voy I go

voz f [bos] voice

vuelo m [bwelo] flight

vuelo nacional [nas-yonal] domestic flight

v is pronounced more like a b than an English v

vuelo regular scheduled flight
vuelta f [bwelta] tour, trip
  a la vuelta around the corner
  dar una vuelta to go for a walk
vuelto m [bwelto] change
vuelvo [bwelbo] I return
vulcanizadora f [boolkaneesadora] vulcanizer, tyre repairs

Y

y [ee] and
ya already; now
  ya está there you are
  ya mero [mairo] right here, right now
yace [ya-seh] lies
yanqui m/f [yankee] Yankee, North American
ya que [keh] since
yerba f [yairba] herb
yerno m [yairno] son-in-law
yo I; me
  yo mismo myself
yucateco [yookateko] from/of Yucatán

Z

zacateco [sakateko] from/of Zacatecas
zafarse [safarseh] to get away, to escape
zancudo m [sankoodo] mosquito
zapatería f [sapatairee-a] shoe shop/store
zapatero m [sapatairo] cobbler; shoe repairer
zapatismo m [sapateesmo] peasant movement led by Emiliano Zapata (1911-19); peasant movement in Chiapas 1994-
zapatista m/f follower of the above
zapatos mpl [sapatos] shoes
zapoteco [sapoteko] from/of Zapotec culture
zenzontle m [sensontleh] mockingbird
zócalo m [sokalo] central square
zona f [sona] area
zona arqueológica [arkehologeeka] archaeological site
zona de servicios [deh sairbeesyos] service area
zona industrial [eendoostree-al] industrial estate
zona monumental historic monuments
zona postal [pos-tal] postcode, zip code
zona (reservada) para peatones pedestrian precinct
zopilote m [sopeeloteh] vulture
zurdo [soordo] left-handed

Menu Reader:
Food

Essential Terms

bread el pan
butter la mantequilla [mantekee-ya]
cup la taza [tasa]
dessert el postre [postreh]
fish el pescado
fork el tenedor
glass (tumbler) el vaso [baso]
  (wine glass) la copa
knife el cuchillo [koochee-yo]
main course el plato principal
meat la carne [karneh]
menu la carta
pepper (spice) la pimienta [peem-yenta]
plate el plato
salad la ensalada
salt la sal
set menu el menú, la comida corrida
soup la sopa
spoon la cuchara
starter la entrada
table la mesa

another ..., please otro/otra ..., por favor [fabor]
waiter! ¡señor! [sen-yor]
waitress! ¡señorita! [sen-yoreeta]
could I have the bill, please? me pasa la cuenta, por favor [meh
  pasa la kwenta]

aceite [asayteh] oil

aceite de oliva [deh oleeba] olive oil

aceitunas [asaytoonas] olives

aceitunas aliñadas [aleen-yadas] olives with salad dressing

aceitunas negras [neh-gras] black olives

aceitunas rellenas [reh-yenas] stuffed olives

achicoria [acheekor-ya] chicory, endive

achiote [achee-oteh] spicy seasoning from Yucatán

acocil [akoseel] freshwater shrimp

adobado tossed in adobo seasoning

adobo red chilli paste used for cooking, in marinades etc

aguacate [agwakateh] avocado

ahumado [a-oomado] smoked

ajo [aHo] garlic

a la brasa barbecued

a la crema creamed

a la criolla [kree-o-ya] in hot, spicy sauce

a la marinera [mareenaira] in white wine sauce with garlic

a la mexicana [meHeekana] with chilli peppers, onions and garlic

a la parrilla [parree-ya] grilled

a la plancha grilled

a la romana fried in batter

a la Tampiqueña [tampeeken-ya] with chilli sauce and black refried beans

a la Veracruzana [bairakroosana] in a tomato-based sauce with olives, capers and chillies

al carbón grilled

al mojo de ajo [moHo deh aHo] in a garlic sauce

al natural [natooral] plain

albahaca [alba-aka] basil

albóndigas meatballs

albóndigas de lomo [deh] pork meatballs

alcachofas artichokes

alcachofas a la romana artichokes in batter

alcaparras capers

al horno [orno] baked

aliñado [aleen-yado] with salad dressing

ali oli garlic mayonnaise

almejas [almeh-Has] clams

almejas a la marinera [mareenaira] clams stewed in white wine

almejas al natural [natooral] live clams

almendras almonds

almuerzo [almwairso] set menu; lunch

anchoas [ancho-as] anchovies

anchoas a la barquera [barkaira] marinated anchovies with capers

anguila [angeela] eel

antojitos [antoHeetos] snacks

apio [ap-yo] celery

arroz [arros] rice

arroz a la cubana boiled rice with fried eggs and either bananas or chillies

arroz a la mexicana [meнeekana] rice with garlic, tomato and coriander

arroz blanco boiled white rice

arroz con leche [lecheh] rice pudding

arroz con mariscos rice with seafood

arroz verde [bairdeh] rice with olives and green peppers

asado roast; roast meat

ate [ateh] quince jelly

atún tuna

avellanas [abeh-yanas] hazelnuts

aves [ab-es] poultry

azafrán [asafran] saffron

azúcar [asookar] sugar

bacalao a la vizcaína [bakalow – beeska-eena] cod served with ham, peppers and onions

bacalao al pil pil [peel] cod cooked in olive oil

baleada [baleh-ada] corn meal pancake filled with beans, cheese and eggs

barbacoa barbecued meat

berenjena [bairenнena] aubergine, eggplant

besugo sea bream

besugo al horno [orno] baked sea bream

besugo asado baked sea bream

besugo mechado sea bream stuffed with ham and bacon

betabel beetroot

bien hecho [b-yen echo] well-done

bife [beefeh] steak

birria [beer-ya] mutton stew

bistec steak

bistec de ternera [deh tairnaira] veal steak

bizcocho [beeskocho] sponge finger

blanquillo [blankee-yo] egg

bolillo [bolee-yo] bread roll

bollo [bo-yo] roll

bomba helada [elada] baked Alaska

bonito tuna

bonito al horno [orno] baked tuna

bonito con jitomate [нitomateh] tuna with tomato

boquerones fritos [bokairon-es] fried fresh anchovies

borracho cake soaked in rum

botanas snacks

brazo de gitano [braso deh нeetano] swiss roll

brochetas kebabs

budín bread pudding

buey [boo-eh] beef

buñuelos [boon-ywelos] light fried pastries; doughnuts

burritos stuffed tortilla parcels

cabeza [kabesa] pig's head (brains, cheeks etc)

cabrilla [kabree-ya] sea bass

cabrito kid

cabrito al pastor grilled kid

cabrito asado roast kid

cacahuates [kakawat-es]
peanuts

caguama [kagwama] turtle

cajeta [kaHeta] fudge

calabacines [kalabaseen-es]
courgettes, zucchini;
marrow, squash

calabacitas courgettes,
zucchini

calabaza [kalabasa] pumpkin,
squash

calamares a la romana
[kalamar-es] squid rings fried
in batter

calamares en su tinta squid
cooked in their ink

calamares fritos fried squid

caldeirada [kaldairada] fish
soup

caldillo [kaldee-yo] stew

caldo de ... [deh] ... soup

caldo de perdiz [pairdees]
partridge soup

caldo de pescado clear fish
soup

caldo de pollo [po-yo] chicken
soup

caldo gallego [ga-yego] clear
soup with green vegetables,
beans

caldo tlalpeño [tlalpen-yo]
chicken broth with
vegetables, chicken strips
and coriander

caldo Xóchitl [socheetl]
chicken broth with

pumpkin blossoms

callos [ka-yos] tripe

camarones [kamaron-es]
prawns

camarones al mojo de ajo
[moHo deh aHo] garlic prawns

camote [kamoteh] sweet
potato

campechana de camarón
[deh] spicy prawn cocktail

canela cinnamon

canelones [kanelon-es]
cannelloni

capirotada bread pudding

caracoles [karakol-es] sea snails

carne [karneh] meat

carne de chancho [deh] pork

carne de puerco [pwairko]
pork

carne de res beef

carne picada minced meat

carnero [karnairo] mutton

carnes [karn-es] meat; meat
dishes

carnitas barbecued pork

carta menu

casero [kasairo] home-made

castañas [kastan-yas]
chestnuts

caza [kasa] game

cazuela [kaswela] casserole,
stew

cazuela de hígado [deh eegado]
liver casserole

cazuela de mariscos seafood
stew

cebolla [sebo-ya] onion

cebollitas [sebo-yeetas] spring
onions

cecina [seseena] sun-dried
pork

cena [sena] dinner, evening
meal

cerdo [sairdo] pork, pig

cereza [sairesa] cherry

ceviche [sebeecheh] marinated
raw seafood cocktail

chabacano apricot

chalupa fried tortilla with
filling

champiñones [champeen-yon-es]
mushrooms

chancho pork, pig

chayote [chī-yoteh] vegetable
similar to marrow or squash

chicharrón pork crackling

chícharros peas

chilaquiles [cheelakeel-es] fried
tortillas in hot chilli sauce

chile [cheeleh] chilli pepper

chile de árbol [deh] dried
reddish chilli pepper

chile guero [gairo] very hot,
white chilli pepper

chile habanero [abanairo] very
hot red or green chilli

chile jalapeño [Halapen-yo]
green chilli pepper, usually
in vinegar with onions and
carrots

chile Pekin small, green, very
hot chilli pepper

chile poblano large green bell
pepper, usually stuffed

chile rubio very hot, white
chilli pepper

chiles en nogada [cheel-es]
stuffed peppers with a sauce

made from walnuts and
pomegranate seeds

chile serrano [sairrano] very
hot, thin green chilli pepper

chiles rellenos [reh-yenos]
stuffed green peppers

chimichanga stuffed, fried
tortilla

chipirones [cheepeeron-es] baby
squid

chipotle [cheepotleh] dark chilli
sauce

chirimoya soursop (a tart-
flavoured fruit)

cholgas mussels

chongos zamoranos
[samoranos] curds in syrup

chorizo [choreeso] spicy red
sausage

chuleta chop, cutlet

chuleta de cerdo [deh sairdo]
pork chop

chuleta de cerdo empanizada
[empaneesada] breaded pork
chop

chuleta de chancho pork
chop

chuleta de cordero [kordairo]
lamb chop

chuleta de lomo ahumado
[a-oomado] smoked pork
chop

chuleta de ternera [tairnaira]
veal chop

chuleta de ternera
empanizada [empaneesada]
breaded veal chop

chuleta de venado [benado]
venison chop

churrasco roast or grilled meat

churros [choorros] long fritters

cigalas [seegalas] crayfish

cigalas a la parrilla [parree-ya] grilled crayfish

cilantro [seelantro] coriander

ciruela [seerwela] plum, greengage

ciruela pasa prune

cochinillo asado [kocheenee-yo] roast sucking pig

cochinita pibil [peebeel] barbecued pork

cocido [koseedo] stew made from meat, chickpeas and vegetables

coco coconut

coctel de gambas [deh] prawn cocktail

coctel de langostinos king prawn cocktail

coctel de mariscos seafood cocktail

codornices [kodornees-es] quails

codornices estofadas braised quails

coles de Bruselas [kol-es deh] Brussels sprouts

corvina bass

coliflor cauliflower

coliflor con bechamel [beshamel] cauliflower in white sauce

comal griddle

comida set menu; meal; food

comida corrida set menu

comidas para llevar [yebar] take-away meals

comino cumin

conejo [koneHo] rabbit

congrio [kon-gryo] conger eel

conservas [konsairbas] jams, preserves

consomé de pollo [deh po-yo] chicken consommé

cordero [kordairo] lamb

cordero asado roast lamb

costillas [kostee-yas] ribs

costillas de cerdo [deh sairdo] pork rib

coyotas biscuits, cookies

crema cream

crema de espárragos [deh] cream of asparagus soup

crema de espinacas cream of spinach soup

cremada dessert made from egg, sugar and milk

crepa sweet pancake

crep(e) pancake

crepes imperiales [krep-es eempair-yal-es] crêpes suzette

criadillas [kree-adee-yas] bull's testicles

crocante [krokanteh] ice cream with chopped nuts

croquetas [kroketas] croquettes

croquetas de pescado [deh] fish croquettes

crudo raw

cubierto menu

cuerno [kwairno] croissant

cuitlacoche [kweetlakocheh] type of edible mushroom which grows on the

253

maize/corn plant

damasco apricot

dátiles [dateel-es] dates

de fabricación casera [deh fabreekas-yon kasaira] home-made

desayuno [desi-yoono] breakfast

dorado type of fish

dulce de membrillo [doolseh deh membree-yo] quince jelly

dulces [dools-es] sweets, candies

durazno [doorasno] peach

ejotes [eHot-es] green beans, runner beans

elote [eloteh] maize, corn on the cob, corncob

embutidos cured pork sausages

empanada pasty filled with meat or fish

empanizado [empaneesado] in breadcrumbs

en escabeche [eskabecheh] pickled

enchilada fried corn meal pancake filled with meat, vegetables and cheese

enchiladas rojas [roHas] stuffed tortillas in red chilli sauce

enchilada suiza [sweesa] stuffed tortilla with soured cream

enchiladas verdes [baird-es] stuffed tortillas in green

chilli sauce

endivias [endeeb-yas] endive, chicory

ensalada salad

ensalada de frutas [deh] fruit salad

ensalada de pollo [po-yo] chicken salad

ensalada mixta [meesta] mixed salad

ensalada verde [bairdeh] green salad

ensaladilla [ensaladee-ya] vegetables and chicken in mayonnaise

ensaladilla rusa Russian salad

entrecot de ternera [deh tairnaira] veal entrecôte

entremeses [entremes-es] hors d'oeuvres

entremeses variados [bar-yados] assorted hors d'œuvres

epazote [epasoteh] commonly used Mexican herb

escabeche de ... [eskabecheh deh] pickled ...

escamoles [eskamol-es] ants' eggs

escarola curly endive

espada ahumado [a-oomado] smoked swordfish

espaguetis [espagetees] spaghetti

espárragos asparagus

espárragos con mayonesa [mī-yonesa] asparagus with mayonnaise

espárragos dos salsas

asparagus with mayonnaise and vinaigrette dressing

espárragos en vinagreta [beenagreta] asparagus in vinaigrette dressing

especia [espes-ya] spice

especialidad [espes-yaleeda] speciality

espinacas spinach

espinacas a la crema creamed spinach

estragón tarragon

fabada (asturiana) [astoor-yana] bean stew with red sausage

fajitas [faнeetas] soft wheat tortillas stuffed with chicken or beef, peppers and onion

faisán [fisan] pheasant

faisán con castañas [kastan-yas] pheasant with chestnuts

faisán estofado stewed pheasant

faisán trufado pheasant with truffles

fiambres [f-yamb-res] cold meats, cold cuts

fideos [feedeн-os] thin pasta; noodles; vermicelli

filete [feeleteh] meat or fish steak

filete a la parrilla [parree-ya] grilled beef steak

filete a la plancha grilled beef steak

filete de puerco [deh pwairko] pork fillet

filete de res beef steak

filete de ternera [tairnaira] veal

steak

flan crème caramel

flan con nata crème caramel with whipped cream

flan de café [deh kafeh] coffee-flavoured crème caramel

flan de caramelo crème caramel

flan (quemado) al ron [kemado] crème caramel with rum

flautas [flowtas] fried tacos

flor de calabaza [deh kalabasa] pumpkin flower

frambuesas [frambwesas] raspberries

fresas strawberries

fresas con nata strawberries and cream/whipped cream

frijol [freeнol] bean

frijoles [freeнol-es] kidney beans

frijoles blancos white beans

frijoles borrachos beans cooked with beer

frijoles de olla [deh o-ya] boiled beans in gravy-type sauce

frijoles negros [neн-gros] black beans

frijoles refritos refried beans

fruta fruit

fruta variada [bar-yada] selection of fresh fruit

frutas en almíbar fruit in syrup

frutillas [frootee-yas] strawberries

galleta [ga-yeta] biscuit, cookie

gallina [ga-**yee**na] chicken

gamba large prawn

garbanzos [garb**a**nsos] chickpeas

garnachas tortillas with garlic sauce, typical of Veracruz

garobo iguana

gazpacho andaluz [gasp**a**cho andal**oos**] cold soup made from tomatoes, onions, garlic, peppers and cucumber

gelatina [Hel**atee**na] gelatine; jelly, (US) jello

gorditas stuffed tortillas

granada pomegranate

gratinado au gratin – baked in a cream and cheese sauce

grenadilla [grenad**ee**-ya] passion fruit

grosellas [gros**eh**-yas] redcurrants

guacamole [gwakam**o**leh] avocado dip

guanábana [gwan**a**bana] custard apple

guayaba [gwī-y**a**ba] guava

guinda [g**ee**nda] black cherry; alcoholic drink made from black cherries

guineo [geen**eh**-o] small banana

guisado [gwees**a**do] stew

gusanos de maguey [deh ma**gay**] maguey worms

hamburguesa [amboorg**e**sa] hamburger

harina [ar**ee**na] flour

harina de maíz [ma-**ees**] cornflour

helado [el**a**do] ice cream

helado de chocolate [deh chok**o**lateh] chocolate ice cream

helado de fresa strawberry ice cream

helado de nata dairy ice cream

helado de vainilla [bīn**ee**-ya] vanilla ice cream

hierbas [y**ai**rbas] herbs

hígado [**ee**gado] liver

hígado con cebolla [seb**o**-ya] liver cooked with onion

hígado de ternera estofado [deh tairn**ai**ra] braised calves' liver

hígado encebollado [ensebo-**ya**do] liver in an onion sauce

hígado estofado braised liver

higos [**ee**gos] figs

higos con miel y nueces [m-yel ee nw**e**s-es] figs with honey and nuts

higos secos dried figs

hongos [**o**ngos] mushrooms

huachinango [wacheen**a**ngo] red snapper

huachinango al ajo [a**H**o] red snapper with garlic butter

huevo [w**e**bo] egg

huevo duro [d**oo**ro] hard-boiled egg

huevo pasado por agua [ag-wa] boiled egg

huevos a la mexicana

[meHeekana] scrambled eggs with peppers, onions and garlic

huevos a la oaxaqueña [waHaken-ya] eggs in chilli and tomato sauce

huevos cocidos [koseedos] hard-boiled eggs

huevos con jamón [Hamon] ham and eggs

huevos con papas fritas fried eggs and chips/French fries

huevos con tocino [toseeno] eggs and bacon

huevos escalfados poached eggs

huevos estrellados [estreh-yados] fried eggs

huevos fritos fried eggs

huevos fritos con chorizo [choreeso] fried eggs with Spanish sausage

huevos motuleños [motoolen-yos] eggs cooked in chillis and tomatoes, served on a fried tortilla and garnished with cheese, ham and chillis

huevos rancheros [ranchairos] fried eggs with hot tomato sauce and tortilla

huevos rellenos [reh-yenos] stuffed eggs

huevos revueltos [rebweltos] scrambled eggs

huevo tibio [teeb-yo] soft-boiled egg

humitas [oomeetas] sweetcorn tamales

incluye pan, postre y vino includes bread, dessert and wine

jaiba [Hība] crab

jalapeños [Halapen-yos] hot green chilli peppers

jalea [Haleh-a] gelatine; jelly, (US) jello

jamón [Hamon] ham

jamón serrano [sairrano] cured ham, similar to Parma ham

jamón York boiled ham

jarabe [Harabeh] syrup

jícama [Heekama] sweet turnip-like fruit eaten with lemon juice or chilli

jitomate [Heetomateh] tomato

langosta lobster

langosta a la americana [amaireekana] lobster with brandy and garlic

langosta fría con mayonesa [free-a kon mī-yonesa] cold lobster with mayonnaise

langosta gratinada lobster au gratin

langostinos a la plancha grilled king prawns

langostinos con mayonesa [mī-yonesa] king prawns with mayonnaise

langostinos dos salsas king prawns cooked in two sauces

laurel [lowrel] bay leaves

lechuga [lechooga] lettuce

lengua [lengwa] tongue

lengua de cordero estofada [deh kord**ai**ro] stewed lambs' tongue

lengua de res ox tongue

lenguado a la plancha [**l**engw**a**do] grilled sole

lentejas [lente**H**as] lentils

lima [**l**eema] lime

limón lemon

lobina sea bass

lomo pork fillet, pork loin, tenderloin

longaniza [longan**ee**sa] cooked spicy sausage

macarrones [makarr**on**-es] macaroni

macarrones gratinados macaroni cheese

machaca shredded meat

macho large green banana

maduro ripe

magdalena sponge cake, (US) muffin

maíz [ma-**ee**s] sweetcorn, maize, (US) corn

mamey [mam**ay**] round, apple-sized tropical fruit

mandarina tangerine

manitas de cerdo [deh s**ai**rdo] pig's trotters

manitas de cordero [kord**ai**ro] leg of lamb

mantequilla [mantek**ee**-ya] butter

manzana [mans**a**na] apple

manzanas asadas baked apples

maracuyá [marakoo-y**a**] passion fruit

mariscada cold mixed shellfish

mariscos shellfish

mariscos de temporada seasonal shellfish

masa dough

mayonesa [mi-yon**e**sa] mayonnaise

mazapán [masap**a**n] marzipan

mazorca f [mas**o**rka] corn on the cob, (US) corncob

medallones de anguila [meda-y**o**n-es deh ang**ee**la] eel steaks

medallones de merluza [mairl**oo**sa] hake steaks

mejillones [me**H**ee-y**o**n-es] mussels

mejillones a la marinera [mareen**ai**ra] mussels in wine sauce with garlic

mejillones con salsa mussels with tomato and herb sauce

melón melon

membrillo [membr**ee**-yo] quince; quince jelly

menestra de verduras [deh baird**oo**ras] vegetable stew

menú [men**oo**] set menu

menú de la casa [deh] fixed-price menu

menú del día today's set menu

menudo tripe; sweetbreads

menú turístico set menu

merluza a la parrilla [mairl**oo**sa a la parr**ee**-ya] grilled hake

merluza a la riojana [r-yo**H**ana] hake with chillies

merluza a la romana hake steaks in batter

merluza frita fried hake

mermelada [mairmelada] jam; marmalade

mermelada de ciruelas [deh seerswelas] plum jam

mermelada de damasco apricot jam

mermelada de durazno [doorasno] peach jam

mermelada de fresas strawberry jam

mermelada de limón lemon marmalade

mermelada de naranja [naranHa] orange marmalade

miel [m-yel] honey

milanesa breaded chop or escalope

milanesa de ternera [deh tairnaira] breaded veal escalope

mojarro [moHarro] type of fish

mole [moleh] sauce made with chilli peppers, chocolate and spices

mole de olla [deh o-ya] spicy meat stew

mole oaxaqueño [waHaken-yo] type of black or green mole sauce

mole poblano rich mole sauce made from nuts, prunes and bananas, a Puebla speciality

mollejas de ternera [mo-yeHas deh tairnaira] calves' sweetbreads

molletes [mo-ye-tes] toasted roll with refried beans and cheese

mondongo tripe

morcilla [morsee-ya] black pudding, blood sausage

morcilla de ternera [deh tairnaira] black pudding made from calves' blood

mortadela salami-type sausage

mostaza [mostasa] mustard

mousse de limón [deh] lemon mousse

nabo turnip

nacatamales [nakatamal-es] corn meal dough filled with meat in sauce and steamed in banana leaves

nachos tortilla chips with cheese

naranja [naranHa] orange

nata cream

natilla [natee-ya] custard

natillas [natee-yas] cold custard with cinnamon

natillas de chocolate [deh chokolateh] cold custard with chocolate

nieve [n-yeveh] sorbet; ice cream

níscalos wild mushrooms

nixtamal [neestamal] maize dough, (US) corn dough

nopalitos chopped cactus-leaf salad

nueces [nwes-es] walnuts

nuez [nwes] nut

ostión [ost-yon] oyster

paella [pa-eh-ya] fried rice
with seafood and chicken
paella valenciana [balens-yana]
paella with assorted shellfish
paleta ice lolly
palmito palm heart
palomitas popcorn
pan bread
pan blanco white bread
pan de cazón [kason] layered
dish of tortillas, beans and
dogfish with a hot sauce
pan de centeno [senteno]
brown bread
pan de higos [deh eegos] dried
fig cake with cinnamon
pan dulce [doolseh] buns and
cakes, sweet pastries
pan integral [eentegral]
wholemeal bread
pancita [panseeta] tripe
papa potato
papadzules [papadsul-es]
tortillas stuffed with hard-
boiled eggs from Yucatán
papas a la criolla [cree-o-ya]
potatoes in hot, spicy sauce
papas asadas baked potatoes
papas bravas potatoes in
cayenne pepper
papas fritas chips, French
fries
papaya papaya, pawpaw
parrillada de caza [parree-yada
deh kasa] mixed grilled game
parrillada de mariscos mixed
grilled shellfish

pasas raisins
pasta biscuit, cookie; pastry;
pasta
pastel cake; pie
pastel de carne [karneh]
brawn, jellied meat
pata foot, trotter
patatas (fritas) crisps, (US)
potato chips
pato duck
pato a la naranja [naranHa]
duck à l'orange
pato asado roast duck
pavo [pabo] turkey
pavo relleno [reh-yeno] stuffed
turkey
pay [pi] pie with a sweet
filling
pay de queso [deh keso]
cheesecake
pechuga de pollo [deh po-yo]
breast of chicken
pepinillos [pepeenee-yos]
gherkins
pepinillos en vinagreta
[beenagreta] gherkins in
vinaigrette dressing
pepino cucumber
pera [paira] pear
perdices [pairdees-es]
partridges
perdices a la campesina
partridges with vegetables
perdices asadas roast
partridges
perdices con chocolate
[chokolateh] partridges with
chocolate
perdices encebolladas

[ensebo-yadas] partridge with onion

perejil [paireh-Heel] parsley

perro caliente [pairro kal-yenteh] hot dog

pescaditos fritos fried sprats

pescado fish

pescado a la veracruzana [bairakroosana] seasoned sea bass or red snapper fillets fried and served with tomato sauce on top

pez espada ahumado [a-oomado] smoked swordfish

píbil cooked in a pit

picadillo [peekadee-yo] minced meat

picadillo de pollo [deh po-yo] minced chicken

picadillo de ternera [tairnaira] minced veal

picante hot, spicy

pichón pigeon

pichones estofados [peechon-es] stewed pigeon

picoso hot, spicy

pierna [p-yairna] leg

piloncillo [peelonsee-yo] unrefined brown sugar

pimentón paprika

pimienta [peem-yenta] black pepper

pimienta blanca white pepper

pimienta de cayena [deh kī-yena] cayenne pepper

pimiento rojo [roHo] red pepper

pimiento verde [bairdeh] green pepper

pinchitos snacks/appetizers served in bars; kebabs

pincho kebab

piña [peen-ya] pineapple

piña fresca fresh pineapple

piña gratinada pineapple au gratin

piñones [peen-yon-es] pine nuts

pipián [peep-yan] sauce of ground nuts, seeds and spices

pitahaya [peetahī-ya] red fruit of a cactus plant with soft, sweet flesh

plátano banana

plátanos flameados [flameh-ados] flambéed bananas

platos combinados meat and vegetables, hamburgers and eggs etc

poco hecho [echo] rare

pollo [po-yo] chicken

pollo al ajillo [aHee-yo] fried chicken with garlic

pollo a la parrilla [parree-ya] grilled chicken

pollo al vino blanco [beeno] chicken in white wine

pollo asado roast chicken

pollo con verduras [bairdooras] chicken and vegetables

polvorones [polboron-es] sugar-based dessert (eaten at Christmas)

poro leek

postre [postreh] dessert

pozole [posoleh] thick broth of vegetables meat and corn

primer plato [preemair] starter, appetizer

puerco [pwairko] pork

pulpitos con cebolla [sebo-ya] baby octopuses with onions

pulpo octopus

pupusa dumpling usually filled with cheese or meat

puré de papas [pooreh deh] mashed potatoes, potato purée

queque [kekeh] cake

quesadilla [kesadee-ya] fried corn meal pancake usually filled with cheese

queso [keso] cheese

queso con membrillo [membree-yo] cheese with quince jelly

queso fresco soft white cheese

queso fundido melted cheese

queso manchego hard, strong cheese

queso Oaxaca [waHaka] soft white cheese used for cooking

rábanos radishes

ración [ras-yon] portion

ración pequeña para niños [peken-ya para neen-yos] children's portion

rajas [raHas] strips of pickled green chillies; sliced green peppers in cream

ravioles [rab-yol-es] ravioli

raya [rī-ya] skate

raya con manteca negra [nehgra] skate in butter and vinegar sauce

rebanada slice

refritos refried beans

relleno [reh-yeno] stuffed; stuffing

remolacha beetroot

repollo [repo-yo] cabbage

res beef

riñones [reen-yon-es] kidneys

riñones a la plancha grilled kidneys

riñones al jerez [Hair-es] kidneys in a sherry sauce

róbalo bass

romero [romairo] rosemary

ron rum

ropa vieja [b-yeh-Ha] shredded meat

rosca round sponge made at Christmas

roscas sweet pastries

rosquillas [roskee-yas] small sweet pastries

sal salt

salbute type of filled tortilla typical of Yucatán

salchicha sausage

salchichas de Frankfurt [deh] frankfurters

salchichón salami-type sausage

salmón [sal-mon] salmon

salmón a la parrilla [paree-ya] grilled salmon

salmón ahumado [a-oomado] smoked salmon

salmón frío [**free**-o] cold salmon

salmonetes [sal-mo**net**-es] red mullet

salmonetes a la parrilla [pa**ree**-ya] grilled red mullet

salmonetes en papillote [papee-**yo**teh] red mullet cooked in foil

salpicón de mariscos [deh] shellfish with vinaigrette dressing

salsa sauce

salsa allioli/ali oli [a-yee-**o**lee/**a**lee **o**lee] garlic mayonnaise

salsa bechamel [be**sha**mel] béchamel sauce, white sauce

salsa de jitomate [deh Heeto**ma**teh] tomato sauce

salsa holandesa [olan**de**sa] hollandaise sauce

salsa mexicana/pico de gallo [me**Hee**ka**na**/**pee**ko deh **ga**-yo] hot sauce made with chillies, onions and red tomatoes

salsa romesco sauce made from peppers, tomatoes and garlic

salsa tártara tartare sauce

salsa verde [**ba**irdeh] green sauce made from tomatillo and chillies

salsa vinagreta [beena**gre**ta] vinaigrette dressing

salteado [**sal**teh-**a**do] sautéed

sancocho vegetable soup with meat or fish

sandía [san**dee**-a] water melon

sandwich sandwich

sandwich mixto [**mees**to] cheese and ham sandwich

sardina sardine

sardinas a la brasa barbecued sardines

sardinas a la parrilla [pa**rree**-ya] grilled sardines

sardinas fritas fried sardines

segundo plato main course

servicio incluido service charge included

servicio no incluido service charge not included

sesos a la romana brains in batter

sesos rebozados [rebo**sa**dos] brains in batter

solomillo [solo**mee**-yo] fillet steak

solomillo con papas fritas fillet steak with chips/French fries

solomillo de cerdo [deh **sai**rdo] fillet of pork

solomillo de ternera [**tair**naira] fillet of veal

solomillo de vaca [**ba**ka] fillet of beef

solomillo frío [**free**-o] cold roast beef

sopa soup

sopa de aguacate fría [deh agwa**ka**teh] cold avocado soup

sopa de ajo [a**Ho**] garlic soup

sopa de arroz rice soup

sopa de fideos [feed**eh**-os]

noodle soup

sopa de frijoles negros
[freeHol-es **neh**-gros] black bean
soup

sopa de gallina [ga-**yee**na]
chicken soup

sopa del día soup of the day

sopa de lentejas [lentee**Has**]
lentil soup

sopa de mariscos fish and
shellfish soup

sopa de pescado fish soup

sopa de tortilla [tor**tee**-ya] soup
with corn meal pancakes

sopa de tortuga turtle soup

sopa de verduras [baird**oo**ras]
vegetable soup

sopa inglesa trifle

sopaipillas [sopi**pee**-yas] sweet
fritters

sopa seca rice or pasta dish
served with a sauce on top

sopa tarasca creamy bean
and tomato soup

sopes [**sop**-es] garnished
tortillas

sorbete [**sorbeteh**] sorbet

soufflé soufflé

soufflé de fresas [deh]
strawberry soufflé

soufflé de naranja [naranHa]
orange soufflé

soufflé de queso [**keso**] cheese
soufflé

taco stuffed maize/corn
pancake

tacos al pastor tacos with
grilled meat

tacos de pollo [deh po-yo]
tacos stuffed with chicken

tajadas [taHadas] fried banana
strips

tallarines [ta-yareen-es]
noodles

tallarines a la italiana [eetal-
yana] tagliatelle with tomato
sauce

tamal filled maize/corn
dough cooked in banana
leaf, tamale

tamarindo tamarind

tapa de ternera rellena [deh
tair**nai**ra reh-**yena**] stuffed veal
hock

tapado stew

tapas appetizers

tarta cake

tarta Alaska baked Alaska

tarta de almendra [deh]
almond tart or gâteau

tarta de arroz [arros] cake or
tart containing rice

tarta de chocolate [chokolateh]
chocolate gâteau

tarta de fresas strawberry tart
or gâteau

tarta de la casa tart or gâteau
baked on the premises

tarta de manzana [mansana]
apple tart

tarta helada [elada] ice cream
gâteau

tarta mocha/moka [moka]
mocha tart

tártar crudo raw minced
steak, steak tartare

tejos de queso [teHos deh keso]

cheese pastries

tencas tench

tencas con jamón [Hamon] tench with ham

ternera [tairnaira] veal

ternera asada roast veal

tocino [toseeno] bacon

todo incluido all inclusive

tomate [tomateh] green tomato

tomates rellenos [tomat-es reh-yenos] stuffed tomatoes

tomatillo [tomatee-yo] green tomato used for sauces

tomillo [tomee-yo] thyme

tordo thrush

tordos braseados [braseh-ados] grilled thrushes

tordos estofados braised thrushes

toronja [toronHa] grapefruit

torrejas [torreHas] French toast

torrijas [torreeHas] sweet pastries

torta filled bread roll with salad, cream and tomato garnish

tortilla [tortee-ya] maize pancake, (US) corn pancake

tortilla de harina [deh areena] wheat pancake

tortilla de huevo [webo] omelette

tortilla española [espan-yola] Spanish omelette with potato, onion and garlic

tostada fried corn pancake topped with meat, vegetables and salsa; toast

totopo thin, fried tortilla

trucha [troocha] trout

trucha ahumada [a-oomada] smoked trout

trucha a la marinera [mareenaira] trout in white wine sauce

trucha con jamón [Hamon] trout with ham

trucha escabechada marinated trout

tuétano [twetano] marrow, squash

tuna [toona] prickly pear

turrón nougat

turrón de coco [deh] coconut nougat

turrón de Jijona [HeeHona] hard nougat

turrón de yema [yema] nougat with egg yolk

uchepos small sweet tamales

uvas [oobas] grapes

vainilla [bīnee-ya] vanilla

venado [benado] venison

verduras [bairdooras] vegetables

verduras capeadas [kapeh-adas] courgettes and cauliflower in batter served with hot tomato sauce and cream

vinagre [beenagreh] vinegar

vuelvealavida [bwelbeh-a-labeeda] marinated seafood cocktail with chilli

yema yolk
yerba [**yai**rba] herb
yogur [yo-g**oor**] yoghurt
yuca sweet potato

zanahoria [sana-**o**ree-a] carrot
zanahorias a la crema carrots
à la crème
zapallo [sap**a**-yo] marrow,
squash
zapote [sap**o**teh] sweet
pumpkin
zarzamoras [sarsam**o**ras]
blackberries
zarzuela de mariscos [sarsw**e**la
deh] shellfish stew

Menu Reader:
Drink

Essential Terms

beer la cerveza [sairbesa]
bottle la botella [boteh-ya], el frasco
brandy el coñac [kon-yak]
black coffee el café americano [kafeh amaireekano]
  (strong) el café solo
coffee el café [kafeh]
cup la taza [tasa]
  a cup of ... una taza de ... [deh]
fruit juice el jugo de frutas [Hoogo deh]
gin la ginebra [Heenebra]
  a gin and tonic un gintónic [jeentoneek]
glass (tumbler) el vaso [baso]
  (wine glass) la copa
  a glass of ... un vaso de ... [deh], una copa de ...
milk la leche [lecheh]
milkshake el licuado [leekwado]
mineral water el agua mineral [agwa meenairal]
red wine el vino tinto [beeno teento]
soda (water) la soda
soft drink el refresco
sugar el azúcar [asookar]
tea el té [teh]
tonic (water) la tónica
vodka el vodka [bodka]
water el agua [agwa]
whisky el whisky
white wine el vino blanco [beeno]
wine el vino
wine list la lista de vinos [leesta deh beenos]

another ... otro/otra ...

agua [**a**gwa] water

agua de fruta fruit drink
made from fruit and water

agua de granada [deh]
grenadine juice

agua de jamaica [Ham**ī**ka]
hibiscus blossom drink

agua de melón melon juice

agua de panela drink made
from water and sugar

agua mineral [meena**i**ral]
mineral water

agua mineral con gas fizzy
mineral water

agua mineral sin gas [seen]
still mineral water

aguardiente [agward-y**e**nteh] a
clear spirit similar to brandy
or white rum

al tiempo [t-y**e**mpo] at room
temperature

añejo [an-y**e**h-Ho] vintage;
mellow; mature

anís aniseed-flavoured spirit

aperitivo [apaireet**ee**bo] aperitif

api thick custard-like drink
made from maize and
cinnamon

aromáticas herb teas

atole [at**o**leh] thick drink
made from maize/corn

azúcar [as**oo**kar] sugar

bebida drink

bebidas alcohólicas alcoholic
drinks

Bohemia® brand of lager

cacao [kak**ow**] cocoa

café [kaf**eh**] coffee

café americano black coffee

café capuchino cappuccino

café con leche [l**e**cheh] coffee
with milk (large cup)

café cortado coffee with a
dash of milk (small cup)

café de olla [deh **o**-ya] coffee
made with cinnamon and
raw sugar

café descafeinado [deskafay-
een**a**do] decaffeinated
coffee

café escocés [eskos-**e**s] black
coffee, whisky/scotch and
vanilla ice cream

café exprés [espr**e**s] strong
black coffee

café instantáneo [eenstan-
t**a**neh-o] instant coffee

café irlandés [eerland-**e**s] black
coffee, whisky, vanilla ice
cream and whipped cream

café negro [**ne**h-gro] black
coffee, usually strong and
often sweet

café perfumado coffee with a
dash of brandy or other
spirit

café solo black coffee, usually
strong and often sweet

carta de vinos [deh b**ee**nos]
wine list

Cava [k**a**ba] champagne

cebada [seb**a**da] drink made
from fermented barley

cerveza [sairb**e**sa] beer, lager

cerveza clara light, lager-style
beer

cerveza de barril draught beer

cerveza negra dark beer

cerveza oscura dark beer

champán [champan] champagne

chocolate caliente [chokolateh kal-yenteh] hot chocolate drink, sometimes sweetened with honey and flavoured with vanilla and spices

coctel cocktail

con azúcar [asookar] with sugar

con gas fizzy, sparkling

coñac [kon-yak] brandy

cosecha vintage

cubalibre [koobaleebreh] rum and cola

cubito de hielo [deh yelo] ice cube

cucaracha tequila and strong, alcoholic, coffee-flavoured drink

destornillador [destornee-yador] vodka and orange juice

Domecq [domek] Mexican wine producer

Dos Equis® [ekees] light Mexican beer

embotellado en ... bottled in ...

espumoso sparkling

gaseosa [gaseh-osa] lemonade

ginebra [Heenebra] gin

gintónic [jeentoneek] gin and tonic

granizada/granizado [graneesada] crushed ice drink

guinda [geenda] alcoholic drink made from black cherries; black cherry

guindada [geendada], guindilla [guindee-ya] cherry brandy

Hidalgo Mexican wine producer

hielo [yelo] ice

horchata [orchata] cold drink made from rice and water

horchata de chufas [deh] cold almond-flavoured milky drink

infusión [eenfoos-yon] herb tea

jarra de cerveza/vino [Harra deh sairbesa/beeno] jug of beer/wine

jerez [Hair-es] sherry

jerez fino light, dry sherry

jerez oloroso sweet sherry

jugo [Hoogo] juice

jugo de damasco apricot juice

jugo de durazno [doorasno] peach juice

jugo de jitomate [Heetomateh] tomato juice

jugo de lima lime juice

jugo de limón lemon juice

jugo de naranja [naranHa] orange juice

jugo de piña [peen-ya]

pineapple juice

leche [**le**cheh] milk

leche de soja [deh so**H**a] soya milk

leche desnatada skimmed milk

licor liqueur; spirit

licor de avellana [deh abeh-**ya**na] hazelnut-flavoured liqueur

licor de manzana [mans**a**na] apple-flavoured liqueur

licor de durazno [door**a**sno] peach-flavoured liqueur

licor de melón melon-flavoured liqueur

licor de naranja [naran**H**a] orange-flavoured liqueur

licores [leek**o**r-es] spirits, liqueurs

licuado [leek**wa**do] milkshake

licuado de fresa [deh] strawberry milkshake

licuado de plátano banana milkshake

limonada fresh lemonade

lista de precios [**pres**-yos] price list

Málaga sweet wine

malta dark beer

malteada [malteh-**a**da] milkshake

manzanilla [mansan**ee**-ya] dry sherry-type wine; camomile tea

margarita cocktail of tequila, lime juice and either grenadine, Curaçao or triple

sec

mate [**ma**teh] bitter tea made from the dried leaves of the yerba mate bush

media de agua [**med**-ya deh ag-**wa**] half-bottle of mineral water

mediana bottle of beer

mezcal [**mes**kal] spirit distilled from the maguey cactus

Negra Modelo® dark Mexican beer

Nescafe® [neskaf**eh**] instant coffee

Nochebuena® [noche**bwe**na] dark Mexican beer

Oporto port

Pacífico® brand of lager

piña colada [**pee**n-ya] rum and pineapple cocktail

posh sugar cane liquor

pozol de cacao [pos**o**l deh kak**a**-o] cool drink made from ground maize/corn and chocolate

pulque [**poo**lkeh] thick alcoholic drink distilled from the pulp of the maguey cactus

puro de caña [deh kan-ya] sugar cane liquor

refresco soft drink, fizzy drink

rompope [romp**o**peh] egg nog, egg flip

ron rum

ron oro matured rum

sangría [sangree-a] mixture of red wine, lemon juice, spirits, sugar and fruit

sangrita orange juice, grenadine and chilli, drunk with tequila

San Miguel® [migel] type of lager

Sauza® [sowsa] brand of tequila

semidulce [semeedoolseh] medium-sweet

sidra cider

sin azúcar [seen asookar] without sugar

sin gas still

Sol® brand of lager

Superior® [soopair-yor] brand of lager

taxallate [taнa-yateh] drink from Chiapas made from maize/corn and cocoa

té [teh] tea

Tecate® [tekateh] light Mexican beer, usually served with lime and salt

té de hierbas [teh deh yairbas] herbal tea

Tehuacán® [teh-wakan] mineral water

tequila [tekeela] spirit distilled from the pulp of the agave cactus

tónica tonic

Tres Equis® [ekees] brand of lager

vino [beeno] wine

vino blanco white wine

vino de casa [deh] house wine

vino de mesa table wine

vino del país [pa-ees] local wine

vino rosado rosé wine

vino tinto red wine

yerbabuena [yairbabwena] mint tea

yerba mate [yairba mateh] bitter tea made from the dried leaves of the yerba mate bush